D1083921

Violence and the Police

The MIT Press
Cambridge, Massachusetts, and London, England

Violence and the Police:
A Sociological Study of Law, Custom, and Morality

William A. Westley

ISBN 0 262 23042 9 (hardcover)

Library of Congress catalog card number: 75-110236

Foreword

Out of their experience men create the world in which they dwell. In this world, illusion and reality merge, and man sees himself in the shadows of his peers.

The policeman's world is spawned of degradation, corruption, and insecurity. He sees man as ill-willed, exploitative, mean, and dirty; himself a victim of injustice, misunderstood and defiled. Hungry for approval, uneasy as to his own worth, wrathful and without dignity, he walks alone — a pedestrian in Hell.

Is he correct? Does the reality justify the illusion? It is of no consequence. We seek only to know his world.

Preface

This book looks back some twenty years to a different time, a different police department, and certainly to a different sociologist. What can I now add to what these have wrought? That the author was a young man hanging on the edge of his first real sociological venture, full of hope, strung tight with the experience but passionately devoted to communicating an understanding of the police and of how their world operated. He was afraid of the police after forcing himself to listen to the tune of violence in their lives, but full of the need to comprehend their humanity within this violence, to understand how the forces of work and community gave this shape to their humanity. He found it hard to so share their point of view that he had rapport with their actions, and yet ask them to bare details of self-incriminating conduct. There was a terrible tension in the flow of this semi-participant research, for to understand, he had to sympathize; but in attempting to sympathize he wanted to be liked. To be liked, he had to play by their rules and not ask too many questions. Thus, the work went in waves of carefully building up confidence and inevitably becoming involved in their regard, then asking questions, sharp probing questions, that soon caused rejection. This proved to be both personally painful, in the sense that thereafter he had to push himself on men who he felt disliked and were afraid of him, and practically disastrous, since if the men refused to talk to him the research would stop.

On one occasion, after asking a series of men probing questions in a very sensitive area, everyone stopped talking to him and failed to meet their interview appointments. Days went by when he would sit in the squad room, and the men would not even pass the time of the day with him. The ice broke only when he observed one day that the hard-bitten patrol sergeant came in, evidently delighted with himself, and explained that he had just helped a lady put some packages in her car. This was so incongruous that the interviewer checked his field notes and found a series of small incidents in which different policemen had expressed what he felt to be excessive pleasure in helping someone. He reasoned that this must be because they felt so rejected by the public that they were hungry for approval. He then tested this hypothesis by going to the sergeant and explaining that he was in trouble, that his career depended on getting the research done and asking the sergeant to help him. The response was overwhelming. The sergeant immediately expressed sympathy, called all the men together the next morning and gave them hell for not helping the interviewer, and then personally vouched for him. Thereafter, all the men talked very freely and were exceptionally cooperative. This was a real gain in insight into the police, achieved, however, at considerable emotional cost to the sociologist.

There were other occasions when, for different reasons, the department became uncooperative and it was difficult to continue the research. The solution was to stay around for such long and continuous periods that it was not humanly possible for the men to keep up the pretense of being the kind of men they wanted the interviewer to believe they were. Sooner or later a major slip was bound to occur, witnessed by the interviewer. After that the men would relapse into their daily routines. Observation of the detective bureau was a case in point. Just as soon as he began talking to the detectives, he was aware that they were maintaining a front. He then determined to wait them out and literally just sat in the detective bureau for days on end. Finally, after ten days of sitting, something broke. They had brought in a small Negro man, and when the detective sergeant, who was a huge, muscular man, asked him what he had been doing that afternoon and the man said something that was obviously considered false, the sergeant slapped him across the side of the head with such force that the man was knocked off his feet. Immediately the sergeant glanced over at the interviewer, then raced over and picked up the man. He did him no more violence, but thereafter all the detectives began to discuss their cases and their tactics quite openly, and the interviewer was invited to go along on raids. This was an alarming incident, since the interviewer found himself in a moral quandary. Observing the violence was upsetting in itself. If they could do that kind of thing to the other man, what might they do to the interviewer should they decide that he was dangerous (because he already possessed a lot of incriminating information)?[1] But if they had continued to hit the Negro man, what should he have done? He felt he would have had to do something. What if the Negro had asked the interviewer to be his witness? Furthermore, how could he possibly sympathize with men who acted in this way? These were very painful conflicts.

These were some of the big issues. Sandwiched between them were a host of less formidable but still significant events. One was the evening when the interviewer was alone in the home of a policeman with a reputation for brutality; the policeman described in detail how he used violence to control sexual offenders. Then, when he was asked what he would do to a man who had killed a policeman, he leaped to his feet, towering above the thoroughly cowed interviewer, and shouted down at him: "I'd beat him to death with a two-by-four." Two weeks later this man wandered into an office in which the interviewer was talking to a sergeant; the sergeant very quickly shoved him out the door, but not before the interviewer noticed that the man's clothes were wet and sticky with what appeared to be blood. A subsequent contact with an informant revealed that the man had that day practically beaten someone to death!

Yet there were *very few* men on the force like this. A surprising number so abhorred violence that they took dull desk jobs to avoid it. Most confessed to the interviewer that brutality brought a bad name to the department. But not one of them was willing to protest openly such violence, and certainly not to report the men who were violent. They all believed that policemen had to use violence at times to protect themselves and that if they exposed the brutality, it harmed the department. The use of violence had deep emotional significance to those policemen, and talking to them about it was always a very delicate matter.

Equally delicate was the problem of letting the men know that one really knew what was going on, so they would feel that they

[1] Evidently there were some grounds for his fears, since his sponsor, Joseph D. Lohman, had warned him to be careful or he might just be found in an alley with his head smashed. Lohman had, in fact, implied to the Chief that he (the Chief) was responsible for the safety of the interviewer. It sounds melodramatic, but for the interviewer it was just plain frightening.

didn't have to protect secrets, while at the same time making them understand that this information would not be used against them. It was widely reputed that in certain sections of the force the men were accepting graft. Because of this, every man on the force was either involved in this graft or he had heard stories about others who were. Naturally, they were very secretive about this and were suspicious of anyone asking questions around the department. In fact, they were often so sensitive about this that they were afraid that if they talked with the interviewer the others might think that they were informers. Thus, the problem was to convince them that they had nothing to hide and that the purpose of the interviews was not to find out about graft. In the beginning, when the interviewer really knew nothing about what was going on, there was no way in which he could indicate that he was knowledgeable. But later, when quite gradually he came to know both what was going on and who was involved, he was able to manifest a sophistication about these matters which was reassuring to the policemen because it made them feel that the interviewer already knew the story and that therefore they had nothing to hide. In fact, some were so reassured that they proceeded to provide facts and figures about graft accepted by their colleagues — much to the horror of the interviewer, who felt that they might later develop guilt feelings about this, or that others would think that gathering such information was the purpose of the research. Again it was often touch and go, but with time and increasing skill the interviewer found it easier and easier to get information.

It is difficult to describe the sense of paradox that he had about the incompatibility between the lives of these men as decent, humble, urban men, usually with wives, children, and small homes, and their lives as policemen in an antagonistic relationship with the community. The resolution of this paradox proved to be the major analytical problem of the study. He felt that he personally had to be able to understand how these men could be both these things, how it would have been possible for him to have held these views. He imaginatively tried to live through what they were living through. He retraced their steps, first in the community, then in the recruit school, then in their early days in the squad cars and on the foot beat. As explanations came to him, he asked the men whether they had had such experiences and feelings. He asked himself what the consequences of having such feelings would be and then went to find out whether, indeed, other men had the same reactions as he. He talked to the rookies, to the experienced men, to their wives and children. Thus, thinking, working, listening, taking detailed notes, and then brooding over them, he came to construct an explanation of their world that made these apparently diverse and contradictory viewpoints coherent.

With an explanation in mind, he constructed a formal interview outline, drew a sample of the men, and began systematic interviewing. The book is a consequence of two personal experiences: first, an attempt to observe, experience, and comprehend the experience of being a policeman — that is, to understand the attitudes and values of the policemen as police, their source in his occupational experience, and their consequences for law enforcement; second, a careful testing of these hypotheses. He kept only the explanations that withstood this test.

The young man who did these things no longer exists, nor does his passionate involvement in that study of the police. In fact, if we are to be realistic, that police department and that city no longer exist in the shape and form that they had then. Thus, in a sense, this book is a kind of fiction. This raises the question of the extent to which it was always a fiction. To what extent could its findings be generalized to other police departments, and how durable are they over time? These questions bring into focus the nature of the community and the department. Let me briefly describe both before dealing with these questions.

The police department was located in a small midwestern industrial city. At the time of the study this city seemed similar to large urban centers in having a slum area, a sizable Negro subcommunity, major traffic problems, a system of political patronage, and a high crime rate. This city was, of course, not representative of major urban centers in the United States, for its size, economic composition, and political influence sharply differentiated it from them. But as far as the police are concerned, it posed most of the major problems encountered by police departments in the larger cities in traffic, in political corruption, in crime, in ethnic relations, and so forth. Its policemen reacted as though they were urban policemen.

The purpose of the study was not to describe the urban police departments of the United States but to articulate the ways in which the occupation and technology of policing gave rise to a set of shared human responses — in the form of attitudes and values. Insofar as we were successful in identifying some of the major components and problems of policing as an occupation and analyzing how these gave rise to police norms, the results should be applicable wherever these conditions hold. Obviously they don't hold for all police departments. Some departments were at that time so corrupt that there was almost no professional core to their activities, and "our" department certainly did not represent them. Other departments were so highly professionalized and controlled by civil service regulations that most of the attitudes we described never developed. In this category would have fallen many of the state police departments and a few of the municipal departments, and again "our" department was not representative of them. But between these two poles of high professionalization and widespread corruption we should guess that most of the major urban police departments in the United States would be found. We should argue that to the degree that any police department was faced with the conditions of public hostility, public pressure, political influence, and opportunities for graft, they would probably respond with the normative system analogous to that described in this book. That many police departments held the same view of their work and of the public was at least partially demonstrated when a California newspaper posed our questions on secrecy to men from seven different departments in the San Francisco area and received almost identical responses.

It also seems clear that time has not entirely eroded these problems of the police. Undoubtedly there have been great improvements in the professionalization of the police, and the police now face problems such as very high racial tension, protests, and riots, which were a relatively minor part of their work in earlier times. However, if I were to hazard a guess, I would say that the pressures experienced by the policeman in 1950 that isolated him from the community have increased since that time. My police-men felt endangered and beleaguered: endangered because they were indeed the victims of violence from time to time, and they magnified the danger in the tales they told each other; be-leaguered because of their antagonistic relationship to society, because of their record of graft, but most of all because their work often made them adversaries of the public. The result was the formation of a conflict group: policemen who said, "We are only a hundred and forty against a hundred and forty thousand." Yet this antagonism, which might have been dangerous to the community, was tempered and controlled by their political vul-nerability. Just because they were subject to the whim of the political machine, which had the effect of making them corrupt, they had to be nice to the public for the sake of that machine. This suggests that the depoliticization of the police, represented in professionalization and in civil service, may not be the panacea it is often thought to be. In fact, the police may be dangerous if the antagonism between them and the public increases, as ap-parently it is increasing, under the prod of racial violence and student protest. Obviously, civil strife of this kind has the effect both of increasing the conflict between the police and the public, and of increasing the physical and social dangers to which the police are subject. It is then reasonable that the police should protect themselves by drawing closer together and becoming more hostile to the public. This is why the police are likely to be at the core of any "backlash" and why they can be a dangerous force in a democratic society.

Thus, it would appear that time has only strengthened the con-ditions that give rise to the defensiveness, the norms of secrecy, and the acceptance of violence by the police. In the 1940's the hope for the improvement of police departments was in their professionalization and in improved public relations. Presumably, by now the police are more professionalized, but it can also be assumed that their public relations have deteriorated.

In 1950, when this study was made, some rookie policemen were so conscious of public disapproval of the police that they refused to wear their uniforms going to and from work. At the same time, the wives of policemen reported that their children were teased because their fathers were on the police force. Many policemen themselves said that they didn't like it to be known that they were policemen because people were always coming up to them and making remarks. These are the reactions of police working in a community in which the police are held in some contempt by most people but really feared and hated by a very narrow segment, usually by people with little power in the community. It seems possible that today, when the police have become anathema to ever-widening sectors of the community, they themselves will have become much more withdrawn and, if not more sensitive to public criticism, at least reacting against it. If the combination of increased professionalization and increased conflict have indeed taken place, we can assume that the police are both more difficult to influence and less considerate of the ordinary citizen.

The dynamics of the relationship between the police and their work described in this study are based on a very simple model of how men handle their occupational lives. If one assumes with Everett Hughes that today occupation is a major badge of identity, then one also assumes that men will act in such a way as to protect their identity and self-esteem. The major problem for the policeman is to deal with pressures and expectations of the public. When the public is hostile, the police will react with hostility and secrecy. When their activities are likely to lead to criticism from the public, they will hide or eliminate these activities.

We found that the public was hostile to the police and that the police were hypersensitive to anything that might affect their self-respect. We also found that in those areas most likely to lead to public criticism, such as the use of force, the police became particularly secretive. If there were no pressures *for* the police to use force, they probably would have abandoned it, but they felt that there *were* such pressures: to protect themselves from violent people, to solve important crimes that they felt could not be solved in any other way, and to control certain types of crimes for which the courts made it difficult to convict or refused to hand out strong penalties. They were in conflict about the use of force because they knew that they would be criticized, and yet they felt they had to use it. Their response was a system of legitimization and a strong emphasis on secrecy.

Like other men, the police were sensitive to the demands of

their occupational audience. Their work tended to make this audience hostile, so they tried to hide what they were doing, to counter the hostility of the public with a negative definition of human motives, and at the same time, wherever possible, to seek ways of getting public approval. The norms of the police (emphasizing secrecy, the use of violence for arrests, and the maintenance of respect for the police) represented a solution to the threats to their self-respect posed by the nature of their occupation.

Within the framework of this model we should assume that, where the police face these problems, they will respond with these norms. Where they have respect from the public, they will have less need for violence and secrecy. Where public hostility grows, so will their utilization of violence and secrecy. At the time of this study, there were differences in the social environments of different police departments. Where the police either had less contact with the public or received a more favorable reception (the two tend to go together), as in the case of the state police departments, they had less resort to violence and secrecy. Yet, at the same time, it seemed that most large urban police departments did face such unfavorable conditions and did respond as our department did.

We have no reason to believe that the passage of time should change this dynamic relationship between the police and the public. Today, with rising public violence and protest and its consequence of sharp criticism of the police, *at the same time that the police are pressured to control this public violence,* we should assume an increasing reliance on violence and secrecy by the police themselves.

This development, which is of serious concern to both the police and the public, may be aggravated, strangely enough, by the increasing professionalization of the police. Professionalization, which has been the major goal of modern police administrators during the past two decades, has the effect of insulating the police from public pressures. In addition, it presumably is accompanied by higher standards and better training (the methods of insuring professionalization). That we want better trained, more competent policemen, insulated from political influence and graft, is evident. Yet we must be wary, since insulation from political influence without other methods of integration, such as a positive relationship to the community, can mean insulation from all of us, and if the goals of the police should vary from those of the citizens, it can become a very serious problem. *This is exactly what is likely to happen* when the public's attitudes toward the police and interaction with the police are hostile, so that they elicit hostile, violent, and secrecy-oriented responses from the police. Today, when policemen are being killed and injured in riots, and openly attacked by large and respectable parts of the community, they are indeed responding with hostility, violence, and secrecy.

Low-status occupational groups like the police do not develop the same professional codes of honor, certification, and internal controls that we expect of, say, the medical profession. In the case of the police, professionalization refers to careful selection, training, skills, and pride in work. The emphasis on this professionalization has the effect of occupational reinforcement, with a development of increasing solidarity among policemen, and the increased use of collective bargaining. It is probably reflected in the increasing strength of police brotherhoods, which in many cities have taken steps to control the conditions of work. This in turn has meant an increased resistance to control by police management, and thus by the police policymakers who are ordinarily the political councils of urban areas.

Under politically stable conditions, the emphasis on the professionalization of the police and the strengthening of policemen's unions would have the effect of improving the standards of police work. They would result in better police conduct and efficiency, higher pay for policemen, and greater respect for the police by the public. They would, in other words, hopefully set into motion a chain of developments making for an efficient and responsible police force.

Under politically unstable conditions, in which the adversarial role of the police is accentuated, in which the police have violent confrontations with the public, in which for real and political reasons pressure groups mount a critical attack on the police, the professionalization and the unionization of the police can have negative effects. The police may use them for defensive purposes, to draw away from the public, to resist public control and accountability.

The police are, after all, only ordinary men, working collectively to protect their interests and self-esteem. They are, however, placed under extraordinary strains, and to compensate for these strains and threats they can become exceptionally brutal and withdrawn. This is a real danger in our time.

I seem to be presenting an insoluble dilemma, in which the social forces arrayed against the police form them into a repressive and undemocratic group. This is probably what will happen unless we alter the course of developments: if we permit the adversarial role of the police to intensify, if we encourage the increasing isolation of the police from the community. It is possible that the police, like the military, are entirely too traditional and isolated from the society. This is apparent when they are contrasted with workers in modern industry. Workers long ago became involved in energetic unions, in bargaining with management, and today they are participating to an increasing degree in decisions about their own work. The police and the military, in contrast, have only the beginnings of union organization, and where they *are* organized, their unions are relatively primitive and rudimentary. This contrast is sharpened when their situation is compared with the demands for participatory democracy being made in universities and to some extent in industry. The psychological consequence of feeling so at odds with the developing climate of opinion may also aggravate the policeman's feeling of isolation and irritation.

Means must be found for integrating the police with the community and for deescalating their adversarial role. To do this, police organizations must be democratized by involving as many policemen as possible in decision making on all aspects of the department's job. Policemen must also be integrated with the community through increased police participation on decision-making bodies, and through public participation in a wide range of police activities. Policemen must have the sense that they have a serious voice in the affairs of the city through participation by many different policemen in a range of public bodies, including the city council. At the same time, citizens should become members of committees and other police bodies within the police department. Paralleling this increased democratization and involvement with the community should be a decrease in the duties leading to violent confrontation with the public, for example, riot control. In these cases, it would be preferable that a broad citizen group like the National Guard (rather than the Army) be called in.

One can hope that if these measures of democratization, involvement, and the deescalation of confrontations are combined with sound training, good pay, and excellent public relations, they would be enthusiastically welcomed by the police and would have the effect of creating truly responsible police departments.

What is printed here is largely identical with the Ph.D. thesis completed in 1951. Minor editorial changes have been made to fit the manuscript for publication, and certain parts of the original manuscript now appear as appendixes. But except for this introduction, nothing new has been added. I cannot write with the impassioned style of the younger and more innocent man who wrote this book. I don't agree with all the ways in which he said what he had to say, but I am sufficiently in his debt to respect fully the way he wanted it said.

William A. Westley
Montreal
June 1969

Acknowledgment

I owe special thanks to the late Mr. Joseph D. Lohman and to Professor E. C. Hughes.

Joe Lohman was generous with his insights into urban life, and the significance of the police therein. He taught me the importance of the police, provided the necessary contacts, pointed out important characteristics of the police, and showed me how to deal with them. Without his assistance and insights this study may well have been impossible.

To Professor Hughes and his understanding of the position of occupations in the social structure and their significance in the self-conception of the members, I owe my orientation in that direction. In addition, his sympathy and encouragement were an asset that is beyond value.

I should like to express my appreciation and thanks to the many unnamed policemen who gave of their time and experience, with a risk to their personal security, to acquaint me with the facts of police life.

Last, I want to thank my wife, whose patience and steadfast appreciation kept me going when things were at their worst.

1. Introduction

Purpose|**The Police as a Public Service Agency**
The police attitude toward the juvenile court;
the need of the police to guard against criticism;
the necessity for maintaining respect for police
authority in the community|**Law, Custom, and
Morality**|**Major Research Objectives**|**Method of
Research** Stages in the research; the choice of a
department|

Purpose

This is a study of a police department, of an occupation, and of the relationship between law, custom, and morality.

Its purpose is the analysis of an institution of great public interest which occupies an increasingly significant position in society, and about which there is surprisingly little information. An analysis of the police in terms of the nature of their job, the way in which they are organized and function, the kinds of men they employ, and their ideology should prove of service.

As a study of an occupation it but adds to an already significant quantity of research in this area. Here the study places its emphasis on the occupationally derived definitions of self, society, and conduct; endeavoring at once to describe and explain the job, the organization, the man, and his actions.

As a study of law, custom, and morality, we are interested in the impact of occupational customs on law enforcement and individual morality. Here our purpose is to indicate the genesis of and describe the norms that the police develop; to demonstrate how these norms function to distort and diminish the force of law enforcement; and to describe the process by which they are internalized and come to constitute a morality.

The Police as a Public Service Agency

The police herein described are the municipal police,[1] a unit in the executive branch of the municipality whose traditional functions have been to enforce the law, to maintain public order, and to protect the community. The municipal police, as such, are a new group, the product of a need for more formalized social controls arising out of the development of the large, anonymous, heterogeneous, urban populations resulting from the industrial revolution. Vollmer, Byrnes, and Fosdick have traced this development to the early part of the nineteenth century in England, notably the establishment by Robert Peel of a metropolitan police force in London in 1829.[2] In the United States the same general

[1] The police function, as such, is that of law enforcement; therefore, any body of men, so constituted by a government, may be called a police force. Many units within the United States maintain police forces, including counties, states, and special branches of the state and federal governments, such as the state liquor control agents, the Federal Bureau of Investigation, the Treasury Agents.

[2] Asher Byrnes (1946): ". . . after 1750 . . . the growing number of landless people made the watch and ward system impossible, and

type of development occurred 15 years later. Fosdick (1920, pp. 61–66) states:

As the nineteenth century progressed and urban populations grew in density the inadequacy of the night watch grew increasingly apparent. The character of its personnel and its organization by wards and districts, each more or less independent of the other, prevented its adaptation to the growing needs of the time. . . . New York took the first practical step to remedy the situation. In 1844 the legislature passed a law creating a day and night police which formed the basis of modern police organization in Amercia.

In the succeeding years most of the major cities in the United States followed suit, and the growth of individual police forces was quite rapid. In those early days the police constituted an organization in name only, for the

department reports of the time indicate a condition of utter lawlessness on the part of the police themselves. Assaulting superior officers, refusing to go on patrol, releasing prisoners from the custody of other policemen, drunkenness, extorting money from prisoners — these were the offenses of daily occurrence committed with impunity under the protection of a political overlord. [Fosdick, 1920, p. 69.]

The *New York Tribune* of that period wrote:

We all know that at present the police seem powerless for good; and that bold and dangerous criminals were never so bold and dangerous; and life and property were never so insecure; that gambling and prostitution and illegal trade were never so open and shameless; that public sentiment of danger from violence was never so acute, nor with so much reason. And why is it? Because the policemen are politicians, getting the places as reward for political service; because they dare not or will not offend the fellows who have fought shoulder to shoulder with them at the polls.[3]

With the passing of the years the organization and discipline of the police improved, and many attempts were made to isolate the police from contacts with the political organizations of the city. However, politics has seldom been severed from the operations of police departments even to this day. Thus, a study of the Chicago police made in 1930 states:

The police force really consists of two distinct sets of hierarchies,

---

beginning with the Stipendary Magistrates Act of 1792 the development of a professional police force was under way."

See also Raymond B. Fosdick (1922) and August Vollmer (1936).

[3] *New York Tribune,* February 5, 1857. Quoted in Fosdick (1920), p. 81.

the one official and the other political. The official hierarchy is clear cut and easily understood. . . . When we turn to the political hierarchy within the Police Department an entirely different situation is presented. Individual patrolmen and sergeants sometimes assume an importance out of proportion to their ranks. An occasional deputy commissioner will, to all intents and purposes, assume the prerogatives of the commissioner, and captains will run their districts as though these were separate corporate entities, with the local political leaders playing the role of political mayors. [The Citizens Police Committee, 1931, pp. 42–43.]

That this situation is not peculiar to Chicago is demonstrated in the recurrent pleas of such prominent police administrators and efficiency experts as August Vollmer (1936) and Bruce Smith (1949) that politics be removed from the police.

Originating as a kind of guard detail, with a responsibility for the enforcement of the law and the maintenance of public order, the duties of the police have proliferated over the years, and today the police have increasingly become a major municipal service organization, used by the community to fill in the lacunae between the controls embodied in the law and those maintained on a primary level. They have become a chief regulator of human conduct in the great metropolitan areas. This is evidenced by their intrusion into relatively private matters such as disputes between husband and wife, and their obviously important positions in the relationship between antithetical groups such as Negroes and whites.

The police have been endowed with powers legitimately possessed by no other group in urban areas. Notably, they are the portion of the state apparatus that maintains a monopoly on the legitimate means of violence. Misuse of this power has occasioned protracted and virulent criticisms of the police by the press, by many groups, and by private persons. These criticisms have been directed at the so-called third degree and other forms of brutality, inefficiency, and graft. An extensive critical survey of the police in the United States was that made by Hopkins (1931), whose book is stated to be a study of the unlawful enforcement of the law.[4] Various state committees have documented the extent of police graft — notably, the investigations of the

[4] Although Hopkins' reports appear to be reasonable and accurate, he gives no documentation for his points and it is therefore impossible to evaluate his material.

Seabury Commission of the New York State Legislature (1932) and those of the Kefauver Committee. Thus, one patrolman in New York City who was interrogated by the members of the Seabury Commission because of his large bank account ($99,000) stated that the "cop" such as himself got only "the crumbs from the table." The news value of police activities and corruption is very high. Thus, there is a considerable volume of material on these aspects of the police in the metropolitan press throughout the nation.

The involvement of the police with graft, brutality, and politics has led to many attempts at reform, such as the attempted reorganization of the Chicago Police Department in the 1930's, following the investigations of the Citizens Police Committee. The most thorough surveys of the police in the United States appeared in a volume called *Report on the Police* by the U.S. National Committee on Law Observance and Enforcement (1931). but its emphasis was on police organization and on law enforcement, and it generally dodged political, psychological, and sociological questions — an evasion, incidentally, which we feel has been a fundamental error. The extent of the error is indicated by a statement made by Vollmer in his section of this report (p. 48):

Eradication of disgruntled agitators, incompetent policemen, police crooks, and grafters, takes much time since it is next to impossible to induce police officers to inform on each other. It is an unwritten law in police departments that police officers must never testify against their brother officer. Viewing it from the inside, it is soon found that as a general rule policemen believe that the average citizen is opposed to them and that they must fight their battles together against the common enemy.

This statement raises basic questions about police organization, customs, and morality, the answers to which are prerequisite to an intelligent conception of the real functions of the police and effective reorganization. Yet most writers have evaded these questions. Thus, works by Vollmer (1936), Smith (1949), Fosdick (1920, 1922), Woods (1919), and others, are directed toward providing information as to the history, formal organization, and duties of the police, coupled with suggestions for improvement, and provide little in the way of information concerning their social characteristics, personal attitudes, and community function.

The police play a significant part in criminal behavior and have an important position in race relations, but they have largely been neglected in the sociological literature. Only two studies have come to the attention of the author which deal with the police at all extensively. The first, Whyte's *Street Corner Society* (1943), describes the activities of the police in Cornerville and provides suggestive hypotheses as to the function of the police in the urban community. His description of the position and function of the police, although undocumented, suggests some important characteristics of the occupation. He states (p. 136):

There are prevalent in society two general conceptions of the duty of the police officer. Middle class people feel that he should enforce the law without fear or favor. Cornerville people and many of the officers themselves believe that the policeman should have the confidence of the people in his area so that he can settle many difficulties in a personal manner without making arrests. These two conceptions are in a large measure contradictory. The policeman who takes a strictly legalistic view of his duties cuts himself off from personal relations necessary to enable him to serve as a mediator of disputes in his area. The policeman who develops close ties with local people is unable to act against them with the vigor prescribed by the law.

This statement undoubtedly refers to the problems of the man on the beat, not the man in the patrol car, but it suggests that the social position of the police gives to them an inherent conflict in motivation. This conflict is more sharply defined in another statement (p. 138):

Observation of the situation in Cornerville indicates that the primary function of the police department is not the enforcement of the law but the regulation of illegal activities. The policeman is subject to sharply conflicting social pressures. On one side are the "good people" of Eastern City, who have written their moral judgements into the law and demand through their newspapers that the law be enforced. On the other side are the people of Cornerville, who have different standards and who have built up an organization, whose perpetuation depends upon freedom to violate the law. Socially, the local officer has more in common with Cornerville people than with those who demand law enforcement; and the financial incentives offered by the racketeers have an influence which is of obvious importance. . . . He [the policeman] must play an elaborate role of make believe, and in doing so he serves as a buffer between divergent social organizations with their conflicting standards of conduct.

Here it is obvious that Whyte believes that the police are integrated with the people of Cornerville in terms of their sympathies and finances, that their primary function is in contradiction to their legal assignment, and that to be a policeman is to be a marginal man.

The only other sociological study of the police is the study by Goldman (1950) of police selection of juvenile offenders in Pittsburgh and environs.

In an effort to explain the differential selection by the police of juvenile offenders for court appearance, Goldman interviewed a large number of policemen in Pittsburgh and surrounding communities. He cites the following attitudes as being significant in terms of the action orientations:

1. The Police Attitude Toward the Juvenile Court. Here he found that "one third of the men interviewed used Juvenile Court referrals only as a last resort, and that the remaining two-thirds had no strong opinions on the matter"; also, that a frequent reason for this was that "the reference of a juvenile offender to court would result in an official record which would interfere in the future with the boy's possibilities of obtaining employment or enlisting in the armed services" (p. 138). As such there is no reason to believe that this attitude in any respect represents an occupationally derived orientation. However, he comments at another point that 43 percent of the men felt that the court was too lenient and that "twenty per cent felt there was no value in sending the boys to the court, because they were immediately released by the intake staff or at best may be removed from the community for a few months" (p. 140). This would suggest that for the police, their experience led them to believe that the juvenile courts did not uphold the law; this might represent an occupationally engendered disrespect for this type of body. However, the percentage is too small to be conclusive.

2. The Need of the Police to Guard Against Criticism. Here he states that "there is a feeling among the police that they must 'cover' or protect themselves against criticism. . . . They feel that they must guard themselves against unfavorable newspaper criticism and censure by the public" (p. 142). He then goes on to point out how the sensitivity of the police to criticism affects their actions with respect to the juvenile offender.

Although Goldman offers no information as to how widespread this feeling is among the police, the fact that he raises the point suggests that he found it prevalent. It would appear, therefore, that there is something about the occupation, something engendering guilt perhaps, that is responsible for the attitude.

3. The Necessity for Maintaining Respect for Police Authority in the Community. In this connection he states (p. 145):

The police officer is concerned with the proper recognition of his authority. An assault on his self-esteem will lead quickly to punitive action. *Almost all* police officials agree that "defiance on the part of a boy will lead to juvenile court quicker than anything else." Such damage to the dignity of the police will lead to court referral even in a minor case.

This suggests very strongly that there is something about the occupation and the social position of the police that engenders a feeling on the policeman's part that no one respects his authority and that he has to *maintain* such respect.

It would appear from Whyte's and Goldman's studies that the police, as an occupational group, find themselves in a marginal and conflicting position in the community, that they tend to sympathize with the underprivileged and criminal, that they are extremely sensitive to public criticism and feel a strong need to "cover" themselves and to force people to respect them. Neither study documents these points to the extent to which they claim them as general characteristics of the cases observed, and they remain as hypotheses to be tested. However, they amplify Vollmer's suggestive remarks about the internal dynamics of police action and together they clearly indicate that an understanding of the police requires an analysis of them as a social and occupational group. Their characterizations stress this need and support our contention that such a study is prerequisite to intelligent reorganization of this important public service agency. Since the attitudes and action orientations of the police seem related to their occupational position, the need for studying them in these terms is suggested. The consideration of this problem follows.

Law, Custom, and Morality

The structure of controls that regulates the conduct of the members of a society or social group was visualized by Simmel (1950) as occurring on three levels: the societal, as embodied in the law; the group, as embodied in custom; and the individual, as embodied in conscience or morality. He saw these three levels of social control as being necessarily related. His discussion raises the questions of what groups function significantly in social control, and what the relationship is between the controls embodied in these groups and the law or controls of the larger society. Finally, like Mead (1947)[5] he pointed out that controls only reached true effectiveness when they became embodied in a morality; that is, when they became internalized by the individual and made a part of himself. The preceding section has suggested that occupations and professions, that is, work groups, constitute some of the most important groups in modern society. Hughes (1951) has stated that "a man's work is one of the more important parts of his social identity — his self."

If this is true, the occupations become centers of group controls. Blumer (1947) and Lohman[6] have suggested that interest groups and occupations certainly fall into this category and are among the most important vehicles of collective action in our society; participation in such interest groups structures the attitudes and self-conceptions of the members. Reitzes (1950) has documented this point in his study of racial attitudes of white workers, when he points out how their attitudes change as the interest basis of participation changes. Durkheim (1947, pp. 1–31) long ago suggested that occupations constitute one of the most important vehicles for collective action in modern society. Mannheim (1938) has stated that small groups, in terms of the interests they represent, are the primary points of orientation and control for the individual.[7]

[5] In terms of Mead's theory, conduct results from the personal interpretation of stimuli, rather than the stimuli itself; and this interpretation is related to the generalized other, or social perspective, from which the person views himself and his situation. The content of this perspective may be said to consist of the system of shared meanings that the individual participates in as a result of his membership in a social group. In our case we would maintain that the policeman as a member of a self-conscious occupation participates in such a system of shared meanings and that the law, departmental directives, and actions of the population are interpreted in terms of such meanings.

[6] Joseph D. Lohman, personal conversations.

[7] Mannheim (1938), pp. 69–70: "Our contemporary world is one . . . in which individuals . . . are compelled to renounce their private interests and subordinate themselves to the interests of the larger social units. . . . Today the individual thinks not in terms of the welfare of the community or mankind as a whole, but in terms of that of his own particular group."

In these terms occupational groups assume a strategic position in the analysis of social control in modern industrialized society. The police constitute such an occupational group and are therefore a suitable unit for the analysis and testing of these ideas. In addition, the police have a unique relationship to the law, or formal social controls, and their study therefore affords an opportunity to study the relationship between these formal control and group customs.

Our thesis is that the customs of the police as an occupational group give rise to a distortion of statutory law, so that the law in force, as it affects the people of the community, can be said to arise in part from the customs of the police. The nature and genesis of the law in force and its relationship to statutory law are questions of great significance in a society that increasingly comes to depend on formalized social controls. There are strong suggestions that this tendency characterizes modern society. Weber (1927; 1946, pp. 338–351) in his emphasis on the increasing rationalization of society and what he has called "the disenchantment of the world," and Mannheim (1938), in his analysis of the trend toward the planned social organization,[8] call attention to this increased dependence on formalized controls. Sutherland and Gehlke (1931), in their analysis of trends in criminal legislation in the United States, state:

The number of criminal laws has increased at an average rate of one to two per cent a year. This increase is approximately the same as the rate of increase on non-criminal laws and of the regulations of private association and appears to express a fundamental attitude in modern society. [p. 1122]

This, then, would represent a concrete and localized substantiation of theories emphasizing the increase in formal social controls.

The position of the police with respect to this structure of formalized social controls — the law — is that of the enforcement agent. However, the police as an occupational group may possess group customs and a system of morality; because of the significance of the occupation in the life of the person, these rules

[8] See his discussion of "functional rationality and functional irrationality." The latter we believe to be endemic to the use of social groups in an instrumental capacity.

should be internalized and come to constitute a part of his morality. Therefore, the significance in studying the police with respect to the relationship between law, custom, and morality, lies in the analysis of the impact of the customs they develop and the occupational morality of the men, or the way in which they enforce the law.

Major Research Objectives

In terms of the preceding discussion, the major objectives of this study can now be stated. They are as follows:

1. To isolate and identify the major social norms governing police conduct, and to describe the way in which they influence police action in specific situations.

2. To obtain an "interpretative understanding" of the relationship between these social norms and the occupation experience of the policeman.

3. To obtain an "interpretative understanding" of the relationship between these norms and the morality of the policeman, through a description of the process by which they are internalized.

4. To analyze the effects of these norms upon law enforcement.

Method of Research

The major methodological orientation of this study has been to make a case study of a small police department through observation and intensive interviewing. The decision to embark on the study in this manner was made with a full awareness of the value of a comparative approach. However, certain important considerations made this impossible:

1. The almost complete absence of substantive materials or previous research on the police made an intensive study imperative. This was necessary to the isolation of the major areas in the occupational experience of the police, which would permit the formulation of adequate hypotheses.

2. The difficulties in obtaining access to the police are immense. The importance of secrecy among the police and their sensitivity to public criticism make them very reluctant to cooperate with anyone. The political entanglements and possible graft involvements of the police make it dangerous for them to have a stranger in their midst. Access to the police is therefore only made with

the reluctant permission of the chief of police, and exceedingly great care must be taken in interviewing the men. The time consumed in just getting to the data is enormous.

3. The case study of one police department offered the advantages of a careful examination of the relationship between all aspects of police work and an interview sample of sufficient proportions so that by chance alone it would include men who would be willing to tell secrets.

Stages in the Research. The research proceeded in three general stages and covered a period of one year, beginning with the autumn of 1949. The first stage consisted of intensive but unorganized interviewing of men in the Chicago police department, with the idea of getting "an acquaintance with" [9] the police. The interviews were with police captains, ex-police captains, and chiefs, sergeants, lieutenants, and patrolmen in both the municipal and park police forces. Contacts with individual men ranged in time from one hour to thirty hours, the longer ones naturally involving several interviews. The data from these interviews have not been used in this dissertation since they were made only with the idea of getting "an acquaintance with" the police that would permit the isolation of significant problems. In addition, this preliminary survey gave to the study a comparative perspective and materially assisted in identifying those elements in police work which would be considered generic to the occupation, rather than the product of specific local conditions.

Stage two consisted of the observation of operations in the department selected for study. The researcher spent time with men on every different job in the police department and often included the observation of one or several full work shifts. The following aspects of the department were observed: the chief of police; the captain of detectives; the captain of patrol; the recruit school (two sessions); the traffic bureau; the desk sergeant and communications men; the detective bureau, including several sessions in the bureau itself and presence on interrogations, raids, and general patrol work; and the patrol division, where the observer spent several full shifts with different patrol cars and the

---

[9] Herbert Blumer (1947) has suggested this as a necessary prerequisite of the isolation of the significant characteristics of any aspect of social life. This becomes particularly important in areas about which previous information is not available.

men on the beat. This stage provided the opportunity to observe the police at work, to interrogate many different men on the job, and to obtain explanations of how and why they did particular things. This period lasted four months, and a detailed picture of the department in terms of its organization, its position in the community, its operations, and its personnel was obtained. "Acquaintance with" police work deepened, and the significant aspects of the operation were isolated. Invaluable contacts were established.

The third stage, which covered a period of six months, consisted of the systematic interviewing of a large and representative sample of the men in the department and the continued observation of the department, mostly to check on new data that appeared in the interviews.

The Choice of a Department. During the first stage of the research it became apparent that large metropolitan police forces were so complex and dispersed and so entangled in graft and politics that it would be impossible to study even one of them completely with the time and finances available to us. In addition, graft and politics seemed such formidable considerations in the behavior of the men that it would be difficult to isolate the characteristics that could be attributed to the occupation as such. Therefore, the decision was made to make a case study of a small police department in which these nonoccupational factors had a less important influence.

Three factors determined the choice of the department to be studied:

1. The department had to be one to which the researcher had geographical and social access. That is, it had to be within traveling distance, and the permission of the chief of police had to be obtained.

2. The department had to be small enough to permit intensive observation of all operations and interrelations and the interviewing of a large proportion of the men; yet it had to be large enough to resemble, in rough outline, the organization of any metropolitan police force. That is, it had to be one in which specialized divisions were established and the usual specialized jobs were carried on.

3. The department had to be located in a city that provided

major problems of police work. We felt these to be a large volume of traffic, race relations problems arising from a large Negro population, organized political machines and the consequent political pressures, a large slum or disorganized area that would give rise to basic problems in the maintenance of order, and the control of vice, gambling, and major crimes.

Access to such a department was obtained through the mediation of Mr. Joseph D. Lohman. The author accompanied Mr. Lohman when he gave a series of lectures to this department on minority-group relations and thus came into contact with the chief of police. The contact eventually resulted in permission to observe all the operations of the department and interview all the men.

The department chosen was small enough to study intensively since it contained only 194 men; yet within the department were many specialized divisions, including traffic, patrol, detectives, training, records, and communications, within which there was further specialization. The bulk of the men in the department had been appointed under civil service regulations and were thus relatively free from political influence. The department was located in an industrial city of 140,000 persons which had a very large slum area, a large Negro population with a history of friction with the white population, a high crime rate, an organized political machine, and extensive vice and gambling. The city was intersected by three arterial highways and had severe traffic problems as a result.[10]

[10] Information on sample and data collection can be found in Appendix A.

2. Within the Department

Responsibilities of the Police Police duties in general; duties Department X; the "dirty work" | **The Community Background** Social statistics; history; political organization; organization of the department | **The Chief of Police** Informal responsibilities; formal authority; limitations of authority; informal source of authority; summary | **Operations of the Police Department** Routine activities; action channels | **The Records and Communication Division** | **The Training Division** | **The Traffic Division** | **The Patrol Division** The beat; the patrol cars | **The Detective Division** Location; assignment of cases; nonpolice contacts; differences between the "dicks" and the patrolmen; the detective's routine of work; competition and jealousy; preferences in assignment; stool pigeons and informants; summary | **Interrelationships of the Divisions** | **Personnel** The choice of the occupation; the selection of the members by the occupation | **Police Work As a Way of Life** | **Summary** |

Men work and live within the frames of organization — that is, of law and norms and morality — but they shape and bend these to their needs. People make up this organization, and their expectations and demands are the voice of its morality.

For the policeman, this organization is the department and the community, and the people consist of colleagues and the public, and they have that order of importance. So we begin with a description of the department, asking first: What are its functions?

Responsibilities of the Police

The exact function of the police within a city is difficult to delineate, ranging as it does from the formal assignment of duties and responsibilities with respect to law enforcement and the maintenance of order to its frequent informal control of the illegal structure of the town, and its adjudication of the differences between section and class moralities. This not only differs from department to department depending on the city in which they are located, but also changes with the perspective in which it is described. Thus, Whyte (1943, p. 138) has described the police of *Street Corner Society* as exercising a careful control over the illegal gambling operations in the town by supporting certain groups and "cracking down" on others; and again he has stated that the police function as a buffer between the values of the middle class and the values of the slum. Lohman has pointed out that the police function to support and enforce the interests of the dominant political, social, and economic interest of the town, and only incidentally to enforce the law.[1] Subsequently, we shall demonstrate that the value structure of the police strongly supports this viewpoint. Otherwise, our material does not permit a testing of this hypothesis for reasons that were stated in Chapter 1. However, even in the formal duties of the police one can obtain considerable understanding of their position and function in society. These formal duties are an intrinsic part of their everyday routine, and without them society would be seriously incapacitated.

Police Duties in General. August Vollmer (1936), a leading police administrator, states that in addition to their better known re-

[1] Lohman, personal conversations.

sponsibilities with respect to the prevention of major crimes and the control of vice and traffic, the duties of the police include:

. . . the enforcement of federal law violations that may come to the attention of the municipal police; all state laws, felonies and misdemeanors that are not included under the classification of major crimes; and the multitudinous city ordinances that cover every variety of subject imaginable; search for missing persons and the restoration to their families of children found or of adults who have wandered away from their homes, the search for lost property or animals, and the delivery of these to the rightful owners.

Besides the foregoing duties, the police are required to take possession of dead bodies found, and to conduct inquiries to ascertain the cause of death. Investigations of this kind must be conducted with extreme care because what appears to be a natural death may later prove to be a murder. Sick and injured persons receive first aid from trained policemen and in many cities these persons are conveyed either to their homes or to hospitals in police ambulances. The police are also responsible for collecting information to be presented at coroners' inquests in suicide cases, and for caring for persons who have attempted without success to end their lives. Handling the insane and feeble minded, and providing for their immediate care or ultimate commitment to an institution, is another form of general police service to which the public gives little thought, but which consumes much of the police officers' time . . . they must take care of riots incident to strikes, subversive activities, or racial disagreements. They must inspect business places which are required to be licensed and investigate conditions incident to the health of the community.

However, even this list is incomplete, for it says nothing of the amount of time the police act as public information bureau, of their attempts to settle family disputes, of the extensive guard duty that they perform in the nightly checking of doors and windows and the inspection of the homes of people away on vacation. Each city will have its additions to Vollmer's list, for each city finds in the police a group who can be assigned that which no other groups can perform.

Duties, Department X. To substantiate Vollmer's material, we quote at length from the Police Handbook given to all policemen in our City X. In this book, a quotation from the law of the state appears as follows:

Section 48–6110. DUTIES OF POLICE FORCE. It is hereby made the duty of such police force, and the members thereof are specially empowered at all times, within such city, to preserve peace; prevent crime; detect and arrest offenders; suppress riots, mobs and insurrections; disperse unlawful and dangerous assemblages, and assemblages which obstruct the free passage of public streets, sidewalks, parks and places; protect the rights of persons and property; guard the public health; preserve order at elections and meetings; direct the movement of teams and vehicles in streets, alleys or public places; remove all nuisances in public streets, parks or highways; arrest all street beggars and vagrants; provide proper police assistance at fires; assist, advise and protect strangers and travelers in public streets or at railroad stations; carefully observe and inspect all places of business under license, or required to have the same, all houses of ill fame or prostitution and houses where common prostitutes resort or reside, all lottery or policy shops, all gambling-houses, cockpits, dance houses and resorts; and to suppress and restrain all unlawful or disorderly conduct or practices and enforce and prevent the violation of all ordinances and laws in effect in such city. The chief of police and each captain, in his precinct, shall possess the power of supervision and inspection over all pawnbrokers, vendors, junkshop keepers, cartmen, expressmen, dealers in second-hand merchandise, intelligence offices and auctions; and any members of such force may be authorized, in writing by the chief, to exercise the same powers. Such chief or captain may, by written authority, empower any member of such police force, when in search of stolen property, of evidence, or of suspected offenders, to examine the books, business or premises of any of the persons named in this section and to examine property in whosesoever possession the same shall be. (Acts 1905, ch. 129, No. 164, p. 219.)

It can be seen from these accounts of the duties of the police that the service functions of the police constitute an important part of their responsibility and the major part of their time. This is not in accordance with the popular conception of the police as a crime prevention and criminal apprehension unit. Such activities are in large measure the job of the detective bureau, as will be delineated later, and form only a relatively small portion of the patrolman's activities. This is in itself a characterization of the police function, for by any measure the patrol and traffic divisions include the bulk of the personnel in any police department. In Department X the detective bureau contains about 30 men, while the patrol and traffic bureaus contain approximately 160 men.

The "Dirty Work." Second, the listings reveal that much of the policeman's job consists of "dirty work." It consists of dealing with drunks, with the insane, with the dead, with the vice-ridden, with the ill. It is a necessary function in any modern community, but an exceedingly unpleasant and in some sense degrading one.

The police, then, can be said to have, in addition to their obvious responsibilities with respect to law enforcement, a tremendous number of service duties, which in themselves constitute an important and essential part of their function in the ongoing life of the community. In an emergency of almost any type — of human relations, of health, of nature — the police are among the first to be called in, and generally people expect them to do something about it. In one sense they can be said to fill in the lacunae between the existent formal control embodied in the law and the agencies of the community and the rapidly breaking down formal controls related to change and transition in society.

The Community Background

A police department is intimately related to the community in which it is located and in which it serves. The personnel of the department are drawn from the community and have a personal involvement in the life and values of the community. The men on the job are responsible to the public definitions of behavior. The nature of the community determines many of the problems that the police department must meet. The political structure of the community may have an important influence on the actions of the department and the areas of law enforcement that it emphasizes. Therefore, it is important that a description of the community should preface one of the department itself.

Social Statistics. Police Department X serves an industrial community with a population of approximately 140,000 persons.[2] The city covers 42 square miles and is located within commuting distance of a major metropolis. During the past 40 years it has expanded at an extremely rapid pace, rising from fewer than 20,000 persons in 1910 to approximately 140,000 in 1950. This rapid growth and its industrial nature have resulted in a large slum area in the center of town, a great mass of unattached workers, and a relative state of disorganization in the city. These characteristics raise problems for the police, since they are fertile ground for machine politics, organized vice and gambling, and juvenile delinquency.

[2] Based on the annual school census taken in that city.

The population in 1940 included a large proportion of foreign-born and Negroes. The labor force at this time amounted to more than 40,000 persons employed, of which more than 60 percent were manual laborers in the steel mills. Median rentals in the city were approximately $30.00 per month, and the median number of years of education completed was about eight years.

History. During its history the city has enjoyed considerable notoriety as a center of vice and gambling and has regularly had one of the highest crime rates in the nation. Politics in the city has always been rough and tumble, and even in recent years votes have been openly bought and sold. Attempts at reform have been made periodically, but the reform governments seldom have enjoyed any real tenure in office. During the periods of reform, and at times when the party in power has changed, there has been a considerable shake-up in the police department, with wholesale appointments and discharges. During those times the police department was at the mercy of political whim, and almost all the men in the department were involved in politics. The advent in 1939 of a strong civil service law applying to the police put an end to the mass changes in personnel, and to the involvement of most of the men in politics. It did not, however, entirely remove politics from the department, since the office of the chief remained a political appointment directly under the control of the mayor, and the chief had sufficient power to swing the department's actions in any direction the political boss desired. For these reasons the police in City X have been and will be closely linked to the political organization.

Over the course of the years, political battles in City X have generally been concerned with the lucrative control over the city's gambling. City officials sometimes get so immersed in the gambling interests and do it so flagrantly that they arouse the citizenry and suffer imprisonment. A number of years back, a good part of the city's administration, including the mayor, was convicted and sent to prison. When the mayor was released from prison he again ran for office on the basis that he wanted to clear the name of his family, and he was reelected. Such was the tenor of public opinion. During the period when the study was being made, the city was again in the throes of an approaching

reform government, and a major reform body had been organized.
Political Organization. In terms of political organization, City X
is an integral part of the county. On the one hand, the county and
the city have overlapping jurisdictions for many public agencies;
on the other hand, the respective party organizations are to a
large measure organized on a county basis. This has important
consequences for the law enforcement agencies, for even within
the city both the county and city elections have an influence on
the legal structure. Thus, the judge of the criminal court and the
county prosecutor are elected on a county basis, while the mayor,
who appoints the chief of police, and the judge of the police
court are elected on a city-wide basis. The implications of this
type of structure are that one party may control half the law
enforcement apparatus and another party the other half. Thus,
the chief and the city judge may be under the control of the
Democratic party, and the county prosecutor may be under the
control of the Republican party. If the Republicans want a strict
enforcement of the law and the Democrats do not, the Democrats
can, through their control of the police force and the city judge,
effectively block law enforcement, and vice versa. Again, if one
party controls all the law enforcement bodies, it can take the
pressure off each from time to time by putting the favors in the
hands of the others. Both these conditions appear from time to
time in that area. During the period when the study was under
way, one party controlled the entire law enforcement apparatus.
Most political favors and protection were extended through the
courts and the prosecutor's office, especially since the police were
under attack for the widespread vice and gambling in town. In
this situation, the pressure was taken off the police and they were
able to make a limited attempt to close up the town; the attempt, in turn, was thwarted by the courts and the prosecutor.

This, then, constitutes the community background in terms of
which Department X operates. The city, basically a working
people's community composed of many ethnic groups and having
a large Negro population, containing a huge slum area, supporting a small army of unattached and frequently unemployed
workers, experiencing tremendous expansion in the past 40 years,
has many of the characteristics of a boom or frontier town.

Organization of the Department. Police Department X may be considered a partial bureaucracy, for in many ways it possesses the characteristics that Max Weber attributed to that form of social organization. Basically, it is a military organization. All power flows from the top of the organization pyramid, and is concentrated in the hands of the chief of police. He, if he so chooses, can then assign responsibilities to the captains of the various divisions, but he can also bypass them if he chooses. However, the outlines of the formal organization divide the responsibilities into five various divisions, each headed by a captain of police. Most of these captains have, in turn, three sergeants who exert direct control over the men on the job. As we have stated, insofar as this administrative structure is not bypassed by the chief, it is a perfect example of the administrative pyramid that characterizes the bureaucracy. In addition, the bulk of the men are appointed, at least in theory, under a system of impartial competitive examinations that determine their relative competence. This is the civil service system. Again, insofar as this system functions, bureaucratic tendencies are apparent. In large measure it does function, although there are apparent divergencies, as we shall subsequently outline. We shall deal with the main offices one by one. Chart 1.1 presents the rough outlines of the organization.

The Chief of Police

The Chief of Police shall be the head of the Police Department at all times but subject to the orders of the Mayor. He shall have the power to suspend any member of the Department for violation of any of the rules and regulations of the Department subject however to the rules of the Civil Service Commission; he must immediately make report of his action to the Civil Service Commission for its approval and subsequent action. He shall have the

Chart 2.1. Organization of Police Deparment X

Mayor				Civil Service Commission
Chief of Police				
Captain, Records and Communication	Captain, Training	Captain, Patrol	Captain, Detective Bureau	Captain, Traffic
3 Sergeants		3 Sergeants, 144 Men	3 Sergeants, 30 Men	2 Sergeants, 16 Men

complete power to control and direct the entire membership of the Department so as to effect honest, efficient and faithful service in the performance of its duties and in the enforcement of all federal, state and local laws.[3]

Informal Responsibilities. The chief is the one political appointee in the department. He is appointed by the mayor of the city and is directly responsible to the mayor and to the Civil Service Commission. The nature of his appointment gives to the chief his basic, though not formal, function in the department. He is expected to function as the departmental public relations man, and to keep the department under control for the political organization to which he is responsible, no matter what their ends. In addition, of course, he is held responsible for the organization of the department, the coordination of all activities, the training of men, and so forth. These consume only a portion of his time and are of little consequence, provided that he stays within the bounds of reason and exercises his other functions well. These functions include a host of detailed activities, among which are the placating of indignant citizens, the fixing of traffic tickets, and the doing of favors for people with influence, such as assigning patrolmen to meetings, prompting the detective bureau to work especially hard on a particular case, and so forth.

In his capacity as a member of the controlling political organization, the chief is required to keep the men in the department in line with the policies of that organization. To do this adequately, he must maintain a group of favorites within the department whom he can depend on to handle delicate assignments. He rewards these favorites by using his influence to see that they obtain the most desirable jobs in the department. They, in turn, keep him informed of any signs of deviation from his policies on the part of the other men. He is constantly on the alert to discern his friends from his foes among the men on the force. On one occasion during the course of the study, a reform group was making a violent attack on the police department, particularly on the chief of police. During this period the chief was on the alert to see who among his men would give information to this reform group. Again, the chief must keep himself informed as to the political affiliations and power of the members of his force.

[3] From the Police Handbook, City X.

Men who prefer the opposing party may aspire to the office of chief come the next election and may be more than willing to provide the enemy with ammunition about the misdemeanors of the chief himself, such misdemeanors being inevitable because as a politician the chief must do favors for the party's constituents, and these favors usually involve some type of exemption from the law.

The result of this political orientation of the chief of police and his consequent need for special friends among the men in the department is to set up an informal organization and informal lines of authority. All the men in the department are conscious of this, although the lower ranks seldom have sufficient information to identify it. The informal organization is not without obstructions, however, since many of the men in positions of power within the department — captains and sergeants — are left over from previous administrations and in some cases are career policemen. Because of this, the chief must be extremely judicious in using his informal organization and must make concessions to the opposition. In Department X the chief has achieved a modus vivendi by trying to stick to the letter of the law and insisting that the department be run strictly according to the rules. The chief could afford to treat most of the patrolmen completely impartially and make them obey the letter of the law in their activities, since he has sufficient power over them to see that they stay in line on the broader questions of political policy. Thus, should his political superiors insist that prostitution and gambling in town be left alone, the chief can keep the patrolmen from interfering with these enterprises. He would merely let it be known that this was his desire and the men would obey.

Formal Authority. The power of the chief arises from the disciplinary rules of the department and his authority to suspend a man for the infraction of these rules. The rules are both manifold and picayune. The rules in Department X, as listed in the Police Handbook, are as follows:

Every member of the Police Department of the City shall be subject to reprimand, suspension, reduction in rank, deduction of pay or dismissal from the Police Department, according to the nature of the offense, for any of the following causes, or for violation of any of the rules, regulations or orders of the Department of Police of the City, now in force, or that may hereafter be issued, after having been given an opportunity to be heard in his or her defense before the Civil Service Commission according to law:

Disciplinary
Rule no.

1. Intoxication while on duty; intoxication while off duty in uniform or when armed.
2. Conduct unbecoming a police officer of the Police Department.
3. Immoral conduct.
4. Neglect of duty.
5. Violation of any criminal law.
6. Sleeping while on duty.
7. Incapacity or inefficiency in the service.
8. Disobedience of orders.
9. Disorderly conduct.
10. Leaving post before being properly relieved.
11. Leaving post or station or being absent from duty without permission.
12. Using coarse, profane or insolent language to a superior officer, to any member of the Department or to citizens.
13. Insubordination or disrespect toward a superior officer.
14. Neglecting to treat officers, members of the department or any other person courteously and respectfully at all times.
15. Wilful maltreatment of a prisoner or any other person.
16. Making false official reports, or making a false report to a superior officer in respect to his sickness or injury with intent of taking time off.
17. Neglecting to wear uniform while on duty.
18. Neglecting to appear neat and clean at all times in public.
19. Smoking in public in uniform while on duty.
20. Receiving bribes in money or other valuable articles.
21. Receiving or accepting any fee, reward or gift of any kind from any person arrested, or from any person in his behalf while in custody or after his discharge.
22. Publicly gossiping about a member of the Department concerning his personal character or conduct to the detriment of the Department.
23. Publicly criticizing the official action of a superior officer.
24. Communicating or giving out information to any person concerning the business of the Department to the detriment of the Department.
25. Communicating any information which may aid a person to escape arrest or to delay the apprehension of a criminal, or secure the removal of stolen goods, or destroying evidence.
26. Destroying evidence or aiding in any way in the removal or destruction of same.

27. Neglecting to pay a just indebtedness, incurred while in the service within a reasonable time. No member of the Department shall permit garnishment proceedings to be brought against him or her while in the employ of the City. In the event such member is lawfully garnisheed, he shall consider that he is in violation of this rule and charges may be preferred against him.

28. Neglecting to wear shield or other emblem of office in proper position.

29. Refusing to give number of shield or name when requested.

30. Neglecting to furnish persons arrested with a receipt for all property taken from them, except such property taken to be used as evidence.

31. Officers must not leave their post until relieved by the officers going on duty. They should give all information they have to the relieving officer on the beat regarding police matters.

32. Officers going on duty must be prompt in going directly to their beats after roll call.

33. Officers making their regular pulls must remain at the pull box for at least one minute with the door open so that the operator can call back if necessary.

34. No member of the Police Department shall communicate, except to such persons as directed by his superior officers, any information respecting orders he may have received or any regulations that may be made for the government of the Police Department.

35. He shall be present at the daily roll calls and attend at the station at the time appointed. If absent without leave, he shall be reported to the Chief of Police or superior officer.

36. He shall make a written report to his commanding officer of all buildings where any noisesome, dangerous or unwholesome trade is carried on, all nuisances and all other matters affecting the safety and convenience of the public or the interests of the City.

37. In case of drunkenness or other violation of the rules and regulations by any member of the police force making him unfit for duty, he shall be relieved from duty by the officer in charge and ordered to report to the Chief of Police or commanding officer.

38. No officer shall engage in pernicious political activity while a member of the Department.

39. Members of the police force must report their residence accurately to the Chief of Police and report all changes of residence and telephone numbers within 24 hours after its occurrence.

40. No member shall, either directly or indirectly, interest himself or interfere in any manner whatsoever in the employment or retainer of any attorney to aid in the defense of a person arrested or accused.

41. Each member of the police force shall devote his entire assigned time and attention to the business of the Department.

42. All property or money taken on suspicion of having been feloniously obtained, or of being the proceeds of crime, and all stolen or other property seized by the members of the police force shall be deposited with the Property Clerk. When the property room is closed, all property shall be turned over to the respective Turnkey on duty and relayed to the succeeding one, as the case may be. The day Turnkey shall turn over to the Property Clerk daily all property turned in as evidence or property to be held for safe keeping.

43. In all cases of suspension, the officer involved shall immediately surrender the police badge and all other property in his possession belonging to the Department to the officer in charge of the station, and a receipt shall be given therefor. Such property shall be delivered to the Chief of Police to be held by him pending disposition of the case.

44. Officers shall not, except with permission of their commanding officers, make arrests in their own quarrels.

45. Officers shall not enter places of amusement while on duty except for police purposes.

46. No officer shall make known any proposed movement of the force without permission of the commanding officer.

47. Officers shall not recommend attorneys, bondsmen, bail brokers or any particular firm or place of business to anyone. Officers shall not obtain attorneys or bondsmen for prisoners unless prisoners request that some particular attorney or bondsman be notified. Attorneys desiring to see a prisoner for whom they claim to be counsel shall be permitted to do so provided the prisoner desires such counsel.

No man in the police department obeys even a good portion of these rules all the time. Therefore, all the men in the department are susceptible to disciplinary action by the chief and are thus under his control in spite of the protection that civil service status gives them. The list is, in effect, an abridgment of the civil service status of the men.

Two points encompassed by the list are of particular significance: first, the presence of a multitude of essentially unenforceable rules such as that against smoking on duty, which keep the men on the force perpetually susceptible to disciplinary action, and therefore under control; second, the intrusion of the police department's control into the private lives of the men, as exemplified by the rule against incurring personal debts while in the service of the department. This represents the legal incorporation of the men into the group, and the elevation of the group over the men. It represents the conception of group ownership of the individual, which only appears in such units as the armed forces. It is amplified by another ruling, which does not appear in the list, that the policeman is on duty 24 hours a day, and is thus susceptible to call at any time. This is not an empty rule and is frequently used, the policeman being called for emergencies, for court appearance, for the whim of the chief, without compensation and without regard for his private interests or for his duty time. It is an effective mechanism for making police work a way of life rather than a job, the distinction being that a job is the sale of one's skills for a specific period of time each day. When one realizes that the policeman is effectively bound to the job by the lucrative pension he will receive at the end of 20 years' service, the degree to which his occupation dominates his life appears to be formidable indeed.

Naturally, the intrusion of the department into the private lives of the men is mediated by the men themselves; and the desk sergeant who is asked to call a man who is off duty into the station will frequently find that he has lost the man's telephone number, or that the man is out of the house. However, in spite of this, the men spend a lot more time on duty than they enjoy during their off-duty hours.

Limitations of Authority. The chief thus has sufficient power to keep the patrolmen in line with the major policies to which he is politically committed. He can keep them out of the gambling places and out of the brothels; he can make them ease up on traffic offenses; he can make them leave the after-hours tavern alone. He cannot, however, make them do particular favors for him. For example, he cannot make them release a prisoner because he has a commitment to the prisoner. He cannot make them work for his political party during the times of election. He can make them work along party lines, but he must exert care not to give them a hold over him. The formal powers of the chief are effective only as long as he prevents the men from getting a hold on him, by having him in their debt for particular services or by obtaining information about his activities that would do him harm. This does not mean that some chiefs do not break this rule; but when they do, they lose a great deal of control over the men.

In addition, the chief has a real stake in making the men stay within the bounds of the law, because then he is able to point to the department with pride before other chiefs and before the public. It is frequently to his interest to keep his department up to date, well trained, well disciplined, and well equipped. This makes a pleasant impression on the public and leaves him free to fulfill his own political commitments. These are the lines of authority of the chief of police. He can use them for whatever ends he chooses. They imply no particular corruption in the department activities, or in the actions of the chief, but they do permit such corruption, and are thus frequently misused.

Informal Source of Authority. The ignorance of the patrolmen as to the affairs of the chief does not characterize the other members of the department — the detectives, the sergeants, and the captains. In order to maintain his authority in this area, the chief is forced to keep his friends in the most important positions. That is, he is forced to tie up the key positions within the department through a series of favors and privileges that keep the men in the key positions under obligation to him. He must place other men of particular prestige or political power in positions where they are innocuous. For this purpose the records and training divisions are favorite areas to which recalcitrant or threatening captains and sergeants can be assigned. These divisions are in large measure cut off from the primary operations of the department.

To accomplish this control over the more powerful members of the department the chief must be able to control both assignment and promotions of the men. This he is permitted to do under civil service regulations. Assignments are at his discretion, and he has a strong voice in the promotions because the examination scores constitute only a part of the final grades of the contenders; the chief's recommendations also are an important part. However, in this he is somewhat limited by the fact that many of the men in the higher ranks are bound to have achieved that rank before he took office, and he can deal with these men only by giving them the type of assignment we have just mentioned. The result is that the department tends to follow a political alignment. The higher the ranks and the closer the men are to the operations of the chief, the more likely the incumbents are to be followers and friends of the chief, and therefore of the political party in power. This is the tendency. The reality is that the structure of the department is a product of many administrations, of compromises the chief has had to make, and of his own desires. The longer a particular administration is in power, the greater is the control of the chief over the members of the department, and the greater is the importance of the informal organization as contrasted to the formal one.

Summary. To summarize, the organization of the police department is formally a bureaucratic one, consisting of a strict hierarchy of authority and responsibility and the impartial selection of the men on the basis of competitive examinations. The department is organized about the office of the chief of police, who possesses enormous power over the jobs and lives of men under him. However, the chief is a political appointee and is therefore responsible to the political party in power and must comply with their wishes. To effectuate these informal ends it is necessary for the chief to draw on informal sources of authority in addition to those formally assigned to him. His formal authority is adequate for the control of the patrolmen, who know little of his activities. For the remainder of the department he is forced to set up an informal organization constructed in terms of a series of informal reciprocal claims and obligations, the chief putting the men under obligation to him by giving them the favored positions and granting them special privileges. It takes time for the chief to construct this informal organization, and unless his party has been in power for a long time, the informal organization is obstructed by the formal, and by conflicting obligations of other powerful men. When the informal organization, which is essentially political in nature, is very strong, it can effectively bypass the formal organization.

Operations of the Police Department

The police department in its day-to-day operations not only completes a scheduled routine of duties but is constantly responding to the demands emerging from the city. Crimes, fights, nuisances, and complaints flow into the department 24 hours a day, 7 days a week, and the department must be ready to respond to these demands. The police station, which can generally be identified as the dirtiest and ugliest building in the city, is the center of these operations.

Routine Activities. The routine activities of the police primarily consist of various types of patrols — foot, car, and traffic, in addition to school crossings. The last activity is gradually being taken over by a special corps of part-time workers who are not officers in the police department.

Action Channels. Requests for action flow into the department from a number of channels. The most important of these are the reports of the men on the beat and the radio patrol cars, and the telephone calls coming in to the desk sergeant. In addition, requests come directly to the detective bureau, and through the office of the chief. In turn, action can originate from any of the captains, the chief, or any of the sergeants. The men on the beat and in the cars tend to handle the problems they face by themselves, with little reference to the station, but frequently they are limited in what they can do and must call in so that some-one else can be put on the job. There is little coordination of activities hour by hour, but reports of the day's activity are kept by the desk sergeant and the central radio man, and policy can be formulated from these.

Basically, any request for action coming into the station or met with by the men on patrol is placed in one of three categories and subsequently assigned to the detective bureau, the traffic bureau, or the patrol division. Thus, should a burglary be reported, both the detectives and the patrolmen will be involved in the consequent action. The desk sergeant will be notified, and he will assign a patrol car to the initial investigation by means of the radio. At the same time, he will notify the detective bureau, where the sergeant in charge of the shift will assign a team of detectives to the investigation. The patrolmen are assigned to make the initial investigation, and they must phone in a report of their findings to the sergeant in charge of the records bureau. He, in turn, will send a copy of the report to the detective bureau where the case will be assigned to a team. The detective team is the formal channel of communication; informally, both the patrolmen and the detectives arrive at the scene of the burglary at the same time.

This description of the flow of action within the department is not meant to be definitive or even perfectly accurate. It has been given to illustrate the way in which the department operates.

The general picture is one of requests, flowing into the station from numerous sources, which are sent out to the field patrols, who immediately speed to the job. Frequently, action can be rapid. A report of a holdup in City X can produce a patrol car at the scene within one minute from the time it is received, provided that the place is not too isolated and is within range of the more intensely patrolled areas. Generally, a patrol car can reach any spot in the more populated areas of the city within four minutes of the time it receives the call.

The Records and Communication Division

Records of crimes, of accidents, of criminals, and of the efficiency of the policemen are kept in the records bureau. The records bureau is responsible for receiving the reports of the patrolmen, typing them up, and sending them to the appropriate action bureaus. It is regularly under the charge of a shift sergeant, who is generally competent to handle the entire procedure. It is one of the quietest places in the police station. Connected with the records bureau is the bureau of identification, referred to as the "B. of I." This is the department's attempt at scientific police work. Its major responsibility is fingerprints.

Records as such constitute an important source of information for the men in the detective bureau, who use them to apprehend, interrogate, and convict criminals. They are also necessary for the court presentations.

The most active section of this division is the communications section. This section consists of the desk sergeant, who is the heart of the police department, and the radio men. The desk sergeant receives all incoming telephone calls and personal requests and assigns men to the investigations. He is in charge of the radio man and the turnkey. He also receives calls from the radio cars and is in communication with the radio cars at all times. For the stranger, he is the principal contact with the police station. His desk is a madhouse of activity, for people are constantly coming to him with all kinds of requests for action and information, and he has to make a record of every complaint and the disposition of every case. Frequently, he is the one man in the station who knows what is going on all the time, since he is in contact with all the patrol and radio car men, and almost every type of information passes through his hands.

The desk, although a fatiguing position, is frequently desired because it is the center of activity and because it offers opportunities for much petty graft. The principal source of this graft, when it is taken, is the so-called bonding and attorney racket. If the desk sergeant establishes connections with bondsmen and attorneys, he can inform them when a prisoner needing their services arrives at the station. They will then give him a percentage of what they make out of the deal. Sometimes this racket can be highly organized, under the control of the chief, with definite men getting a specific split. Thus one ex-desk sergeant informed the interviewer that at one time many years ago, the chief had issued a listing of the names of "qualified bondsmen and attorneys," who had to pay the chief a set percentage of what they made, and in turn the chief paid the desk sergeant and perhaps the arresting officers a regular monthly stipend.

The Training Division

The training division consists entirely of one man, a captain, who is responsible for the recruits' training school, which lasts two weeks, and for planning in-service training courses of various kinds.

The Traffic Division

This division consists of a captain, two sergeants, and 16 men. Its responsibility is to patrol the main arterial highways that cross the community and to regulate the speed on these highways. The men work on two shifts, during the day and in the evening. They patrol the highways in cars and on motorcycles. They are called to the scenes of vehicular accidents and must take charge and make a report.

Many men in the department refer to the traffic division as the lazy man's paradise because it does not work the midnight shift, and because the men can loaf on the job with relative ease. At times the traffic division has also been considered a desirable job because it offers the easiest access to the traffic shakedown. This is the form of graft in which the policeman accepts a sum of money and releases the traffic violator. The traffic division, in patrolling the highways, comes in contact with the out-of-town violator, who is the logical victim for the traffic shakedown because he is susceptible to a large fine or bond, and because it is not likely that he will have connections in town. For the men who wish to participate in this racket, it can mean a lucrative return. However, because it establishes a bad reputation for the department, and because the total financial returns are inconsequential relative to other possibilities, the chiefs of the department seldom favor such activity, and the men who engage in it do so at considerable risk to themselves. During the period of this study, one man was suspended from the force for such activity.

The Patrol Division

This is the major division in any police force, and it performs the basic service functions of the police. Two types of activity or assignments take place — walking a beat or patrolling a district in a squad car. The best men are generally assigned to the business section of town, where during the daylight hours it is their responsibility to keep the traffic moving, to maintain order, and to give information. Each beat is approximately 20 minutes long, and at each end of the beat the patrolman is required to report into the station through the police call box. During the night hours his principal duty is that of a watchman. He checks the doors and windows of the buildings in his area to see that they are locked and that there have been no break-ins.

The Beat. The beat man is the traditional cop. He is the man who becomes integrated into his district, who comes to know most of the people there and to respond to their values and ideas. Men who like the beat say that they like it because it is healthy and because one gets to know people and seldom has to deal with emergency situations. The beat man prides himself on being able to know all the people in his area and to spot any strangers walking the streets, especially during the evening hours.

As the beat man walks his beat, he is constantly stopping to talk to people who are passing by, to exchange the time of day. He goes in and out of the stores, speaking to the owners and lingering over the counters. He becomes a community information center and principal problem dealer for the people on his beat. As problems come up, he must make a decision himself and deal with them rapidly. Generally, these are confined to such minor affairs as fights, drunks, and trucks blocking the street, which seldom require serious action.

The Patrol Cars. The experience of the men in the patrol cars is very different from that of the men on the beats. Most of the city is covered by the patrol cars. They even cover the areas covered by the beat men. Most of the police action takes place through the patrol cars. Each car has an assigned territory to cover, and they do this by driving up and down the street, slowly in the more populated areas and rapidly in the less populated. They are in constant contact with the station through the radio, which they listen to all the time and through which they can tell exactly what is happening in the city. They are required to call the station whenever they go into action and whenever they leave the car. As they patrol the streets they are on the alert for signs of disturbance, for fights, for crimes, for traffic offenders, and so on. What they see they take action on.

In contrast to the man on the beat, the man in the car is isolated from the community. He has no regular, informal contacts with the people in his territory. Most of the time, when he does have contact, it is some type of an emergency. Most of his contacts with the public are unpleasant ones in which he is trying to make them do something they don't want to do.

It is through the radio that the patrol car men obtain most of their assignments. Hours will go by with absolutely nothing happening, and then everything will break loose. They will start out with a shooting at such and such an address, a reported robbery at another, a family quarrel at a third. This is the action to which the men look forward through the monotonous hours of driving up and down the streets. Through these hours the radio is the only break in the little world of two inside the car — the radio is their link with the larger organization both from a physical or action perspective and in a personal, psychological sense. Through it they are in contact with the action of all the other cars and they listen with half an ear to the reports of the life of the city as it is presented to them in its disorganized and more sordid aspects. This picture of the life of the city is of importance to them, since the year-in, year-out repetition of what happens in the city works a powerful alchemy on the way in which they themselves picture it. Life and the city become cheap and sordid through the ears of the radio — and it is to this characterization that they begin to react.

The more serious policemen among those assigned to the cars take pride in hard work and alertness in emergencies. A pleasant personality is highly valued, for the long hours in a car can easily drag. Thus, in a popularity poll conducted by the interviewer among 27 of the men, 41 percent of the men gave alertness and competence as the qualities most necessary in a good policeman, 37 percent gave hard, consistent work as a major characteristic, and 30 percent felt that a good, likable personality was of importance. The policeman who received the majority of the votes as the best policeman on the force was considered to have all these characteristics.

The Detective Division

The detective bureau — or "upstairs," as the men say — is where policemen feel the "real" police work is done. It is also where the prestige is obtained. It is the center of information about police activities. The men working here know what is going on in the chief's office; they know what is happening in every case. Many of the chief's friends are in the detective bureau.

Location. Located on the second floor of the police station, the detective bureau in Department X has a radically different atmosphere from any other part of the station. In it one will always find men lounging about, reading the newspapers, talking to prisoners. At the beginning and at the end of every shift the room is crowded, for the men from both the incoming and the outgoing shifts are there. The crowd talks of the news, sports, and their cases. It is a period of orientation for all the men in the bureau, for it is then that they bring themselves up to date on what has been happening while they were off duty.

Assignment of Cases. Incoming cases derived from the reports of the patrolmen, telephone calls, and personal complaints, come to the shift sergeant, who either assigns the cases to the men immediately if they are there or puts the assignment in the detectives' box. The cases are assigned to the men who specialize in the particular area, such as stolen automobiles, homicide cases, casualties, juveniles, vice and gambling, embezzlement and fraud, and general crime. This is the theory of the assignment as the captain of detectives in Department X conceived it. In reality, the cases were assigned not only on this basis, but also on the basis of the preferences of the shift sergeant and the needs of the chief. Thus, if the shift sergeant had a preference for one of his men, that man was likely to be given the good cases, the cases that either were easy to solve or would bring the detective a lot of publicity and prestige. Upon receiving their assignments the men generally leave the station slowly to begin work on their cases, the work consisting either of slow, hard, and routine questioning of all the witnesses and other possible informants, or of checking with personal stool pigeons and informants. If a prisoner is obtained, he is brought to the bureau and interrogated. Interrogation takes place either in the closed and relatively soundproof locker room or in a small open cubicle, depending on the nature of the case and what the detectives think they will have to do to get the prisoner to talk. When the case is disposed of, a detective will write a report of its disposition, which will then be filed and sent to appropriate persons.

Nonpolice Contacts. Since the detective bureau is the center of what is happening in the area of major crimes, it tends to attract the outsiders. Court personnel such as the judge and the prosecutor, members of the Federal Bureau of Investigation, police reporters, attorneys, and politicians are constantly coming and going from this room. The detectives know all of them and generally converse with them. The reporters naturally want to find out what is happening and to get inside information on the cases which will be of news value. The people from the court, the judge and the prosecutor, come in to discuss cases that will come up with the chief, the captain of detectives, and the sergeants. The detectives may ask the judge to go easy, to suspend sentence, or to give a light sentence to one of their regular or prospective stool pigeons. The judge and the chief want to consult on cases of political importance. There may be deals in which the prosecutor tells the police what he thinks they can convict the man on, thus suggesting what the man should be charged with. All such dealing was quite in the open, and the interviewer was able to overhear it. The court referred to here is the police court, which handles misdemeanor cases: traffic violations, fights, intoxication, vice and gambling, cases in which the "fix" is particularly prevalent. Somewhat the same thing is likely to happen in the judge's chambers in the county criminal court, but to a relatively minor degree and probably with a great deal more secrecy.

F.B.I. men come into the detective bureau to get information on cases that involve the federal law and to work out joint operations with the police department. They are always treated with respect, for the police have a great deal of admiration for them.

Through the contacts in the bureau, the detective becomes familiar with most of the legal apparatus of the city and the county. He comes to know who has influence in these areas, and he is in touch with the attitudes of the dominant political party. He comes to know a great deal about what favors the chief is doing. He is "in the know" in a way that is never true of the man in the patrol division.

Differences Between the "Dicks" and Patrolmen. Being "in the know" is one of the three major differences between the work of the detective and that of the patrolman. In addition, the detective (1) works on criminal cases, can follow the case up at his leisure, and obtains prestige from breaking the important cases; and (2) tends to work individually, alone, and according to his own dictates, with little routine. The patrolman, on the other hand, performs service activities and tends to follow a relatively routinized day.

The Detective's Routine of Work. The individual detective looks over his assignments as he comes on duty; if he has any assignments, he figures out how to work on them and leaves the station to follow this course of action. If he has no assignments, he will either hang around the bureau waiting for something to break or will cruise about the town checking up on various things and waiting for an assignment to come over the radio. When he is working on a case, he may go to the scene of the crime, search out witnesses and talk to them, or just drift about the town in and out of bars and brothels, pool halls and gambling places, talking to the people he knows, his stool pigeons and his informants, trying to get information about the crime. When he gets suspects, he generally brings them to the station, where he holds them on suspicion until he can interrogate them. Although the work frequently involves long hours and extra time in court, the detective can work at his own pace. He can loaf when he chooses, without being noticed; he can spend a great deal of time over a leisurely drink in a bar or a long dinner in a restaurant. He can always write these activities off as "obtaining information."

Competition and Jealousy. Among the detectives there is a great deal of competition and jealousy. Every good case that is assigned by the sergeant is regarded as the result of the sergeant's preferences. Every man is anxious to get and solve the big cases. The competition for these cases is cutthroat. Each detective keeps his information to himself and refuses to share it with his fellows, even though it may involve cases to which they are assigned. The captain of the detectives informed the interviewer that this posed one of his most difficult problems since he could find no way in which to make the men cooperate. Unlike the patrolmen, there is little in the way of group identification among the detectives, largely because of this very competition for making the "good pinch." All the detectives tend to be suspicious of one another's purposes and methods, and in conversation with the interviewer they frequently accused one another of using unfair tactics to obtain information. They tend to write off the successes of the other men as due to the fact that the sergeant gives them breaks, or that they give protection to drug peddlers and serious criminals in order to obtain information from them.

Preferences in Assignment. The detectives place a differential evaluation on assignments which is based on the access they give the incumbents to graft, and the degree to which they enable the holders to obtain big cases. Thus, they feel that both the automobile detail and the vice and gambling squad are good positions because the auto detail enables the holder to cash in on the rewards, and the vice and gambling detail enables him to collect a lot of graft.[4] All the major crime details are desired because of the attendant possibilities of publicity and prestige. The juvenile assignment was desired only by those men who had a particular interest in that area, and generally it fell to their lot. Interviews with these men indicated that they particularly liked the juvenile detail because they didn't have to use any rough stuff, and they had asked for it for that reason. Other assignments such as

[4] At the time the study was being made, vice and gambling were being closed down in the town, and the men on that detail disliked it because they had to enforce the law, but it was difficult to obtain convictions and everybody criticized them.

casualties and minor assignments such as the investigation of broken windows were considered to be a kind of Siberia, the reward for inefficiency or unpopularity in the front office.

Stool Pigeons and Informants. The stool pigeon and the informant are the life blood of the good detective in Department X. The detective who was most frequently named as a good detective by the other men was given this title because he "had more friends than anyone else" and "had plenty of connections" and because he was unscrupulous and used "dope peddlers and gunmen to get his information." Everybody seemed to dislike this man. All the detectives felt that stool pigeons (people whom they have something on or whom they pay) and informants (people who act for the good of the community and tell them things) were the most important ingredients of successful work. Discussions with them about stool pigeons and informants evoked statements such as the following:

1. In towns this size stool pigeons are essential because the hoodlum element in town knows all the policemen. The way to get stoolies is by picking up something you have on them and constantly holding it over their heads or try to give them a break by getting a suspended sentence for them.

2. Good stool pigeons: Those are fellows in pool rooms and hotels. You should make friends with them. They see things and tell you a lot. The shoplifter is not a good stool pigeon, because he works alone. Neither are dope peddlers. They are pretty clannish and all they know about is dope. They only get close to the cheap characters and then they don't learn anything because the men who need dope are pretty shrewd and pretty well in control of themselves. The prostitute is generally a good stool pigeon.

3. You get them by arresting them for minor cases and doing them favors like charging them with one out of five offenses. Prostitutes are especially good because they get around a good deal. Some of them sometimes give information for a buck or two.

There's a difference between stoolies and informants. Informants are public citizens telling you something you can take into court and use as evidence or use to testify. You can't take stoolies into court.

4. Most pigeons are not worth anything. *A good informant is worth a dozen pigeons.* Pigeons are out for personal benefit. The informant has the interest of the city at heart.

5. To get informants you should cultivate friendships. You should associate with them — with the person, and find a chance

to give them a break along the line somewhere. Get him out of a jam or cover up for him in some way, or help him financially. Sometimes a small amount of money or giving him a chance to make money in some way. Hold something over his head.

One of the ways to work with them is to get them in jail and have one of your partners play the tough guy and the other the nice guy.

6. Pigeons account for the solution of between 40% and 50% of the tough cases. The way you get pigeons is to bring them in for a minor crime and give them the idea you are bargaining with them. Then you can go to them for information when you need it. We keep our pigeons quiet. If a man has a source of information, it is better that he keep it to himself. If too many men get in on it, they are likely to spoil it.

7. I don't know how the pigeons are paid. I just go around and try to get the information. I have to figure out in each particular case some way of getting information. You have to build up a person's ego.

8. A detective is as good as his stool pigeons. To get pigeons you got to get in contact. It's a trading proposition to a certain extent. It's a nasty proposition all the way through. There are some that want that green though.

9. A dick is as good as his pigeons. We have no money to pay the pigeons and since the first of the year that makes it hard. You can't let them have a game or anything like that and as for me, I wouldn't let a fellow peddle drugs or anything like that. Some of the police do it but I don't have any part in it. You have to get the confidence of those people and you have to have something on so-and-so.

Once in a while I will have a couple of the police pick up one of my pigeons and they will tell him they want him for purse-snatching or something and I will come up and say that I know the fellow and they will say that they are going to take him in and they will put him in the car. And then I will talk to them for a while — a long while, and then they will let me put him in my car and then I will let him go. That always works pretty well.

But you gotta get to know these people. Now take Frances. She's been stooling for years but she has been getting away with an awful lot. Why, she could get away with anything, but I don't take that. When we tell all the girls they have to stay inside she just sits on the step and whistles at the guys. But now she knows I am tough and she gets adjusted to it.

If I could pick up a little money from a crap game we break up I can use a little of it to get information. It's a town where money talks. Sometimes you can get in with the pigeon by pretending to do favors for them which are really not favors, like letting them go when you never have anything on them anyway. They don't know what the law is and you do.

10. In the case of informants, nine out of ten times you have got something over his head. The first time he gives you bad information you push him around a bit. You have to do that with them before you can get their confidence.

11. If I knew that one of my dicks was using a dope peddler or stickup man for a stoolie it would be his ass. But you got to have stoolies. One of the important ways to get them is you talk to the judge and have the person put on parole. Then you tell the guy that you took up for him and try to make him feel grateful to you.

The above materials have been quoted at length both to present the significance of the stool pigeon and informant in the work of the detective and to give an example of how the detectives talk and think to some extent. The statements reveal the amount of reciprocity and bargaining that characterizes crime detection in City X. They indicate that the detective believes that the goals of apprehension justify the sufferance of some types of crime. The detectives can thus be seen not only in competition, and as jealous and suspicious of each other, but also as slightly afraid of each other. They fear that the other fellow will find out what they are doing and hold it over them. The methods offer a significant commentary on the impact of scientific crime detection, and on the popular conception of the detective as a Sherlock Holmes who figures things out. In his tactics the detective is much closer to the overwritten hero of the modern crime story, the tough private detective. His experience is one of violence, bargaining, and a drive toward prestige. His attitude is pure cynicism.

Summary. The detective bureau is the center of most of the criminal detection and apprehension operations of the police department. It is the place where one gets to know what is going on in the department and the city, from both a political and a criminal viewpoint. It is the center of prestige for the men in the department, and prestige and publicity are among the most important drives of the detectives. It is the center of much of the good graft in the department. The men are jealous and suspicious of each other; competition among them is very strong. A detective is made or broken by the kinds of cases given to him by the shift sergeants. The solution of cases is largely the result of bargains that the detective makes with the underworld in which he gains stool pigeons and informants. The detectives feel that the possession of many good stool pigeons is the most important element in the success of a detective in crime solution.

Interrelationships of the Divisions

The only relationship of prominence and significance in the operations of Police Department X was that between the patrol and detective divisions. All other units seemed to work together harmoniously. There was considerable antagonism between the detectives and the patrolmen, especially from the patrolmen. The patrolmen felt that the detectives were hogging all the credit, and that they stole the credit from "pinches" which legitimately belonged to the patrolmen. Many patrolmen recited cases in which they had made the initial apprehension and the detectives had taken over for the interrogation and then claimed the credit for the solution of the cases without even mentioning the patrolman. The patrolmen felt very bitter about this since these good "pinches" are their only source of demonstrating their competence as policemen. The patrolmen also felt that the detectives were in on the graft and that they were cut off.

The detectives, on the other hand, did not reciprocate this antagonism. They seemed to feel that the patrolmen misunderstood them. This would seem a natural development since all the detectives had previously been patrolmen and looked with some tolerance on the attitudes of the patrolmen. They also experienced a shock, upon being detailed to the detective bureau, when they found that getting either the prestige or the graft was not as easy as they had thought it would be.

The great differences in the nature of the detectives' and the patrolmen's jobs tend to increase the gulf between them. The detective's job is more clearly important according to the values of the police, and is very much an individual matter; the patrolman does what can be considered the dull routine work and has to work in a set pattern. Communication between them thus tends to break down except as the formal structure dictates.

Personnel

The personnel of any voluntary social or occupational group will be the result of two general processes of selection. First, there is the selection of the occupation by the men; second, there is the selection of the members by the occupation. A thorough analysis of occupational selection of personnel would therefore require the widespread use of case histories indicating the preoccupational experience of the candidates for the occupation, and an explanation of how they came to arrive at their choice of occupation. Second, it would require a familiarity with the exact process by which the occupation chose from among the candidates from both a formal and an informal viewpoint. Our materials do not permit such a thorough analysis. However they do contain information that is suggestive of answers to the questions of selection. We shall treat of these two processes separately, although at times the choice of the data to be included in either category has been somewhat arbitrary.

The Choice of the Occupation. The policeman's choice of his occupation is related to his occupational aspirations in high school, his age at joining the department, his social mobility, and his stated reason for joining the police force. A sample of 90 policemen chosen to be representative of time in service, race, and position within the department indicated that the majority of the men came from working-class families in which their fathers had done laboring work, were one of an average of five children, either had no aspirations while in high school or wanted a professional or semiprofessional job, joined the department at a mean age of 28.6 and a median age of 26.9 years, joining for reasons of security or because they felt it was a better job. Details and explanations of these factors appear in Appendix B.

The Selection of the Members by the Occupation. The present personnel in Department X are selected in one of two ways: by political appointment — therefore with regard to their political power or work, or both; or by civil service appointment. Most of the men fall into the latter category. No significant differences were noted in the two groups.

Under civil service standards applicants for the police force take a competitive oral and written examination. Their grades on the examination form an eligibility list, and the men are chosen from the top of the list as vacancies occur. All candidates are required to have a minimum of a high school education, must be between 23 and 33 years of age, must meet with certain physical standards, which seem to be very lenient, and must be of good moral character as determined through an investigation by the detective bureau.

Police Work As a Way of Life

The policeman in City X has a steady job; he has settled down to a life's work. His civil service status assures him of a steady income, and his pension makes the job something worth sticking with. He receives a pension upon retirement after 20 years' service. It is worth approximately $140 a month for life. He figures it is as good as a $35,000 retirement policy.

The average man out of a sample of 91 is married and is raising a family. He owns or is buying a house, and he keeps up with the world through numerous newspapers and magazines, and through his television set. He frequently finds that his salary is not sufficient to meet all the costs of his growing family and thus he works at other jobs during his off-duty hours. He is the member of at least two voluntary associations, one of which is a policeman's association. He claims membership in some church, but if he is a Protestant he doesn't take it seriously enough to attend the services.

Summary

This chapter has presented an impressionistic description of Police Department X, based largely on the personal observations of the author but supplemented by documentary material and interview data. A summary of the results follows.

Police Department X performs a large number of services for the community. These services are so extensive that they can be said to constitute an essential part of the community's successful operation. Among them are many which can be called "dirty work," which are quite necessary, but which tend to place the police in a low position in the community.

The police department is intimately related to the community in terms of its personnel, in terms of the problems it faces, and in terms of politics. The community has long been under the domination of a well-organized political machine, which controls the police department through the chief of police, who is a political appointee and therefore an important person in the dominant political party. Because he is a political figure, the chief must run the police department along political lines and use the department to do these favors necessary to a successful political career.

From an organizational viewpoint, the department is *formally* a bureaucracy, with a well-defined division of authority and responsibility; appointments and promotions are given impartially on the basis of competitive examinations. However, *informally*, the department is organized around the chief of police, from whom all power and authority flows, who uses this power and authority to keep the men in the department in line with the policies of the dominant political party. His control over the patrolmen arises from the fact that the disciplinary rules are so extensive and detailed that it is impossible for the patrolmen to abide by them; thus, the chief always has something he can pin on them. In the other divisions of the department the chief maintains control by keeping his friends in the important positions.

The two most important divisions in the department are the patrol and the detective divisions. The patrol division has as its major concern service activities, and it does little in the way of criminal apprehension. Patrolmen have two general types of assignments: foot and car. The foot patrolmen are on what is called "the beat"; they act mostly in a routine fashion as guards, problem solvers, and information agents. Men on the beat are likely to develop personal relationships with the people in their territory. The car patrols cover wide stretches of territory, over which they operate as deterrent agents and a traffic control device. They maintain constant contact with the police station by two-way radio, and it is through this radio that they get most of their assignments. In contrast to the men on foot, the men in the patrol cars generally meet people in an emergency, and their social contacts with the public are in a large measure confined to this type of activity.

The detective bureau is the criminal apprehension unit of the police. As such, it constitutes the source of prestige. The detectives are aware of what is going on in the station and in the city and thus it is necessary for the chief to keep control of the detective bureau through placing his "friends" there. Individual detectives obtain prestige through obtaining the important or easy cases, the assignment of which is up to the shift sergeant. Among the detectives there is a great deal of jealousy and competition. Each detective has his stool pigeons and informants whom he obtains by making deals with people engaged in criminal activities. The more contacts of this type a detective has, the more cases he solves, and the better detective he is considered to be. Use of stool pigeons represents a case in which the police encourage minor criminal activities in order to obtain information on the big cases, the solution of which will bring them much favorable publicity.

The men on the patrol division are hostile to and jealous of the detectives, who they feel cheat them of credit for cases that they brought to the detectives' attention, and who they feel are getting a lot of graft. The detectives feel that the patrolmen just don't understand them.

The majority of the men in Department X come from families in which the father has been engaged in manual labor; they are one of an average of five children, either had no aspirations in high school or wanted a professional or semiprofessional job, and joined the department at a median age of 26.9 years, for reasons of security or a better job. Irregularity of previous employment and the need for security appear to be the dominant factors in their choice of the police as an occupation.

The personnel in the department were appointed on two bases: as a political favor or through competitive civil service examinations. The majority of the men fell into the latter category. About half the men in the sample were from families in which one or both parents were foreign born, but no particular national origin was dominant. Sixty percent of the men had previously worked as skilled, semiskilled, or unskilled laborers. The median year of education completed was 10.6. Seventeen percent of the men had one or more years of college.

The majority of the policemen in the sample were married and raising a family. They owned or were buying a small house, frequently had a television set, and concentrated their reading on newspapers and magazines. Almost half the men did extra work to supplement their income. Almost all the men belonged to at least two voluntary associations, one or both of which were concerned with police work.

3. The Public as Enemy

Public Opinion Lawyers; social workers; Negroes; union stewards; summary|**The Policeman's Contact with the Public** The nature of the relationship; uniform versus plain clothes; traffic cases; family quarrels; sex cases; criminals; the businessman; the fight; the courts; juvenile delinquents; contacts in general; summary|**The Policeman's Definitions of the Public** The public are antipolice; some are for, some against; public is for the police; ignorance is responsible; the newspaper is responsible|**The Different Publics of the Police** Children; the "better class" of people; the people in the slums; the Negroes; the criminal; summary|**Summary and Conclusions**|

It is with the public that the policeman is most concerned. He is its hero, its aid, its servant, its disciplinarian, and its avenger. It is the public that the policeman must differentiate, define, protect himself from, and contend with. The most important part of his time, the greatest part of his energies, his future, and his prestige are involved with the public.

The duties of the policeman bring him into contact with greatly varied portions of the public. On the beat he meets the pedestrian, the drunk, the bartender, the merchant, the prostitute, and the priest. In the car he meets the driver, the injured, the family, the thief. As a detective he meets the complainant, the accused, the rapist, and the raped. In the court he meets the lawyer, the judge, the politician, and the city hack. In the hospital he meets the nurse, the doctor, the insane, and the disquieted. Sooner or later he meets them all and finds in them the range of human sentiments and human problems. Mostly he meets them in their evil, their sorrow, and their degradation and defeat.

He sees this public as a threat. He seldom meets it at its best and it seldom welcomes him. In spite of his ostensible function as protector, he usually meets only those he is protecting them from, and for him *they* have no love. The fight in the bar, the driver in a hurry, the bickering mates, the overtime parker, the cutters of edges and the finders of angles; the underworld — bitter, sarcastic, afraid; none of these find the policeman a pleasant sight. To them he is the law, the interfering one, dangerous and a source of fear. He is the disciplinarian, a symbol in brass and blue, irritating, a personal challenge, an imminent defeat and punishment. To him they are the public, an unpleasant job, a threat, the bad ones, unpleasant and whining, self-concerned, uncooperative, and unjust.

The theme of an enemy public that threatens and criticizes binds the policeman's group to isolation and secrecy. It is an occupational directive, a rule of thumb, the sustenance and the core of meanings. From it the definitions flow and conduct is regulated for the general and the particular. To it our inquiry is directed.

Public Opinion

Although our interest is not centered here, the reality should have content, so we inquire as to the public and its definitions of the police. The sample is bad, but the cases are illuminating. We selected the lawyers, the Negroes, the unionists, and the social workers. Their opinions vary but have one thing in common — condemnation.

Lawyers. Twenty lawyers were contacted and interviewed by inexperienced interviewers. The group was not representative of the lawyers in the city and interviewing situations were not stabilized. The following material is therefore not trustworthy in a representative sense and should be regarded merely as illustrative. Our interest lies in the types of response that these lawyers gave to the question: What do you think of X Police Department? Most of the lawyers were slightly evasive; several refused to answer the question. (See Table 3.1.)

Considering the fact that the lawyers who refused to answer the question were probably against the police, the picture given, even considered conservatively, is extremely derogatory. They are characterized as brutal, inefficient, grafting, corrupt, and controlled by corrupt politicians, by close to 50% of the men interviewed. Only two men made positive statements about the police, and these were known to have business connections with them. This is the policeman's most aggravating court audience.

A few of the lawyers waxed more eloquent and described cases in which clients of theirs were involved with the police. The following are illustrative of these stories.

A middle-aged, well-known lawyer stated:

On the other hand, a friend of mine was driving north on Virginia Street one evening when he noticed that a couple of police officers were beating up a Negro on Eighth and Virginia. The Negro was taking a severe beating from the officers and had no way of protecting himself. My friend drove immediately to the police station, where he reported the incident and wanted something done concerning this type of treatment. He was ignored completely. While he was making his complaint, the two officers involved walked into the station and my friend was immediately thrown into jail without a chance to call his lawyer or family. The young man was jailed about 7:20 in the evening and was not released until about 10:30 P.M. This release came about because from his jail window he was able to call to his companion, who was still waiting for him in the car outside of the jail, in the alley. The friend got in touch with the young man's family and lawyer and they in turn had the fellow released. The charge the police were holding him on was disturbance of the peace. Another

Table 3.1. What 20 Lawyers Think of Police Department X

Opinion	Frequency
Brutal and inefficient	9
Grafting and corrupt	11
Controlled by corrupt officials	8
Ignorant	2
Think the victim (theirs) is always guilty	2
Uncooperative	2
Cooperative	1
Need assistance from civilians	1
Self-preservation is their philosophy	1
Better than they were 10 years ago	1

time, another client, who became my client after the incident, was taken to jail for questioning, and was not allowed to get in touch with his lawyer or any member of his family. He was kept in jail for sixteen days before anyone was able to find out where he was. During this period he was beaten unmercifully, having his nose broken, ribs broken and bruised severely. This man was a Negro. When I took over the case the client could not identify the officers, as they (the officers) were too smart to let their identity be known to the man during the beatings. Therefore, these same officers are still on the force. No doubt the same officers are the ones who constantly use force on a suspect. These officers are sadistic in their attitudes toward the people who are picked up by the police.

This lawyer was unable or unwilling to give any instances in which the police appeared in a more favorable light.

An ex-county prosecutor stated that after he and his two helpers started to clean up the city, he asked for help from the police department. The chief agreed that he would supply the men needed for the various raids and such that the prosecutor had in mind. The attorney said that they would call on the police and inform them where the raid would take place and the police always promised to have men there. However, when the attorney and assistants arrived, the police were nowhere in sight and the intended place to be raided was closed tight. He could only jump to the conclusion that there had been a tip-off as to the raid and knew that the police were not there and would not cooperate with them. The attorney did state that when they did make a raid (he and his helpers) and called upon the police to assist them in bringing the arrested people to the station, the police did respond, probably because this was within the law to them. He also stated that if the police officers or captains did not help him in this instance, he would appeal to the chief, who would issue orders to follow through on the order, and in this particular instance to obey the attorney and assistants.

Interviews with some of the older men on the police force confirmed the fact that the police had actually tipped off the gambling places.

Social Workers. Fourteen social workers were asked what they thought of X Police Department. Like the lawyer interviews these were done by inexperienced interviewers and thus are not too reliable. Generally, the social workers felt less strongly about the police than did the lawyers. Even so, they made only a few really favorable remarks, and generally their replies indicate a weak but definite condemnation. The points that they raised are as follows.

Social workers tend to find the policeman, that is, to be in touch with the policeman, in situations where his soft spot shows: amid the poverty-stricken and the young. They are, however, also in a position where they can obtain much information about the more disreputable behavior of the police. The characteristics that they attribute to X Police Department are indicative of this type of contact (Table 3.2). Although they have all

Table 3.2. The Social Worker's Characterization of the Police

Opinion	Frequency
Graft-ridden and corrupt	5
Give too much amateur psychological advice to workers	2
Spend too much time on petty things	3
Cooperative	2
Not scientific	1
Desire to feel important and authoritative	3
Aggressive and brutal	2
Detective bureau good	1
Too uneducated	1

heard bad stories, they also know of cases in which the police were solicitous and helpful. Nevertheless, we feel that the given characterization is obviously in the nature of condemnation.

The following quotations taken from the interviews with the social workers are characteristic of the bulk of the interviews:

1. The police department is adequate in its own realm. Such things as graft and corruption exist in all police departments and X is no worse than other cities of the same size.

2. I've never had any difficulties in my relations with the police. I feel, however, that they spend too much time investigating parking meters and traffic violations and not enough time investigating the more important things.

3. X Police Department is typical of police departments in all large cities; however, they take too much authority upon themselves. Usually they show aggressiveness while wearing the uniform. [The respondent then related an incident in which a policeman severely beat up a man who refused to take care of his family. She felt that this was taking undue liberties and that his correction should have been made in more orthodox channels.]

Negroes. Thirty-five Negroes of prominence and influence in the Negro community were interviewed. They included lawyers, politicians, clergymen, teachers, businessmen, and the head of the numbers racket. They were asked to give their conception of an ideal police department and to assess the police department in City X. They were extremely cautious in their replies. The interviewers were inexperienced and the results are not representative, but they are regarded as reliable. What follows represents the statement pro or con about X Police Department as found in the interviews.

Most of those interviewed confined themselves to saying such things as that there was a need for more civil service, that the policemen should have more education. (See Table 3.3.) Only one man gave a complete and open endorsement which can be regarded as enthusiastic. This was the policy king.

Several of the respondents told stories about the police. A welfare worker stated:

One evening when I was downtown I wanted a cab. I noticed two white people in a cab as it was ready to pull out. I asked what direction they were going and they said ———, so I asked if they minded if I rode to ——— with them and they replied that it would be okay. When the cab driver noticed me in the cab

Table 3.3. The Negro's Conception of the Police

Opinion	Frequency
Doing an excellent job	9
Use too much brutality	8
Rude and use bad language	8
Corrupt, get paid off	7
Controlled by the political machine	7
Doing a fair job	7
Negro policemen have no authority	4

he exploded and called the cops and all. The cops took me to the station and hit me as we rode to the police station.

Another respondent stated:

Not long ago a fellow was shot in the back on the other block. The wound was quite visible, as was the blood on the floor. The cops came rushing in and one of them began to kick the guy, using profane language, ordering him to get up. Tell me, could you get up if you were shot? No, I don't think you could, but I guess the cops think a person can. Well, finally the captain came in and the officers changed their attitude, and began to act like gentlemen in a way. However, I still think they waste much time with formality. They shouldn't waste time, but act as fast as they can, as in this case for instance. This shot-up soul could have died while they were going through the formality of the investigation. First aid first and formality later, I say. This is one incident which I have witnessed.

These stories typify the type of experience that passes by word of mouth through the Negro community. Negro friends have assured the writer that had the respondents not been so afraid of the police the interviews would have been much more strongly worded and would have contained even a greater abundance of antipolice stories.

In all, it is clear that among even the more prominent Negroes rough treatment at the hands of the police is not unusual and that in the Negro community no love is lost on the police force. **Union Stewards.** Eight union stewards were interviewed. The interviews were very badly done by an inexperienced interviewer. The interviewer was propolice and got into arguments with most of the stewards who had declared that the police were bad. How-

Table 3.4. Union Stewards' Opinions of the Police

Opinion	Frequency
Graft-ridden and crooked	5
Doing their job	3
Out to get those whom they dislike	1
Brutal	1
Drunk on duty	1
Play around with the women too much	1

ever, as Table 3.4 indicates, the sentiment was strongly anti-police.

Summary. These four areas of the public constitute an important part of the policeman's public audience. Three are definitely threatening, one is more conservative. In City X the unions are a powerful political force and there has been no union-police trouble in a decade. The lawyers represent the policeman's most prominent inferiority experience. In the courts the lawyer tries to make the policeman look like a fool and frequently succeeds. It is the lawyer who takes the policeman's suspect away from him when he would like to hold him for a few more days. It is the lawyer who can get the policeman in trouble for graft or brutality. The Negro in City X represents the slum dweller. City X has a history of bad relations betwen the Negro and the police. However, the Negro is gaining in political power as he forms an ever more significant portion of the city's population. The social worker is a trained observer who has frequent contact with people's troubles and listens to their stories. Together, we feel that these reports constitute a significant representation of public feeling toward the police. Therefore, we see the universal condemnation as the reality of public opinion that the policeman senses and faces in his everyday contacts with the people.

This reality is not our primary concern, however; rather, it is the policeman's definition of the public and his self with respect to the public which we are interested in identifying. Operating on the assumption that this is a product of his interaction with the public and the conclusions he draws from this interaction, we shall describe the major occupational references of the policeman.

The Policeman's Contact with the Public

The contacts that the policeman has with the public form the basis for what we will refer to as the occupationally engendered definitions of behavior and audiences. For purposes of clarity, we would like to present these experiences point by point, choosing those which observation and interviewing have indicated as being the most significant. Before doing so, it is necessary to describe certain objective characteristics of the relationship.

The Nature of the Relationship. The policeman is a symbol of authority and interference. His uniform assures him of this symbolic status and makes for a high degree of identifiability. He is defined as low and degraded, yet he must frequently give orders to those with prestige. He does the dirty work for the community: handling the insane, the intoxicated, the diseased, and the dead. He has easy access to corruption and graft, for who is to catch him? He expects rage from the underprivileged and the criminal but understanding from the middle classes: the professionals, the merchants, and the white-collar workers. They, however, define him as a servant, not a colleague, and the rejection is hard to take. What he does makes news. It is exciting and interesting. It concerns those who break the rules; and the people are interested in them. Whether the interest arises from the ritualistic punishment or identification and guilt cannot be determined. Perhaps it is both, perhaps neither. Whatever it is, the policeman is in the public eye. Condemnation and his uniform stereotype him. Condemnation and his work make of him a pariah.

Uniform versus Plain Clothes. The experience of the policeman must be differentiated between the patrolman and the detective. The former wears a uniform, and frequently as not is a restrictive or punishing figure. The latter can be identified only by the sophisticated and more often appears helpful. In all cases when a complaint is issued it is the detective who will follow up the case, who will retrieve the stolen goods and catch the thief. The detective thus experiences more gratitude than the patrolman.

In either case the most significant experiences are those which the policeman remembers, for these are the root of and the index to his definitions. Our material is not confined to these cases, however, for such were far too scanty to do justice to the problem. We include, therefore, the results of our observations.

Traffic Cases. Today the direction and control of vehicular traffic constitutes a major part of the policeman's job. However, interaction occurs most significantly with respect to the traffic violator: the speeder, the light passer, the reckless driver, and the drunken driver. It is the policeman's job to apprehend such persons. The apprehension represents a crisis situation for the violator: he finds himself in the wrong and this is unpleasant. He may be fined or confined. For the policeman the traffic violator represents an unpleasant experience, or an opportunity for grafting — perhaps excitement and danger. Policemen frequently get injured in accidents resulting from chasing speeders. The job tends to be specialized, with the same men assigned to it for long periods of time.

For the men on this detail interaction with the public is very frequently in the nature of an argument. The motorist, anxious to evade a court appearance and a fine, tries to legitimate his error with an excuse, or by claiming that the policeman is in error. He may try to buy his way out, which is insulting to the policeman's integrity. In spite of this, most motorists are allowed to go free with a warning. Unless a shakedown is contemplated, or unless the case is of an extreme nature, a warning is all that the policeman generally contemplates giving the man. Among themselves the men on the traffic patrol see the arrest of all violators as an impossible task, and the warning without arrest as a good public relations policy. Frequently, they see the apprehension as a kind of game in which they pit themselves against the motorist: if the motorist gives them a good chase and is a good driver, they will comment on the fact; if he is reckless and therefore dangerous, they will become angry. In the sense that they see it as a game they expect the man who gives them a chase to capitulate gracefully, but this seldom happens. They usually meet with whining or a threat. If there is no chase, there is the problem of breaking down the excuse. Seeing what kind of excuse the violator will give is in itself a game. Good excuses are something to tell the other fellows at the garage or in the squad room. If the excuse is good, they may let the man go even though they know he is lying. Too often, however, the policeman is deprived of any satisfaction in the interaction. Typically, the motorist will first argue that he wasn't going that fast, then change his tune and admit his error when he sees that the policeman is only going to give a warning. This leaves the policeman with an unpleasant feeling. On the other hand, had the motorist admitted his error initially, taken his warning, and thanked the policeman, the officer would leave with the sense of being a good fellow and having done his duty.

Thus, a traffic officer states:

The thing I dislike is the arguments that you have with the average citizen. On traffic violations they are always innocent.

The following situation, in which a policeman attempts to arrest an out-of-town speeder, tells the tale from the policeman's viewpoint. Although it has obviously been selected to place him in an advantageous light, it nevertheless illustrates the difficulties inherent in the interaction. The interviewer brought up graft, and the respondent said that he didn't believe in it.

I had a case recently where I caught this couple that was speeding. Well, I chased them quite a long way and finally caught them just at the city limits. I told them to follow me into the station. They kept lagging behind. Finally, I pulled over. I was going to tell them that if they didn't keep up with me I'd get a tow car and tow them in. At that point the fellow jumps out of the car, runs over to me, and says, "Here's ten dollars. Forget it. If I had more I'd give it to you. We were just in a hurry. We gotta get someplace. Just keep the ten bucks, officer." I just told him to come on into the station. When we got into the station the woman began to fuss and called us everything. She told us we couldn't pinch him. She kept yelling and hollering. He began to fuss too and told us we couldn't pinch him. To give back his driver's license, it was their private property.

I just walked in to the turnkey and told him to book him for speeding and disorderly conduct. Told them to book him for disorderly conduct and attempting to bribe an officer. At that point that calmed them down right away. He said, "Well, we will pay our fine and get right along." I told him it was no fine. He said, "How about a bond?" We said $10,000 for a bond — and cash. So they put them in the lockup.

When the case comes to trial they reported that the man had a bad heart. He couldn't come to trial, so we had to have a session in the judge's chambers. The man and his wife, my buddy and I, the judge and the prosecutor. The prosecutor explained to them that they were up for these various charges and for attempting to bribe an officer, they would be subject to a thousand dollar fine and/or two to ten years in jail. When that guy heard that he just turned white and so my buddy and I we took the prosecutor aside and said that we would just drop that attempting to bribe an officer charge. We would drop that charge. When the judge heard that he turned to me and said with a twinkle in his eye, "You would let this man go? You would drop that charge after the way he has treated you? How can you find the kindness in your heart to treat a man so nicely who has treated you so badly?" Then he said about the same thing to the man. Finally, the case was closed. [*Note:* The respondent mentioned that the car was a Cadillac with Michigan license plates.]

What is of sociological importance in this contact with the public is that it represents an interactional situation in which the policeman tests and is constantly testing his integrity, his pride, his competence, and his good or bad nature. That he generally comes out the worse for wear is indicated by the great reluctance of the officers even to chase the violators, and it is only with great pressure that a traffic drive can be inaugurated in City X. Left to their own devices without special pressure from the chief, the traffic division becomes the division of loafers. The parked car is the symbol.

Out of this interaction with the motorist the policeman divides the public into two major categories: the town driver and the out-of-town driver. Little effort is made to arrest the town driver since the men on the one hand feel some degree of identification with him, and on the other recognize that the case may be fixed. The out-of-town driver, however, is legitimate prey. A violation is a personal challenge and the violator frequently a good shakedown. Expecting the excuse, the argument, the evasion, the officer tries to get tough first, to treat them tough, to make them respect the law, a particular judgment of the law. This is one origin of the "get tough, make them respect you" thesis, which predominates throughout police work. Here it is important to realize that the officer thinks of himself not as an instrument of the government, but as a person in interaction with another person. He tends to feel that the derived power is in himself and that by withholding it he himself is doing the other person a favor. He therefore expects gratitude for his personal favor, gratitude and acknowledgment of his own competence. The man who typifies the antithesis of both these reactions is the "wise guy," again a recurrent character in the drama of the police versus the public. It can be seen that the situation is intrinsically productive of ill feeling. The officer and the violator have little in the way of common ground, conflict is imminent, each acts personally, each can easily become offended. The policeman thus meets a public which in interaction defines itself as unpleasant and the policeman as ill-willed. When the game can be indulged in, when the deed can be performed, the policeman emerges pleased and confident. Much more frequently, ill will and unpleasantness are the only result. The policeman emerges suspicious of himself and intolerant of the public.

Family Quarrels. Domestic discord is a tale that the police tell with distaste. For them it is an all-too-recurrent event in their occupational lives. It is a problem to which there is no solution, in which the policeman is ill at ease, in which the public appears in a most unfavorable light.

Family quarrels, disputes between man and wife, in which the police are called generally are violent and take place in the most deteriorated areas of the city. These are areas in which the police are particularly feared and despised. The police are called in by one of the participants or by one of the neighbors. When called in by one of the participants it is generally with the idea of engaging the police on his side, to increase his own power, but since the policeman is forced to act according to law and not as a partisan of the caller, even the caller will object to his actions. Should a neighbor be the caller, the appearance of the policeman is inevitably distasteful to both participants. Furthermore, since the quarrel is in an area where the police are a particularly ominous and disrespected group, the stage is well prepared for unpleasantness. The result follows the prediction. Both parties frequently turn on the policeman and reinforce the policeman's tendency to see the people as being no good. Thus, one of the men said that he finds family arguments the most disagreeable part of his job. He stated, "I run into them all the time; we get them by the dozens. There isn't really very much police work there. You can't do anything, but they seem to feel that the policeman can settle everything."

One of the higher officers in the department indicated this problem well when he stated:

You get calls that there is a family quarrel, and according to the law you are not supposed to interfere in a family quarrel unless one of the members asks you to, but people expect us to. So we go. You know, there are some funny incidents. I remember a time I went out on a call in a family quarrel. The wife had called us. Her husband was drunk and ugly when we got there and he had been beating his wife, and boy, when he saw us he looked like he was going to tear her limb from limb after we left. We didn't know what to say. We figured we couldn't leave him there or he would do damage to the woman, so we asked him to come along. He took a swing at her. I started to grab him and struggled with him and the first thing I knew I felt an aluminum pan pounding on my head and there is the little woman who ten seconds ago was standing there trembling at what the husband would do when we left, beating me on the head with an aluminum pan and saying, "You are not supposed to hurt him. Let him alone." Well, we figured that he would probably feel a lot better towards her after that and that things were quiet between them, so we left. But boy, I could feel that aluminum pan ringing in my head for the next two blocks. You know, if there is one thing these men hate more than anything else it is to go out on a call for a family quarrel. You ought to see their faces when they hear that call come over the radio.

The uncertainty of this police problem forbids definition. Different men handle it differently. Some take satisfaction in a paternalistic role and tell stories of how they advised families and kept them together. Most try to detach themselves and keep away from any involvement, refusing to advise and insisting on a warrant before arrest. They feel that the family quarrel only means trouble.

We refer to this area not because it explains a particular definition of conduct, but to indicate again what the policeman sees in the public and the public's reaction to him. The acrid words, the petty and sordid claims, the intolerance, the bitterness of the family dispute in slum areas hardly characterize the participants favorably. The hostile reception that he receives he feels is uncalled for, unjustified; he feels that he has just been doing his job and thus is martyred.

Sex Cases. The sex case[1] forms an unusual and perplexing portion of the policeman's job. We include here rape, exhibitionism, homosexuality, peeping toms, and sex delinquency by juveniles. For the policeman this represents an area of intolerance and of

[1] We are indebted to Professor Albert Reiss for calling our attention to this problem and for suggesting aspects to be investigated.

difficulties. Their intolerance arises perhaps from personal definitions, from public approval of intolerance. It manifests itself in
extremely rough treatment of the offender, the "take him out in
the alley and beat him up" attitude. Interviews indicate great
variations in personal attitudes toward the offender but indicate
a consistent belief that rough action is the socially approved form
of behavior both by the men on the force and by the public.
Extramarital relations and juvenile offenses do not fall into this
category. The important thing about the orientation of the police
toward sex cases is not the actions, past or contemplated, by the
men, but rather the belief that personal and brutal action is
sanctioned. This permits those men with inclinations toward
brutality in this area to satisfy themselves without fear. An additional factor making brutality safe is that the sex offender
has no recourse and therefore tends to fear public exposure more
than the beating.

The difficulties in sex cases lie (1) in the community demand for
action by the police, (2) in the difficulties in obtaining witnesses
or complainants, and (3) in the great quantity of false alarms or
claims. Should a peeping tom or an exhibitionist be working
through the city, public fear and indignation results in tremendous pressure on the police, who, being a politically sensitive
group, must get into action. Public imagination and the sug-
gestibility inherent in collective behavior intensify the pressure,
and unless the police act they suffer in the area where they are
most sensitive. The difficulties become multiplied, however, since
it is always difficult to get evidence against the offender: the
parties won't testify, the offender is elusive. The police, knowing this, are in a conflict between the desire for action and the
pacification of the public, and resentment against what they feel
are unjust claims of incompetence, since they know they have no
evidence and feel that if the public really wants to apprehend the
offender they should cooperate by filing complaints and testifying.
In addition, they have to be very careful, since many complaints
are made to the police as a camouflage for other actions or needs.
Thus, the young girl or woman who wants some publicity may
claim to have been raped. A mother who is angry at one of her
daughter's boy friends may claim that he has attacked the girl.
A woman anxious to hurt some man may claim that he raped her.

Women may imagine any prowler is a peeping tom. Cases like this are multitudinous. Should the police arrest such a man, and the complaining party fail to swear out a warrant or testify, the officer in question will be subject to lawsuits for false arrest. The police are conscious of this and exercise great care in these cases. But they are also conscious of the fact that the refusal to testify may be because of embarrassment. Thus, the complexity of the situation is apparent.

The solution of this problem has not completely crystallized. However, the group acceptance of harsh treatment for the sex offender is permissive of brutality, and brutal treatment is frequent. The following quotation illustrates both the thinking and the treatment on the part of the men inclined toward violence.

Now take a woman like Mrs. B. A respectable woman in the community. Some guy comes down the sidewalk and starts wagging his prick at her. She is not going to come into court and prosecute that man and say if he took out this long white thing and it looked like this and it was approximately so long, or to answer the prosecutor's questions and the prosecutor would probably ask her as to whether or not the foreskin was pulled back and then there are a lot of people like that. And there's peeping toms — they just like to look through people's windows and see things. Guys like that never get punished unless the policeman does it.

Now in my own case when I catch a guy like that I just pick him up, take him into the woods, and beat him until he can't crawl. I have had seventeen cases like that in the last couple of years. Then I tell the guy that if I catch him doing that again I will take him out to those woods and I will shoot him. And I carry a second gun on me just in case I find guys like you and I am going to plant it in your hand and say you tried to kill me and no jury will convict me.

It should be repeated, however, that many officers refuse to follow the dictates of the group with respect to the problem of sex. They either treat the sex delinquent gently, or take him into the station. Nevertheless, they do not condemn the use of force in this area by the other men.

The investigation of the sex crime, which is usually the function of the detective bureau, requires the most careful interrogation of the complainant. Frequently, the interrogation is harsh, the detective firing questions at the complainant and asking him or her to give a full account of the most intimate details. Most complaintants find this unpleasant, and are not prepared to answer the questions that are posed to them. In the complainant's account of the details of the crime, the sophisticated detective can generally identify the false complaint and break the complainant down. The final step always is to ask the complainant to swear out a warrant for the arrest of the accused.

We would like to summarize the important factors in understanding the definitions and the actions of the police with respect to sex crimes. These we see as factors making for brutal treatment and factors making for care. In the first category should be included (1) great public pressure and the consequent need for action upon the part of the police; (2) the difficulties in obtaining evidence that would stand up in court; (3) the position of the sex delinquent, i.e., great fear of public exposure and therefore no recourse in the case of brutal or unfair treatment; (4) the public acceptance and endorsement of brutal treatment of the sex criminal; and (5) police prejudice against sex crimes. These factors are of sufficient power so that today the sex criminal is the object of brutality and blackmail upon the part of the police, and the accusation of immoral conduct is one of the most accessible forms of framing a man.

On the other hand, the difficulty in differentiating the false from the true claims, the recognition of the seriousness of accusing a man on a morals charge, the difficulty in obtaining evidence or a warrant, and the threat of a false-arrest suit from persons who they know will be righteously indignant make for caution, for cynicism, for a tendency to treat the sex criminal with kid gloves. Thus, there are alternative lines of action which are sanctioned by the group. Individual men make their choice according to the situation and their own inclinations.

Of greater importance to this study is the way in which the policeman's perspectives on the public are refined by this area of interaction. Here we feel that two factors are of particular importance: first, the sense the police have of unfair public demands, i.e., the demand for action and the refusal to testify, which in itself would suggest an adverse definition of the public, particularly in its relationship to the police; second, the conception of a weak, not too moral group which emerges from the collective hysteria and the calculated vengeance motive, respectively.

Criminals. The criminal, in the parlance of the men of Department X, is the felon. He is the object par excellence of police activity. He is the legitimate prey of the sleuth and the cop as romantically defined in story, radio, television, and on film. He is the source of publicity and prestige. He is the "good pinch" of which we will say more later. His importance to the police for self-justification is enormous. Yet only a minor portion of police activity, if not thought, is devoted to this overpublicized phenomenon.

Amidst the graft and political involvement characterizing American police forces, the robber, the killer, and so forth, have been selected as evil, as something to be rubbed out, and police action against the felon has generally been defined as legitimate and good on the part of the police. This has represented a change in police orientations over the years, as in the early periods police linkages with the mobs: the booster mobs, the pickpockets, and so forth, was renowned. Observers such as Lincoln Steffens and early personal accounts such as those of Wilemse substantiate this point. The change we suggest has been due to the present greater significance of vice and gambling, their power and lucrative returns, and the threat which the more violent forms of criminal activity represent to these more organized interests. Furthermore, public attitude toward the felon is ambiguous, and he is the subject of great interest. Thus, the police have found in the felon an easy source of favorable publicity and justification. The result has been a great decline in mob activities of this type.

Of further interest to us is the way in which many of the policemen define the felon as being exceedingly smart and capable, in spite of the fact that in the next breath they will tell us that the old-time felon is gone and now they have only the stupid young punks. Their tendency is to attribute these better characteristics to the felon, which undoubtedly enables them to feel a greater sense of satisfaction with themselves for having overcome him.

Thirty-eight men were asked: "What kind of person is the criminal anyway?" Their replies can be classified into four general categories. Sixteen, or 44%, saw the criminal as the average man gone wrong, as a victim of his environment. They gave such replies as the following:

1. The criminal is the average man who has gone wrong. He

thinks he can beat it. The younger element is led into it by the older people.

2. It depends on a guy's childhood. If he is kicked around as a kid, and I saw the way it happened in my family, he is likely to turn that way.

3. Just a kid after a fast take. They are a lot of teen-agers these days.

4. They are just like everybody else but they want to get out the easy way. Lots of times they just don't like the policeman. Some when they were younger were brought up that way. Lots of them just want that easy money.

5. He is mostly uneducated. They become criminals because they do not belong to any church or any other organization or have anybody to tell them what the truth is.

Nine, or 28%, saw the criminal as morally weak or deficient. They characterized him thus:

1. A drunkard to start with. This causes him to take a down path. He gets in with a bunch of punks and starts to pull capers.

2. The criminal is usually a liar and he is somebody who wants an easy living and to live high. They become criminals when they want something and are unable to get it without resorting to crime.

3. Well, it's all according to background and training. In a real criminal, it's in the workings of his mind. He has an idea that he can get away with certain things and that is when he commits that crime. He may get away with it the first time but on the second or third, sooner or later, he will be caught and locked up. A criminally minded individual is a real criminal.

Six, or 19%, saw him as somehow biologically deficient, a born criminal or a mental case. They stated:

1. Born that way. It seems like it's just born right into them.

2. Not fully mentally developed. A person becomes a criminal because they can't get the things they want in any other way. They like to see whether they can't get by the easy way and they don't want to work.

3. I don't think a criminal is very intelligent. There is something wrong with them mentally. There must be if they believe that they can get along without working.

Six, or 19%, saw him as a shrewd, intelligent opponent, and gave such characteristics as the following:

1. In general the criminal is a high type and shrewd. They don't want to work and they will find fifteen different ways to avoid it. All the felons have at least a high school education. They have got brains but they are running in the wrong channels.

2. The crook just looks for money. The ones I have run into

are pretty well-educated boys. They know better. The average burglar or robber is of well-to-do people. The purse-snatcher comes from a lower class of people.

In an attempt to isolate the factors that identified the criminal to the police, ten men were asked whether the bookie and/or the pimp were criminals. Their replies were inconclusive on the points on which they were questioned, since many of them had definite reasons for saying what they did (the town was currently engaged in a vice drive) and thus camouflaged their own opinions. However, the reasons they gave for their answers are significant characterizations of what they consider the criminal act.

Thus, the bookies are not criminals because "They are not taking it away from you, you are bringing it to them," and "They don't cheat you, you go there of your own accord." The pimp is not a criminal because "They don't twist a man's arm," and "If a man wants it he is going to get it." The pimp *is* a criminal because, "He usually ends up rolling the party," and "When the town is wide open they just laugh at you and make you mad."

The reasons would indicate, to the extent that they are representative, that for the policeman crime lies in the relationship, not in the act (as it does in the law). If the action upon the part of the so-called criminal party is performed with the real acquiescence of the victim, it is not a criminal act. However, should the illegal action be against the wishes of the victim, it does constitute a crime.

We have dealt with the policeman's characterization of the criminal because a great part of his time is spent dealing with persons whom other people think are criminals and about whom he has to make a decision. If the above account is true, he makes his judgment partially on the basis of the nature of the relationship between the parties concerned. Thus, we feel that his actions should be characterized as being on a moral rather than a legal basis, although it should be understood that the arrest is only made within the framework of the law — the arrest being only one form of police action.

The contacts between the police and the criminal occur principally in the apprehension and interrogation situations, although it must be added that probably the most irritating contacts occur with known criminals, when they are free and in the streets. In either of the first situations the policeman is the dominant person and feels justified in almost all of his actions. He expects no love from the criminal, recognizing that the criminal will naturally resent and hate the police as the logical enemy. He tends, however, to treat the criminal in terms of a freedom to express his own (the policeman's) otherwise suppressed resentments at the rejection by the public. He is in a position where he feels that he is acting in the public interest and the ends justify the means. He is in a position where he is challenged to prove that the criminal is guilty, where his own competence is at stake. Thus, one policeman justifies police brutality in the following way:

If we were damned sure that he was the guy who did it we wouldn't quibble over the justification for getting rough with him. There is a case I remember of four Negroes who held up a filling station. We got a description of them and picked them up. Then we took them down to the station and we really worked them over. I guess that everybody that came into the station that night had a hand in it and they were in pretty bad shape. Do you think that sounds cruel? Well, you know what we got out of it. We broke a big case in Chicago. There was a mob of twenty guys, burglars and stickup men and eighteen of them are in the pen now. Sometimes you have to get rough with them — see? The way I figure it is if you can get a clue that a man is a professional and that he won't cooperate, tell you what you want to know, it is justified to rough him up, up to a point. You know how it is. You feel that the end justifies the means.

This, however, is one area in which the policemen obtain satisfaction from their social contacts and the interaction issuing therefrom. The contacts generate a set of definitions that operate around the concepts that this is the real job of the police and that "the end justifies the means," thus condoning anything they think they can get away with to obtain their confession or conviction. The relationship is almost always one of conflict, in which the ends of the criminal and those of the policeman are in opposition, the criminal seeking to prove innocence and the policeman to prove guilt.

The need that the police have for the apprehension of felons renders actions and judgments in this area of greater significance than the time devoted to them would ordinarily indicate. As we have pointed out, the apprehension of felons is one area in which the police can create a favorable public impression, and therefore one from which they derive considerable gratification. Thus, there is a tendency to look for the felon in every suspicious character, and the underlying willingness to use illegal methods to identify a person as a felon. This can be seen individually and collectively. Each man obtains prestige and a greater chance for promotion by the publicity that attends the apprehension of the felon. The force as a whole is justified as an existent body. What public judgment of the police does occur is seldom in regard to the extensive time and activity they devote to their mundane service activities — preventive cruising and walking of the beat, traffic regulations, supervision of all kinds of public events, and so on — but rather in terms of how they behave in the more dramatic and newsworthy areas, of which the apprehension of the felon is outstanding. The public, and for the purposes of our case we will represent it as the middle-class clubwoman, in City X long condemned the laxity in the enforcement of vice and gambling laws in City X yet did nothing extraordinary to indicate their dissatisfaction in this area. However, when the police failed to apprehend immediately the murderer of one of their group, they raised a public outcry and organized and financed a powerful committee to investigate the police and politics in their city. The incident is illustrative of the way in which the public directs its attention and gives a reaction to police service. Thus, the felon, in terms of whose apprehension the public tends to judge the police, has assumed an importance well out of proportion to his activities and effect on the community. The police thus need to apprehend felons (criminals) to insure their position in the city, and for individual prestige. The statement quoted earlier (p. 68) indicates the way in which the policeman tends to act and to vindicate himself. The interviewer was not informed of any cases of a similar nature in which the beating failed to produce results, although common sense would suggest that these are even more frequent than the given case. We feel that the lack of such cases was a matter not of concealment but rather of a convenient memory. Their retention in the minds of the police and in the stories of the past would tend to destroy a definition of criminal treatment, which although unjust is of great assistance in the achievement of their ends.

Police contacts with the criminal, whom they define as the felon, thus produce orientations different from the contacts with other parts of the public. The importance of the criminal to the police individually and collectively has made him an object of primary concern to them and has led to an acceptance of the use of violence to obtain evidence against him. Generally, the police feel that the criminal is like everyone else but has had bad breaks or bad upbringing. They define the criminal as a felon, as the person who illegally takes advantage of another; they define the crime as a relationship between social beings, not in terms of the law.

The Businessman. Most police contacts with the businessman are confined to the small businessman — the merchant, the bartender, and the owners of places of recreation. Among these the contacts tend to emphasize the businesses in the more disorganized or slum areas of the city. In these areas business is likely to be slightly on the shady side; businessmen are apt to be cutting the corners of legal regulations, not to be meeting the requirements of their licenses. They don't like to be looked into too closely. They have more need and less fondness for the police than the more prosperous middle-class business. Theirs is the place where the drunks, the prostitutes are found, and where fights and burglaries take place. They cater to the police, serving them food and drink, giving them tips and presents, actually paying them off very frequently. They dislike but fear the police. They often help the police to apprehend the felon.

The businessman in the better-class section of town tends not to fear the police, and tends to think of them more as servants. He may, however, establish a regular friendship with the policeman who has been on the beat for a long period of time.

The policeman is suspicious of the businessman. He feels him to be friendly but is cynical about the friendly gestures, feeling that behind them is a request for a favor. The policemen in City X had many stories about how businessmen had tried to take advantage of them or tell them their business. Illustrative of these stories is one told by a policeman assigned to walk the beat along a business street.

When I was a rookie first on the beat I was always being called into a bar to pinch some drunk who was making trouble. I'd pinch him and take him in. One day I got wise to what was going on. I saw some young fellow go into this bar and I saw a couple of others there beside him. I waited for a little while and I pulled my box and went in and waited some more and he was still drinking. I could see him getting pretty drunk and that kept up for a couple of hours. And then one time when I came back to talk to the bartender he was throwing him out on the street. The guy was all beat up. The bartender told me that he had started the fight. He wanted me to pinch him. I really told that bartender off. I told him, "So you want me to pinch him. I'll pinch him all right, I'll pinch the bunch of you and I will close this place of yours down. That's a fine thing. That guy starting a fight. You people have just taken all his money away from him." And I went on like that. I was really mad. And after I had done that a couple of times they didn't bother me any more. They didn't pay any attention to me.

In this case the policeman started out with faith in the actions and requests of the bartender, then realized that he was being taken advantage of and lost faith. Such stories define the policeman's relationship to the businessman. He begins to define the relationship as one in which the businessman is only out for his own interests and only supports the law when it is convenient to those ends. He sees the businessman as looking upon the policeman as an instrument to further his business and profits.

What is interesting about the relationship between the policeman and the businessman is that the policeman welcomes the friendship of the businessman in spite of the fact that he believes the businessman is trying to take advantage of him. Thus, policemen spontaneously make statements about businessmen being *for* the police, although they add that this is probably because they have need of the police. They make such statements as:

1. There's a difference between the way the businessman and the average public treats a police officer. The businessman is for the police officer. I guess maybe he needs the protection but at any rate he is for the police officer.

2. Well, I guess it depends on how they need you. Some of the restaurants feed you and give you a cup of coffee. They do it just to have you around. You will find that many of these restaurants that are open late at night, like Thompson's, have only a couple of women working in them and they have got a lot of drunks and toughs eating there and they appreciate having a policeman around. I know they do at Thompson's.

3. Storekeepers are with the police. I mean businessmen and a few of the church people. They will come to your aid. Then there is a certain group who is afraid of policemen and that won't say anything against the policeman because they are afraid. Then there's the cagey type. The type that are always getting into something, but knows all about the laws.

This conflicting definition of the businessman arises out of a mixture of feelings and experiences. On the one hand, the policeman experiences friendly relationships with the businessman. He is greeted cordially — the businessman likes to have him around. He spends much time in various business establishments, talking with the salespeople and the owner, to break up the day; he goes into the bar and the restaurant to warm up in cold and rainy weather. He manages to get his meals, his drinks, and many of his personal household needs free or at a considerable discount. He likes the feeling of being wanted and being useful. On the other hand, he recognizes that the businessman does these things with a reason, and that every time he accepts something from the businessman he in indebting himself to that man. This, to the policeman, carries an adverse moral connotation, which he finds unpleasant. Again, his experiences with the businessman are such that he remembers or has heard about occasions when the businessman appeared to be making a fool of the policeman. It appears to be a relationship of false love and therefore is unpleasant, but apparently even false love is better than none.

Out of these contacts and this relationship between the policeman and the businessman, the policemen in City X have on the one hand defined the businessman as having a positive attitude toward the police and at the same time have become increasingly conscious of the relationship as essentially Machiavellian, a strictly business proposition, in which the idea is that you get what you pay for. They become cynical of the middle-class morality, since as they see it the middle class feels free to abridge its own code.

The Fight. A frequent police call is to the fight in the bar, the street, the restaurant. Generally, such fights involve persons who are intoxicated and as a result have become aggressive. This is of importance for the police, since the belligerent drunk is at once incautious and at the same time likely to feel a necessity to flaunt the law. The result is that the policeman frequently has to use force to quell the fight and to subdue the drunk. He uses force to protect himself from the attacks of the drunk and to keep his uniform from being torn, in addition to the actual need of force to make the drunk obey his orders. Therefore, the drunk, like the professional criminal, becomes a source of legitimation for brutality. And, in a similar fashion, those policemen who have tendencies in that direction are inclined to take advantage of the permissive situation. Add to this the fact that in City X the bulk of the drunks are Negroes toward whom the police generally feel an antipathy, and the amount of unnecessary brutality undoubtedly rises sharply.

The fight is also the source of a great deal of unjust public accusation of the police. Many policemen in City X recited tales of how they were having a difficult time with some drunk who started a fight with them, and how some pedestrian reported the matter to the chief. While the number of such incidents is undoubtedly much smaller than the policemen's reports would suggest, it is of importance to us that the policemen tend to define the situation this way. Their attitude is indicative of their consciousness of a public definition of the police as an essentially brutal group of men. They choose the areas of the drunk and the professional criminal to defend themselves against this felt accusation since they feel that in these areas the use of violence is necessary to their work and therefore justified. One policeman, an essentially gentle and quiet person, told the interviewer the following story, which involves violence on his part about which he felt justified but nevertheless embarrassed.

Another fellow and I were working on a squad car. We were eating lunch. We got a call. There was supposed to be a disturbance in a cleaning shop. It was only a couple of stores away so we walked there from the restaurant. Outside there was a lady who was crying. She was frantic.

The window next door was broken. There was blood around the place. The lady told us that her husband was drunk. That he was throwing her clothes around.

We went in. He was there. He was a big fellow. He asked us what the hell we wanted. He then said, "I don't have to tell you punks anything." Well, I told my buddy I would get the car and as I walked out I heard the lady scream. She said that her husband had the other policeman and when I looked around I saw that he had a bear hug on my partner.

Well it just so happened that we had left our clubs in the car so I pulled my gun and told him to let my partner go. Twice I told him, but he didn't pay any attention. So I took the butt of my gun and beat him over the head. He was yelling and cursing and everything. After I hit him he released my buddy and dropped to his knees. I noticed blood coming out of his cut. He sprang to his feet and said he had had enough. He was really bleeding. My buddy was covered with blood.

We called for an ambulance and took him to the hospital where he refused treatment. He was still bleeding bad and was swearing that he would get me and kill me for what I had done. Since he refused treatment we just took him to the station.

A couple of hours later they took him to the hospital where he agreed to get treated. After it was over we had to get our clothes cleaned on the way. In court the case was suspended. We never heard about it since.

You see, when we first approached that fellow we didn't want to make a pinch but the way he acted we had to. The fellow was sitting in the turnkey's room when the chief happened to come by. He asked us what had happened and whether either of us had been hurt. When he found out that we had not he just told us to go home and change our uniforms.

You know, the original call turned out to be a family argument at a cleaning shop.

In this case it is clear, as it was told, that the use of force by the respondent was necessary to the defense of his partner. It is illustrative of the type of situation the policeman faces in his contacts with the fighters. It is the type of story that the police-men pass from one to another and that justifies the use of force for them.

In spite of the experiences of violence in the policemen's con-tacts with the drunk, they tend to treat the drunk with some sym-pathy, and it is within the framework of their definitions that the drunk who is not disorderly should be sent home if possible. Thus, violence with respect to the drunken fighter is permitted.

The contact with the drunk and the fighter has, however, more important connotations in our understanding of the police; for these experiences are flavored with criticism, from both the fighters and the observers. The agitation produced by the strong emotional involvements of the fighters and the bystanders seem to occasion a real antagonism to the police, and produce remarks to that effect. It is therefore a situation in which the policeman can expect and does experience outright public criticism and the expression of strong and probably exaggerated remarks about the deficiencies of the police. Typical of the stories the police seem to remember and tell each other about is the following tale a policeman tells of his experience at the hands of the sister of a drunken girl.

For example, the other day a woman asked me to make her sister go home since her sister was drunk. I said no, that was not my authority. Then I saw the sister standing by a light post and the drunk sister began to cuss everybody and throw things around and scream. So I went over and talked to her and when I got there she cussed me out, so I grabbed her and led her to the box and called a car, and right there in the street while I was waiting for the car she called me every name in the book. So I took her in and do you know that for the next week or so all that I heard was how I mistreated that poor woman.

One of the things the public does that riles me up is to talk to me about other policemen and I always tell them don't tell me anything unless it is good because I know that they are not in sympathy with the police and that they are not going to tell you anything good about them.

Here is an allegory of injustice, which the respondent takes care to make explicit after he finishes the story. The policeman receives a request, he is hesitant to act, he finally does act, and for his action he receives only injustice, although his intentions had been good. So it is seen by the men. From it they derive the conception of a public hating the police.

Out of this conception of a hostile public and out of this sense of injustice comes a need to strike back. This is illustrated in the following description of a street fight, the intrusion of the bystanders, and the policeman's description of his feelings.

Another fellow and I were talking. I was on the beat then. We saw a fellow come running out of a door across the street and right after him there were three Puerto Ricans. They jumped him and threw him down. One sat on him and another kicked him in the face and the third twisted his ankle. We came running over. One of them tried to run away. My buddy caught him and I held on to the two others. We took them all over to the call box. The victim was bleeding. All three said they had nothing to do with it. Another fellow came running over and said we couldn't arrest them, so we arrested him too. We took them all in the squad car. We booked the three for assault and battery and one for interrupting an arrest and took the victim to the hospital. We told him to swear out a warrant.

Now in that case we didn't use force although I wanted to beat hell out of them.

"I wanted to beat hell out of them." That expression is strong and real, but it doesn't answer to the situation. It is the expression of other injustices that seem to be symbolized in the situation. The policeman sees a situation that calls for police action. The participants try to defy him — they have no respect for the law. A friend or bystander tells the police they are incompetent — "He said we couldn't arrest them." The policemen act within the framework of the law, but they are looking for an excuse for more stringent and personally satisfying measures.

Through stories and experiences like these, the definition of the public is refined and strengthened. It is abstracted to a symbol of intolerance, hatred, and injustice. It becomes the lens of interpretation, and reality is shaped by it. The experiences then become ever more frequent and the exceptions more scarce. Memory selectively reinforces the conviction, and the tales passed from man to man constitute an expression of the feelings and a support against the hostile world.

One should be careful, however, in asserting that the use of violence among the police is frequent and extensive. That it is present, and that every working policeman has occasions (one or two a year) to use force, is not to be doubted. The policeman is conscious of the public condemnation of these practices, however, and he makes an effort to keep them to a minimum.

The significance of the policeman's contacts with the drunk and the fighter is that they represent an experience which for the policeman reinforces the legitimation of violence developed in his interaction with the professional criminal and stated in the law — a legitimation that is an integral part of the policeman's definition of conduct in a specific situation. In addition, it should be emphasized that these experiences strengthen the policeman's conception of the public as malicious and hostile.

The Courts. The policeman's experience in the courts represents at once his frustration, his triumph, and his crucifixion. Fundamentally, the appearance in the courts is an unpleasant chore which the policeman has to perform. In City X the policeman frequently has to appear in court on his own time and without remuneration for these services. In fact, if he is diligent, he has to spend a great deal of time in court. The court there is under stern political control. The result for the policeman is that he constantly is forced to battle with the court itself, in addition to the defense attorneys. Should he be persistent in prosecuting a case, the case will be postponed one, two, and maybe up to eleven times. Each time the policeman will be forced to leave home, or bed, to appear in court. When he fails to appear, the case is heard and dismissed for lack of prosecution. This needless waste of time, at his own expense, is one of the most frequent gripes of the policeman in City X. Thus, one man stated:

Suppose you make five arrests. You come in and make reports. Suppose it is midnight shift. Next day you got to go to court. One case is called, you may have to wait three or four hours in court, on your own time, this is, and then the case is continued, which means you have to come back another day. With the vice cases, like as not you will get five continuances, which mean five more days in court. Why, I have been to court up as high as eleven times on one case. Why, if you make from fifty to seventy-five arrests in a month you will spend every day in court and then, even then, lots of times you are not finished with a case. Fifty percent of them will be appealed to the criminal court. And then there will be more continuances and more time in court and for all this you get no overtime pay or time off. You know, when you come down to brass tacks there is not much you can say for police work. Not much good about it. About the only thing you can say of it is it's a good steady position.

Another states:

The worst gripe of the policeman is his long hours of work. He has to spend a lot of extra time in the courts and he is lucky if the court is called during the period when he is on work. Most of the time he is off duty and he has to go to court and he doesn't get paid for it. If a man is a vigorous policeman he has to put in about forty days a year over and above his regular duty just in the courts.

In these cases it is clear that the policeman, who works six days a week anyway, has a real source of irritation in the extra unpaid time he has to spend in the courts.

Additionally irritating is the existence of the "fix." One policeman describes the fix as follows:

The first time it dawned on me that there was such a thing as a "fix" was in a flea trap in ——— Street. Some Italian woman caught her husband in bed with a blonde and she was chasing him down the stairs. My partner got the husband and I got her. We charged them with disorderly conduct. I thought it was a good pinch, but when we came to court my partner took me aside and said that somebody had put in a good word for them. That I could go ahead and prosecute the case if I wanted to, but it was no use because when the fix was on they would not be found guilty. That's the way it is all the way around, now, I have learned. When a policeman considers arresting some local yokel, the first thing they think about is how much drag the guy has got.

In this case one observes the type of experience that makes the policeman at once suspicious of the courts and gives him a feeling of helplessness with respect to them. "I thought it was a good pinch" . . . "somebody had put in a good word for them" . . . "they would not be found guilty" . . . "now I have learned." These thoughts and words signify bitterness and resignation. The case is without much effect, however, since the policeman evidently had little stake in making the pinch stick. In the case that follows, the fix occurred even before it got to court. In this case the officer felt that the pinch was a way of asserting himself, a way of punishing the culprit.

Well, yes and no. There was a case where we picked up a guy who got involved in an automobile accident and he started asking us lots of questions and then telling us what to do. And he kept it up for so long that the older policeman finally pinched him for disorderly conduct. On the way back in the car he kept abusing us, saying things like "You guys aren't so big," and "Just put your badges here and I will knock the s--- out of you." I could just see the older fellow counting to five but he didn't touch the guy and then when he got him to the station, he says, "I am a guy under arrest. I am not going to open the door for you, you open the door for me." I could see the other fellow's pressure was beginning to go up but he opened the door for him and then just as we got inside the station the other guy raised his hand like he was going to strike one of us, but then he looked around the room and saw there were a lot of other policemen there, so he didn't do anything.

Well, we hadn't been out more than a half hour when I had to call in for something else and the sergeant said, "You know that fellow you just brought in?" and I said, "Yeah," and he said, "Well, the mayor just came down and bailed him out." I don't know whether that is the fix or not but I do know that it has been two weeks and the case has not come up in court yet. I learned later that he is one of the city employees.

Some of the officers say that there is not much use in making arrests for minor offenses because the judges do not follow through on it, but that is all I know about it. I don't think they would tell me much, my being a captain's brother and everything.

Here the arresting officer was most conservative in telling of the incident and took great care not to give an expression of his feelings with respect to what he obviously felt to be an injustice. The officers had been insulted, they had used great restraint, had followed the legal rulings, had been deprived of satisfaction. In a sense they had been punished for not punishing the man themselves.

We introduce this case at this point not because it demonstrates anything with respect to the court experience itself, but because it is part of the type of political dealings the policeman involves himself in when he brings a case to court, and it illustrates the types of situations that make him lose faith in the courts and find the experience unpleasant.

Another policeman, when asked whether he got much satisfaction from making a good pinch, replied that he didn't because

Half the time you make a good pinch and the case never turns up. You find that the turnkey's sheet is red-pencilled. One time I picked up a man on intoxication. He had no driver's license. The next day when I looked at the turnkey's sheet the name was just scratched off. No word said to the policeman. If they would just call us in and tell us that the guy was a friend of the mayor and had a little dough we wouldn't bitch so much, but it's never telling us anything that makes us mad.

These people with friends. Why, one day I picked up two guys. One of them had a gun that was sticking out of his pocket. The other also had a gun on him. The guy with the gun sticking out of his pocket had sentence suspended. The other guy who wasn't even showing the gun got thirty days and a hundred-dollar fine.

This man felt that if they were going to fix a case they should at least let the policeman in on it and not do it behind his back. He expresses the injustice of the court.

Another policeman gave expression to the more general feeling about the uselessness of bringing cases to the courts when he replied to a question as to whether he ever had a case which was never brought to court. He said:

Well, I got one like that right now. It has been two months and I have never seen the guy. It makes the policeman hate to make any pinches. That's the way it is. I remember in school one of the captains told us that there are two kinds of people you arrest: those who pay the fine and those who don't.

This policeman remembers learning about the fix in school, and in learning about the fix he is absorbing a definition of the courts as an agency that fails to do justice, that is discriminatory and subject to partisan pressures. He learns that the court is not a dependable institution of punishment, one that will uphold him in his judgments.

The actual experience of the policemen in the courts tends to substantiate his feelings about them. Here he finds himself the supposed expert who does not know his business. The defense attorney at once points to him as an authority on the law and demonstrates his inadequacy in this respect. One policeman stated that he disliked lawyers; when asked why, he replied:

Well, I think you will find that most policemen feel the same way about it. You work on a case, you know you got a conviction, and then the damned lawyer will do anything to get his fee. They accept cases and I know they accept cases plenty of times when they know the man is guilty. They just set out to confuse you on the stand. Why this fellow ——— in ———, you probably heard about him, famous criminal lawyer. Took the case one time where I was testifying about a drunken driver. He had driven into another car, broken two people's legs and the back of a woman in the process. When we got there we found him behind the wheel, stinko. He was out. Just sleeping there behind the wheel. Snoring. We hauled him in.

Well, this lawyer, he starts out and he asks me, "Did you ever work twenty-four hours a day in a shift?" and I said, "Yes, I have worked twenty-four hours in a shift." He said, "Anybody ever wake you up after being asleep like that after you have worked twenty-four hours?" I said I didn't recall anything like that, but I have been waked up out of a sleep. He said, "Did the telephone ever ring while you were asleep?" I said, "Yes," and he said, "And when you got up to answer it maybe you didn't know exactly what you were doing?" I said "Yes."

He said, "Maybe you didn't walk so straight, you staggered a little," and I had to say, "Yes." Well, he never did ask me what the man's breath was like, or anything like that. Of course not, and I'll be damned if they didn't let the guy off.

Well, now, you can't tell me this lawyer didn't know that the guy was drunk. They are all like that. Boy, that's the last thing in the world I would want my kids to be is a lawyer, and there is not one of them would want to be one.

In the defense attorney the policeman finds a source of irritation, one who manages an interpretation of the law that makes his head swim. Again, the defense attorney often has connections that cause the prosecutor to give at best a futile and weak support to the policeman. The policeman is insecure about his knowledge of the law; he may know that a man is guilty of some transgression but when it comes to a matter of interpreting the law, as the lawyer does, he finds himself the helpless victim of a facile and confident man. The prosecutor is his only protection in this situation, but as we have pointed out, the prosecutor also has his political responsibilities and thus sometimes only offers token aid to the testifying officer. Thus, the testifying officer is likely to emerge embittered, bewildered, and suspicious of the whole court procedure. As in the example cited, he is made the fool and does not enjoy the part.

To protect themselves, the policemen in Department X are carefully instructed by their superior officers before they appear in court. They are told what to say and when to keep their mouths shut. Generally, the idea is to get one good straight story and stick to it through anything. The men themselves appreciate the threat of the court and frequently tell of spending the night before with the case on their minds, carefully planning how to outwit the defense attorney.

The policeman's triumph comes when the court vindicates his judgment by a conviction. For the policeman this represents the conclusion of a case he has been working on. If he has defined his relationship with the suspect as one of competition, the conviction represents a victory. At any rate, a conviction reassures him of his own competence and at the same time of the worth of his job. It makes him feel that he is actually achieving something. It thus gives meaning to his life and his work. It provides for him a reassurance as to the correctness of his judgments. This last point is of more consequence than one might think.

The policeman, being essentially a man of action, must have the confidence to make quick, sure judgments. Frequently, he is in situations where he must judge the guilt or innocence of a particular person. To make such a judgment, he has to be certain of himself. Once he has made such a judgment, he finds it difficult to admit that he is wrong, for this would indicate uncertainty. This fear of uncertainty thus forces him to stick to his initial judgments, in the face of contrary evidence and in spite of the decisions of the court. In this connection the court poses a double threat. On the one hand, the court may not uphold his judgment as to the guilt of the party, and on the other hand, should the court find the man not guilty, the man can then turn around and sue the policeman for false arrest. The policeman, needing the security of past judgments for future judgments, tends to rationalize away the decisions of the court. This is easy to do by saying, "The man was guilty all right, but we just didn't have enough evidence to make it stick," or "The fix was on."

The threat of a false-arrest suit is one aspect of the uncertainty for which the policeman has found some recourse. Many of them are taking out insurance from Lloyd's of London. One policeman stated:

By the way, I am taking out insurance by Lloyd's of London against the false-arrest suits. It's six dollars in the beginning and then three dollars a year and they protect you up to five thousand dollars. That will take a weight off my mind. The only trouble is that they don't protect you against assault charges.

The anxiety that is expressed here with respect to the possibility of false-arrest suits adds to the general unpleasantness that the policeman feels about the courts.

To summarize, the policeman's experience with the courts is one in which he finds an unjust and tiresome chore because of extra time and lack of pay. Because of the defense attorney's interrogations, he often feels that he is being tried rather than the culprit. He is made to play the part of the fool. He is often frustrated in his attempt to make a pinch stick by the political machinations of the courts and the existence of the fix. He tends to lose faith in the course of justice and in obtaining the support of the courts for his judgments. He may feel that the only way in which the guilty are going to be punished is by the police. He has anxieties about the results of court action, for if the prisoner is declared innocent, he, the policeman, may be subject to a suit for false arrest. He sometimes gets great satisfaction from his court appearances, for when he obtains a conviction he has at once a sense of having accomplished something and a proof of his own competence.

Juvenile Delinquents. "We are just waiting for them to grow up" is probably the phrase that best expresses the policeman's irritation with the juvenile delinquent. But the police in City X are fond of children and sympathetic with the delinquent. The conflicting ideas with respect to the delinquent represent differences in attitude toward individual delinquents, and differences in orientation among the members of the force.

In City X the delinquent has to be treated with "kid gloves." This is because he is protected by the juvenile courts and by the social agencies. He also represents one area in which the police are particularly vulnerable to public attack. The result is that police treatment of the juvenile is the treatment of the professional criminal in reverse. While, as we have pointed out, there is a tendency for the police to feel that "anything goes" in obtaining a conviction for the professional criminal, they also tend to feel that one has to be mighty careful in the treatment of the juvenile delinquent. Whereas a public outcry and public pressure will appear if they fail to apprehend the criminal, there is likely to be public outcry if they are too tough on the juvenile delinquent. There is much in the nature of community feeling in City X which directs responsibility for delinquency to the social agencies, to the slum, and to the school, rather than to the police. There is little in the way of allocating responsibility for delinquency to the police, as there is in the case of crime. This would seem to be a simple problem, except that juveniles often commit major crimes, and here the crime tells nothing of the age of the criminal. The police apprehend the juvenile delinquent and then turn him over to the juvenile courts. The courts then generally release the delinquent. The crimes that the juvenile is engaged in create public pressure on the police. In City X a great many of the housebreakings and robberies are due to teenage boys' gangs. When such a wave of robberies does occur, there is public criticism of the police. However, when the police do apprehend the robbers and the robbers turn out to be juveniles, the police have to turn them over to the juvenile authorities, by whom they are frequently released. The police in City X feel that most of these delinquents then just resume their former activities and again become a police problem.

The problem of the juvenile delinquent and public opinion is illustrated in the following incident, which took place in the police station of City X one evening.[2]

---

[2] From the research diary of the author.

Two uniformed officers came in, bringing with them two children about sixteen years old, a boy and a girl. A uniformed officer reported that they had chased this boy in a car about three miles on one of the roads running into town. That he finally had stopped in front of a drive-in cafe, but when they got out of the car the boy drove away immediately, leaving them behind, and that they had given chase again.

The boy had driven into the center of the city, around and around the block, through lights several blocks in a row, through filling stations, and so forth, at a clip between seventy and eighty-five miles an hour. The officer was white and shaking as he reported this and that they had opened their siren wide in order to warn people in the streets that something was coming and they had been lucky that they had done so because the boy had just barely missed killing several people.

The sergeant then turned to question the boy. He asked to see all his identification. The boy explained that he had once lived in City X but that now he lived in ——— City, and was coming to visit someone in City X. That the reason why he had run was because he was scared. The boy was very calm. The girl was crying.

The sergeant was very quiet, didn't yell at the boy in any way, but continued to question him about who his father was and whether he had permission to use the car, how much money he had with him, and so on. After some questioning along these lines he turned to the patrolman and said that the only thing they could do was to call up the boy's father and tell him to come on over and get the boy. The patrolman was angered at this because he felt that he had risked his own life in catching the boy. The sergeant then went upstairs and called the boy's father. I was amazed at the amount of "kid glove" handling the police had given to this boy, so I asked the sergeant about it. He told me that juveniles were an awful problem, that if you mistreat them in any way, even to the extent of yelling at them, you were liable to be in court yourself instead of having the boy in court; that they were very seldom able to pin anything on these boys, aside from taking their licenses away from them. [*Note:* It turned out later that they finally did manage to book the boy on three charges, so that his father had to post a bond of some eighty-five dollars to get him out.]

Although this case does not fall into the juvenile delinquency category to which we have previously referred, it illustrates the type of problem the delinquent poses for the police. He is a problem in the sense that the crimes he commits must be curbed, and again a problem in the sense that he is just as dangerous to the policeman as is the adult criminal. In one sense he is even more dangerous, he is more likely to shoot the policeman because he cannot understand the consequences. However, the police really have no way to deal with this problem. They cannot inflict punishment themselves, and they can seldom obtain punishment by way of the courts. They do, of course, have the alternative of letting the juvenile go with a warning or of sending him to the juvenile courts. Goldman (1950) has devoted extensive research to this problem. Such material as we have substantiates his analysis of police attitudes. With the child from a good family, or with the quiet, repentant, fearful child from any family, the police will attempt to deal with the problem themselves. They will take the child to his home, speak with the parents, leave him and them with a warning. They deal with the child from the slums, who is sarcastic and rebellious, by turning him over to the juvenile authorities and getting him off their hands. By doing this, however, the police do not solve their own problem. They look forward to further depredations from the same boy.

In the sense that we have just outlined, then, the juvenile is a source of frustration to the police. He poses a problem of crime prevention and solution and is a source of personal danger. Yet the means for handling this problem are not at the disposal of the police. Many men in Department X pointed out that the juveniles they brought in had long records and that they were just waiting for them to reach 18 when they could take them to the criminal courts and finally send them up.

The juveniles recognize the protection they receive from the juvenile courts and flaunt this in the face of the police. This is naturally an additional source of irritation. One patrolman summarized his feelings about juveniles in the following statement:

I think the biggest problem in this town right now is the juvenile problem. There's too much delinquency and the courts are too lenient. If you get a kid and they let him off, all the kids go right back to it again. The kids will sass you up and tell you, "I am a juvenile and you can't touch me." I think that's the fault of the parents. They don't know where their children are.

This man felt that the leniency of the courts made delinquency a problem to the police, and that the leniency of the courts created a situation in which the kids would sass the policeman back.

The really tough little boy, alone or in a gang, occasions much suppressed wrath on the part of the police. The policeman feels that no good will come out of the lenient treatment by the courts, and that sooner or later he will have to deal with the child as an adult delinquent. One policeman, pointing to how tough even the young ones get, stated:

There is a little Negro boy I met recently. I saw him down there one day and had gone to talk to him and he said to me, "Brother, you got a gun but some day I will catch you without it." He began to curse me out. I said, "Boy, I just wish you were a little bigger," and he says, "Brother, just stick around. I will be bigger soon." Twelve years old, mind you.

The older delinquents, those who are 16 and 17 and thus just under the line, become a threatening group for the policeman. Many find that they can no longer treat delinquents of this age group as children, since boys of this age are particularly obnoxious to the policeman. Those boys seem to derive real status in their group from challenging the policeman and insulting him. They are old enough to engage in serious crimes and to constitute a source of danger to the men on the force. Therefore, gangs of these boys are a sore spot in the policeman's routine. One policeman, while talking about such gangs, stated that in his area he had a lot of trouble and that "we have to rough them up once in a while to keep them in line . . . if we could only use a little real force I think a good kick in the pants would really keep them down for a while."

The policeman's relationship to the juvenile delinquent constitutes for him a source of satisfaction when he finds a mild delinquent and can act as a corrective influence, and a source of irritation when the delinquent is sarcastic and/or old enough to be insulting and threatening. The necessity to treat the delinquent with kid gloves, and the failure of the juvenile court to deal out what the policeman feels is necessary correction, give the police a sense of helplessness and rage toward the delinquent problem and the juvenile courts.

Contacts in General. The preceding sections have been directed toward specific areas in which the policeman has contacts with the public. Although the listing is not exhaustive, it does cover the most important areas as they appeared in the research. In one sense, however, the previous accounts are specific to the point of introducing a bias in the picture. In an attempt to correct this bias, it is necessary to describe briefly some of the contacts that the policeman has in his job which do not fall within the areas previously described, and his reactions to these contacts.

Among these should be listed the multitude of casual contacts that every policeman has with the public. Contacts with the pedestrian in the street, the children at the schools, the people at parties and gatherings, the passengers in the bus or on the train, the city employees around the police station and in the city hall, and many others. In contacts of this type the policeman, while on duty, can play the role of the interested and helpful participant in casual social interaction. He frequently enjoys giving information about the city and other subjects to the pedestrian; he likes the children at the street crossing and in the school yard; he is greeted with cheer and responds in the same manner to persons at parties and other gatherings; he carries on conversations about topics common to everyday life with the passenger in the bus; he finds a sympathetic listener in and listens sympathetically to the city employee about common gripes. This type of social contact fills the gaps between the incidents of work and constitutes an important part of the policeman's routine. In it he can act as a person apart from his duties. In contacts like these he keeps his touch with the affairs and values of the community. Through them and because of them he can never completely dissociate himself from the values of the community, and they are an important ingredient in making him a responsible person.

These casual social contacts occur at every level of the community. The policeman, especially the detective, is interested in the life experience of the prostitute and the bum. He can sympathize with them. He often carries on a joking relationship with them. He sometimes makes friends with them. The man on the beat in the more affluent section of the business district comes to know the people and the merchants. They inquire into his family affairs and he into theirs. He tends to pass the time of day with these people. He gets to know the schoolchildren and appreciate their respect for him and is interested in their activities. He comes to know the criminal, and they often have a half-threatening, half-braggadocio kind of friendship.

Strewn amidst these casual contacts there are some which can be identified as primary rather than secondary relationships. In them the participants experience a real involvement in the emotional reactions of each other. To the extent that the policeman establishes such primary relationships he finds himself identified with the values of those to whom he relates himself. This is illustrated in the case of a policeman who, upon being assigned to a beat in a slum area, found that when doing a favor for somebody he had to allow them to reciprocate the favor: to buy him something — a hat, a pair of shoes, a meal; and that when he refused to accept the return favor the people looked upon it as an attempt to hold something over them. In the slum, jungle law is particularly prominent and reciprocal incrimination is regarded as a prerequisite to friendship. The policeman entering into such a relationship may easily see nothing wrong in it and may defend it, although it later may be ground for his legitimation of much petty graft. On the other hand, the policeman in the better residential district may well consider such petty graft as essentially immoral. The threads of such relationships are woven through the more apparent and powerful fabric of group definition of behavior and thus introduce at times behavior which is unaccountable in terms of these group definitions. Their persistence in the life experiences of the policeman would lead one to suspect that they have more influence than they do, except for one outstanding characteristic that they possess. This is that they tend to be individualized, to depend on the particular circumstances and the personality of the particular policeman. This is in contrast to the community of experience evoked by the nine major contact areas previously outlined. In addition, the bulk of these contacts are casual and do not engage the policeman in his role as an agent of the law and in his publicly and self-defined capacity. The result is that they become dissipated, and few, if any, group definitions of values or conduct develop from them.

Our purpose in describing these contacts is to indicate that the policeman's life is not empty of warm and satisfying relationships as our previous descriptions would imply, and at the same time to point out that although they are casual and without particular importance in analyzing the policeman's perspectives, they do constitute an important part of the policeman's daily activity.

This is particularly true of the man on the beat, who, incidentally, is of all policemen least affected by and involved in the group definitions of conduct, but is at the same time in a minority on the force.

Summary. In the preceding sections we have briefly described the nature of the public contacts of the policeman: in traffic cases, family quarrels, sex cases, and fights; with the criminal, the businessman, the drunk, and the juvenile delinquents; and with the lawyers and judges in the courts. In each case we have tried to indicate the meaning these contacts have for the policeman.

In the traffic case the policeman meets the public and finds them lacking in respect for his judgment and his morals. He finds them ready to give obviously false excuses, to try to bribe him, to threaten him, to insult him. He treats them as they tend to treat him; although initially he adopts a tough attitude, he frequently will be lenient if they are respectful and penitent, provided that he is not out for a shakedown and that the case is not of too serious a nature. He will pinch or otherwise severely treat the "wise guy" who talks back or pretends to know more about the law than the policeman does. He finds little in the way of gratification from traffic arrests. He emerges with a feeling that the only way to treat the public is to make them respect you by getting tough. He senses that they dislike him, and correspondingly has a low regard for them and their judgment.

The family quarrel poses a situation in which the policeman is likely to feel insufficient and in which it is often impossible to do the right thing. Here he sees the public at its worst, with its hair down, so to speak. He finds people intolerant of one another, vulgar in their words and gestures, jealous, and lacking in human dignity. He meets with a poor reception, frequently being insulted and almost always being made to feel that he himself is an intruder.

Sex cases pose a difficult problem for the police. The presence of the sex criminal in the community results in great pressure for police action. However, people often refuse to give testimony or swear out a warrant, and it is difficult for the policeman to make an arrest. He is angry with the public for what he considers unjust treatment. He is ready to do anything to get out from under the public pressure, and often uses illegal measures to get rid of the sex criminal without the dangers of bringing him to court and a false-arrest suit. Here he finds a justification for the use of force, for brutality. The men on the force tolerate such actions by their fellows, the public seems to think the sex pervert deserves it, and the sex criminal, as defined by police, has little recourse. The sex criminal thus provides a sanction for brutality in one area, and at the same time the source of police resentment of the public.

The criminal is a source of public justification for the police force, and a source of personal prestige for the individual policeman. As a result, the police tend to devote an amount of attention to the criminal well out of proportion to the effect he has on the community. Policemen define the criminal as the felon and the crime as an illegal action in which one individual takes advantage of another. They see the criminal as an unfortunate product of chance. This does not generate sympathy, however, for the criminal is too important to the ends of the police. This importance gives rise to a tendency to feel that catching and convicting the criminal is of such importance that the end justifies the means. Thus, the police find in the criminal another legitimation for the illegal use of force, for brutality. The apprehension of the criminal is, for the policeman, perhaps the most important source of gratification on the job.

The contacts that the policeman has with businessmen — merchants, bartenders, restaurateurs, and so forth — are friendly on the surface but contain an undercurrent of mutual distrust. The policeman feels that the businessman favors him only to demand a favor in return. He finds in the businessman a representative of the community who is also anxious to evade the law in many ways. In the sense that the businessman represents the community, the policeman comes to believe that the people in the community hold their morals only for others. Nevertheless, the policeman appreciates the businessman because he likes the feeling of being wanted and being useful, and because the businessman's gestures of friendship are lucrative and among the only persistent gestures of this kind in the community.

In the drunk and the fighter the policeman finds aggression, insults, and trouble. The drunk, the fighter, and the bystanders seem to feel that the intervention of the policeman is done maliciously. Thus, they tend to attack the policeman and/or insult him. He, in turn, finds in these attacks justification for the use of force. He finds that the public uses these occasions to reinforce the conception of the policeman as an essentially brutal person, overauthoritative and power-happy. The policeman feels that he is doing his job, feels that these public accusations are unjust, feels bitter toward the public.

In the courts, the policeman finds that he is frequently frustrated and often made to play the part of the fool. He feels that the city is taking advantage of him in making him go to court on his own time and at his own expense. He is threatened in an area of great importance to him — the correctness of his own decisions. The court, for good or bad reasons, frequently repudiates the policeman's judgment of the guilt of the defendant. The policeman rationalizes by saying that the man was guilty but that they didn't have enough evidence against him, or that the fix was on, or that he didn't care what the courts did. Basically, court is an unpleasant experience for the policeman. It uses up his free time, it frustrates his desire to make a good pinch stick and have his own judgment upheld, and it causes him to lose faith in the law itself. On the other hand, it is in the courts that the policeman obtains great satisfaction when his judgment is upheld by a guilty verdict. He finds that felons are the most easy to convict. Because of this, the courts exert an influence that cannot be neglected in selecting for the policeman those areas that are defined as criminal and in which he will give his best efforts.

The juvenile delinquent is a constant source of trouble for the policeman. His depredations bring community pressure on the police, but at the same time the community will allow the police to do little in the way of preventing these depredations. The community says that the juvenile is to be treated carefully, and people are easily aroused if the police act otherwise. Again the police feel that the community is doing them an injustice. Furthermore, the free delinquent is a great source of irritation to the police; knowing that the police can do little to him, he makes the policeman the butt of his jokes. The policeman is frustrated and feels that he should be given the freedom to punish these delinquents and keep them in line.

In every case it is clear that the policeman's contacts with the public tend to be unpleasant and to generate a feeling on the part of the police that they are a hated group. In many cases the contacts are such that they are frustrating and productive of anxiety. Among them the policeman finds grounds for the use of force, in addition to his legal privileges in this respect.

This section has emphasized the interaction of the police with the public in various areas that entail action on the part of the police. In each case the emphasis was on the interaction and the development of definitions of conduct arising from this interaction. No attempt was made to indicate the various lines of action that the police adopt in these areas as the definitions arise, or in response to a particular definition of conduct called forth by the specific situation. This problem will be dealt with in a later section. Our purpose in presenting the foregoing material was to indicate the background of experience that is responsible for the police definitions of the public, which we now propose to delineate.

The Policeman's Definitions of the Public

The policeman's attitude toward the public is at best anomalous. On the one hand, he recognizes the political responsibilities of the department and is thus cognizant of the necessity for acting in a fashion that will meet the public approval. He frequently will use what he considers to be the public's attitude as a measure of how he should judge various actions. Thus, he tends toward leniency in law enforcement in those areas in which the public seems to require leniency. In addition, he never detaches himself from the judgment of the public as it is expressed in the newspapers and in day-to-day comments. His most important sources of prestige are the newspaper and the gossip. Thus, his emphasis on the apprehension of the felon and his ruthlessness with the sexual offender are justified. On the other hand, he is extremely sensitive to the hostility of the public, and tends to see himself as a victim of injustice, unappreciated for his sterling efforts, and without friends. From this perspective he defines the character and the judgments of the public as being poor and not worth giving attention to.

The experiences that the policeman has with the public indicate grounds for a severe detachment from and criticism of the public. In order to determine the extent of this feeling, 85 policemen, representing all ranks and degrees of experience within the department, were asked the following question: "How do you think the general public feels about the police?" The great majority of the men felt that the public thought that the police were, respectively or in combination: racketeers, power-crazy, parasites, bums, brutal men, no good, looking for trouble, and ready to abuse them. They felt this was because: "They just don't like us," . . . "They are afraid of us," . . . "They think we are going to take their privileges away," . . . "They don't appreciate the good we are doing." Also: "They watch us all the time," . . . "They are always trying to get a policeman in trouble," . . . "They are against us."

The replies to the question, which were sorted into three categories, are summarized in Table 3.5.

Typical of the responses were the following:

The public are antipolice

1. The public believes that the police officers are grafters and power-happy; that they like to have the badge so they can show people around and they are not so far from wrong. The trouble with it though is that when a policeman makes a mistake everybody knows about it. But he can do twenty good things and you never hear a word about it. Police are just like everybody else.

2. The average person doesn't like us. We restrain their movements. The average public is afraid of you. Now that's wrong because take the average jailbird. He isn't afraid of a policeman.

3. The public don't like the police. You can tell because of their attitude when you come to the door for information. They will say things like "I don't want you," . . . "You got no business here," and then slam the door. Or they will look out the window and watch a policeman being beaten up and never lend a hand.

4. The public does not like a policeman. They think he is just a hard head, that's all. You take your average person. The one

Table 3.5. Policemen's Conception of the Public's Attitude toward the Police

Presumed Public Attitude	Frequency	Percentage
Against the police, hates the police	62	73
Some are for us, some against us	12	13
Likes the police	11	12
Total	85	98

who says he is a good citizen. But when I pinch him I am just an ass hole. He wants to know why did I arrest him. They just want you to arrest everybody else but not them.

5. Well the public demands action but they don't cooperate. They don't give you any information. You can run into a place where a guy is shot and there are twenty people there in a little room and nobody saw it. They figure that you are the cop and you should figure it out. But when something happens to them they scream bloody murder.

6. You catch hell if you do and if you don't.

7. Well, the better class of people pretty well realize that you are doing a job a lot better than the shadier class of people. Of course, a big percentage of the people feel that you are putting your nose in looking for trouble. They figure that you are just marching around looking for somebody to get out of line so that you can arrest him and exercise your powers.

8. The only time the public cares for the policeman is when they are in trouble. Otherwise they have no use for them.

Some are for, some against

1. The attitude of the public is fairly divided. Some are for you one hundred percent but to others you are something to be spit at.

2. Fifty percent are suspicious and prejudiced. Fifty percent are cooperative and want them as friends. But being a policeman — you know it's hard on you at times. Your kid has strikes against him. If he climbs a tree in front of somebody's house they call the police. Whereas if any other kid did it they would just tell him to get down.

3. One half looks on the policeman as a friend. That is the half that has nothing to be afraid of. I think there is a lot in the way a person is raised. My parents told me that if I got into trouble I should go to the policeman and he would help me. I think that a lot of the lower class people tell their kids that the policemen are bad and will get them in trouble, but it is the policeman himself that gives the people the impression. If one policeman looks bad the department will look bad.

Public is for the police

1. The law-abiding element likes the police. They think you are pretty decent fellows and are glad to see you. They like to see you come into their stores and things like that. I think they really do.

2. The majority of the public likes the police but about twenty percent think you are a prick.

3. Well, the people that are settled down are polite to the policeman but the floaters — people who move around — are entirely different. They just don't like the police because they have got

lots of bad days which they can't help sometimes and they think we are after them.

These cases were selected to be representative of each category and thus give the range of opinion within each category. We feel this will permit the reader to evaluate the distinctions.

It should be noted that many of the replies which were not categorized as indicating a feeling that the public was against the police contained a recognition that some large part of the public was antipolice, which would indicate that even these men felt somewhat persecuted.

Frequently, the respondents tried to explain why the public was against the police. In general these explanations were in the nature of indicating to the interviewer that the public conception was false. Three general explanations were advanced: (1) that the public was ignorant of present police work and needed to be educated; (2) that the town newspaper was misleading the public, its publisher being antipolice and not giving them a fair coverage; and (3) that the public had good grounds for being against the police.

The following were typical explanations:

Ignorance is responsible

1. Well, in the first place the police are underpaid. In the second place they are too openly criticized by the public. There should be some way to inform the public as to the policeman's job. The public feels badly towards the police. They seem to think you are their enemy, that you are out to beat them up or to abuse them.

2. I don't care what the public thinks of me. If I have a good job I don't care. They are ignorant of police work. If you could educate them then you would have the public on your side.

This theme of the need to educate the public was repeatedly expressed in many different contacts with the policemen in Department X.

The newspaper is responsible

1. The way the public thinks about the policeman depends on the section you are talking about. It's only natural for them to be prejudiced against the policeman. The newspapers don't tell about the things the police accomplish.

2. The public in this town have no use for the policeman. You know why that is. The local paper. That paper has got a policy of being down on the police and the results have always been bad.

Many policemen felt that the newspaper thought that an attack on the police was good news policy and that the paper didn't give the police any good publicity. To some extent they were correct but they actually received a lot more positive publicity than they thought they did, since every apprehension of a felon was news, and the police frequently received good publicity in this connection.

The Different Publics of the Police

The policeman's sensitivity to the public and his concern about the impression he is making on the public form the basis for a general division of the public into five groups. The groups form a rough continuum which corresponds to the degree of respect that the policeman has for the group and the care with which he deals with it. They range from children, whom the policeman respects and treats kindly, to the criminal, whom he does not respect and treats roughly. The five groups are children, the "better class of people," the slum dwellers, the Negroes, and the criminals. Policemen seem to distinguish and define these groups on the basis of their supposed attitude toward the police, their values (what will make them respect the police), their political power, and their relationship to the ends of the police. In their concern for public approval they analyze these groups in terms of the degree of influence they have over the police and the way in which they must be treated in order to obtain respect and other social goals of the police.

It is not intended that the continuum that is presented here be considered scientifically demonstrable; rather, it should be thought of as a descriptive device meant to convey in a rough, impressionistic fashion the major elements in terms of which the police differentiate the public. It is derived of many observations and casual conversations and, unfortunately, a minimal amount of interview documentation.

Children. To the policeman, the child is the approving innocent who is to be guided and taught. His contacts with the child in the streets, the parks, the schoolyards, and the crossings are frequently ones in which he experiences a feeling of respect or at the worst fear on the part of the child. He himself feels solicitude for children, frequently identifying them with his own children. The police department or the lodge in City X have sessions in which the police speak to the schoolchildren or sponsor marble contests for them. Most of the men approve of this program.

The community defines the child as a privileged citizen, and police mistreatment of the child would arouse vehement protests. Thus, although individual policemen may have prejudices against children, the social definition of the force is such that they wouldn't dare mistreat a child. This is one of the rare categories of people that the police define as requiring good treatment; the men, individually and collectively, would feel clear resentment should any member of the force mistreat a child.

Juvenile delinquents, many of whom fall in the child category (roughly everyone up to high school age), receive a differential definition. They are liable to minor forms of mistreatment. However, even here the policeman is inclined to view the child offender as a child, and only considerable brashness and sarcasm, serious offenses, and recidivistic tendencies on the part of the child will lead the policeman to define him in the category of juvenile delinquent. The positive definition of the child explains, in part, the conflicting attitudes that the police have toward the delinquent. Goldman (1950) has presented extensive documentation of these attitudes.

To summarize, the child is in the lone category among the policeman's public to which he can attribute a positive, or at least the absence of a negative, definition of the police. The child is thus one of the few sources of prestige for the policeman, and represents an area in which he can derive satisfaction, on a positive emotional level, from his social interaction. The child is also the potential citizen who may someday make a judgment of the police. The child has political power, since his mistreatment will easily arouse the community. The child responds to kindness and guidance. These ways in which the police see the child serve to explain their attitude toward the child.

The "Better Class of People." These are, in essence, the people who live in the better residential neighborhoods, or who should live in those areas. They include everyone from the skilled worker with a home in a good area up through the professional people and the rich people.

One of the most significant differentiations that the policeman makes is between the way people in the well-to-do areas and people in the slum areas should be treated in order that the police may be effective. Thus, one policeman states that "in the better districts the purpose is to make friends out of the people and get them to like you. If you react rough to them, naturally they will hate you." Another states that with the people in M, a better residential area, "you just pass the time of day with them. But with these hill billies you got to talk rough with them to make yourself understood to them." Thus, the following attitudes are expressed:

1. In the police department you deal with two types of individuals. In the residential neighborhood you take that kind of individual. We don't handle him as you would the habitual criminal where you have to use force to keep him in line. But you have got to remember that the commission of crime by an individual is not enough to classify him as a criminal.

2. In the good districts you appeal to people's judgment and explain the law to them. In the south side the only way is to appear like you are the boss. You can't ask them a question and get an answer that is not a lie. In the south side the only way to walk into a tavern is to walk in swaggering as if you own the place and if somebody is standing in your way give him an elbow and push him aside.

3. The difference between good districts and the north side is that in the good district you have to be nicer because they are nicer. In the central district they don't know half the facts. You have to try to explain. You have to try to be tougher.

The distinction indicates that for the more affluent and better educated the policeman believes that the friendly attitude is the proper one, that one should use a polite approach and never be rough, and that "that is the way to make them respect you." The "better class of people," then, are those who dislike violence, who think of the policeman as a servant, and who react positively only to the humble, the positive, and the polite approach. However, the policeman does not regard this group with the same tolerance that he displays toward the child. He feels that most of them look down on him and are ready to define him in the role of a racketeer. He resents their patronizing attitude; he likes to arrest them if he can. Nevertheless, he recognizes that they have influence, and in his need for approval and his sensitivity to disdain he feels forced to act the role they assign to him; that is, to act toward them in such a manner as to obtain their approval. He sees these people as within the law — that is, as being within the protection of the law — and in his treatment of them, as a group with which he has to observe the letter of the law. Their power forces him to do so. On the other hand, there is no particular distinction to be obtained from the apprehension of such a person. Essentially, they do not fall into the category of potential criminals.

The People in the Slums. These are the people who live in the more deteriorated areas of the town: the bums, the migrants, the immigrant groups. The policeman sees them as lacking in morality, ready to commit a crime, ignorant of the law.

The distinctions indicated in the previous section show that the policeman believes that the people in these areas understand and respond only to fear. He feels that in order to elicit respect from these people he must force them to respect him.

The individual in this category is seen as lacking in political influence. He is, in fact, regarded as a potential criminal because of his moral weakness and his great needs. This leads to a feeling that the use of rough treatment not only elicits respect but can be gotten away with, and may lead to a confession, which will result in a criminal apprehension. Besides, they feel that if rough treatment is not used these people will get out of hand and take advantage of the police. They may even "try to push the policeman around." The policeman feels superior to this public and wants them to recognize this superiority. Deviations from this expected response are liable to arouse violent action. This is the area of focus for the "you gotta make them respect you" attitude, which the rookie is carefully instructed in.

Thus, the policeman expects open hostility from this group; he recognizes their potential weakness; he feels that they respect only through fear; he sees them as the potential criminal.

The Negroes. For the police the Negro epitomizes the slum dweller, and he is considered inherently criminal both culturally and biologically. Individual policemen sometimes deviate sharply from this general definition, but no white policeman with whom the author has had contact failed to mock the Negro, to use some type of stereotyped categorization, and to refer to interaction with the Negro in exaggerated dialect when the subject arose.

Fifty white officers of all ranks and positions in the police force of City X were interrogated as to their feelings toward the Negro. They were asked (1) what they would do in specific situations in which they would have to protect the Negro's rights; (2) how they would feel about those situations; and (3) how they account for the high Negro crime rate. All the men were not asked the same questions. Some responses were introduced spontaneously. The materials that follow are not therefore statistically valid or susceptible to generalization about the whole force. However, they do offer an excellent qualitative index to the way in which the policeman in this department tends to define the Negro.

The results should be interpreted in the light of recent emphasis on race relations in the police department. This emphasis was the result of a course in race relations given to the top officers of the department (captains and sergeants), an emphasis on race relations in the recruit school, and the filtering down of some of these ideas to the men in the department. Always conscious of the political temper of the department, the men on the force were undoubtedly aware of this emphasis on the police handling of minority groups. Therefore, it should be realized that the anti-Negro statements were made in spite of the men's consciousness of this departmental emphasis, and in spite of the fact that the interviewer was suspected slightly of being a stooge for the chief.

Of the 50 men interviewed 38, or 76%, expressed ideas indicating that they had a prejudice in this area. Most conservatively, this

Table 3.6. Policemen's Opinions of the Negro

Attitude	Frequency	Percentage
Anti-Negro	38	76
The Negro is biologically inferior	22	44
The Negro has become morally deteriorated because of the way in which he lives	7	14
No particular reason	9	18
Pro-Negro	12	24
Total	50	100

prejudice can be expressed as the feeling that relationships between whites and Negroes should be kept to a minimum and that the Negroes should keep to themselves. Many opinions were much more violent, however. Table 3.6 gives a breakdown of these opinions.

Most of the explanations of their position on the Negro came from the questions that asked the men to account for the high crime rate among the Negroes. None of the men denied the veracity of the high crime rate, probably because it was so obviously true in this particular city. Their responses to this question were categorized, and appear in Table 3.6, as anti-Negro when they indicated some feeling of aversion. Otherwise they were considered to be pro-Negro. Thus, although some men felt that the high Negro crime rate could be accounted for by sociological causes — poor housing, poor upbringing, and so forth — they yet felt that through this the Negro became morally weak. Responses of this type were considered to represent anti-Negro feelings. In addition, all responses characterizing the Negro as inherently morally deficient were characterized thus.

In all, some thirty-six men were asked, "Why do you think the Negro crime rate is so high?" Their replies, which give a rough indication of the way in which they characterize the Negro, are summarized in Table 3.7.

Thus, 61% of the men felt that the Negro was somehow inherently (biologically) inferior and possessed characteristics that would lead to criminal activity. Of the remaining 39%, many of the replies were not truly expressive of the policeman's picture

Table 3.7. The Negro as Characterized by the Police

Characteristic	Frequency	Percentage
Corrupted by living conditions	14	39
Naturally lazy and irresponsible	9	25
Still savages — just out of the jungle	7	19
Born criminals, they love crime	3	8
Naturally lacking in sense of morals	2	6
Not fully developed mentally	1	3
Total	36	100

of the Negro, since at the time the interviews were made it was the explicit policy of the department to make the men acquainted with the sociological basis of the Negro problem in the city and many of these men were doing their best to make a good impression on the interviewer.

Since these materials may be of interest to other research workers, and in order to substantiate the above categorizations, we will cite at length a sample of the replies in each category.

The Negro is corrupted by living conditions

1. Well, things are pretty tough. The trouble is that these Negroes are getting into politics. These politicians, they go around to the Negroes and try to make a deal with them for votes and this gives the Niggers a pretty high idea of themselves. Then they tell you to your face that that white fellow was lower than they or else who would want to cater to them that way.

2. I think that the high colored crime rate is hard to pin down. Probably the conditions they have to exist in down there have something to do with it, but you know it seems they live for today and not for tomorrow. If they have money it is spent right away but of course that is changing.

3. I imagine that it is due to lack of economic security, poorly paid jobs and things like that. I don't doubt that they are easier on morals than the average white person but that in turn could also be pushed back to lack of education and stuff like that.

4. I'd say that a quarter of the population of X is colored. The crime rate is high. It's not that I like the colored, I think they are that way because of conditions they live in. It's very hard for them to spread out. They get used to these conditions.

5. The high Negro crime rate is due to home environment, poor education, and poor recreation facilities, and the fact that they grow up around vice and crime.

The Negro is naturally weak and irresponsible

1. I'd say they get the same opportunities as the white fellow but they won't work for small money and wouldn't work if they had to work.

2. The colored crime rate is high because they don't have any sense of responsibility. They don't want or have any education. They live beyond their means. They buy a Cadillac and they have to starve to pay for it.

3. The colored — well I guess they commit so much crime for their living. They live packed together. They live fancy though. Drink, for example. That's their nature, I guess. You know, every person in the central district plays the numbers game. I can't see anything in this numbers game.

4. The high colored crime rate is due to home environment. They get to expect a lot for nothing. They don't like to work. It comes from a general lassitude of the whole race. They will buy a Cadillac car and live in a box.

The Negro is a savage just out of the jungle

1. They are just jungle people. They are not all there mentally. They will steal and cheat and spend a dollar as soon as they get it. You can tell they are jungle people because you know how the natives in the jungles use drums to communicate, to spread the word. Well, if anything happens down in the colored area the word spreads just as fast like in the jungles. They are still jungle people at heart only they don't do it with drums.

2. It's high. Of course, they are only a hundred years from being savages. They haven't had a chance to develop.

3. The colored — I don't think they are educated enough. They come from poor families and surroundings and want to get something for nothing. Just as soon as they get a few drinks under their belt the savage comes out and they want to do bodily harm to the other party.

4. The high crime rate among the colored is due to the fact that they still have one foot in Africa. They go savage when they get mad and they want to kill. When they are mad you can't handle them. You gotta let them cool off in the lockup for a couple of hours before you can talk to them.

The Negro is a born criminal, he loves crime

1. The nigger women are all whores. When the old man goes on the night shift they try to pick up a few bucks to supplement the family income. They just love crime, they're naturally criminals.

2. The colored crime is just due to ignorance. Where the people are bad they are born bad. If you educate them they are still just bad.

The Negro is naturally lacking in a sense of morals

1. The high crime rate among the colored is because they are still living in shacks, eat sourbelly and beans, but always have nice clothes and a big car. I can't understand why they do it that way. Me, I haven't had a car in thirteen years but I always eat well.

2. Most of the colored are not working. As soon as they get the stuff they pawn it and buy cars. I don't know why they don't work, there is plenty of work for them in X.

The Negro is not fully developed mentally

I think the colored people are not developed mentally. They are equal to the way we were in the Western days. You know, I was raised in an Irish Catholic family and we were brought up to hate the Jews and the Negroes. I don't like that, and when I got into high school I thought now's my chance to stick up for them. So I read some books. I wanted to defend them. But I wasn't on the police force three months, in the central district, when I grew to hate these people.

The police place the Negro between the slum dweller and the criminal. Many of them seem to feel that every Negro is just waiting to commit a crime or has already committed a crime, and all you have to do is make him confess. Except in the case of a relatively few Negro professionals, the policeman tends to shout at rather than speak to the Negro, feeling that this will make him stop lying. Among the policemen there is a growing consciousness of the increasing political power of the Negro, particularly with regard to the efforts of the NAACP and the Urban League. However, as yet this does not appear as a real threat to them and they feel free to treat the Negro as they choose. Their feeling that the Negro has inherent criminal tendencies leads the police to treat the Negro with more roughness than the white man in situations where they are under suspicion.

To summarize, the police feel that the Negro dislikes the police and will only respect them if they put the fear of God into him; that the Negro has little political power, and that therefore there is little danger in mistreating him. And finally that the Negro is a criminal who is yet to be found out.

The Criminal. The criminal is thought of by the police as a felon. He is thought to hate the police. No attempt is made to gain his respect; compliance is forced. He is regarded as being completely without political power and therefore eligible for any type of treatment the police feel they can get away with. His apprehension and conviction are a major value of the police and in this task they feel that the means justify the end. We have dealt previously with the policeman's conception of the criminal at length[3] so we will not document these attitudes at this point.

Summary. The policeman divides the public into five general categories, according to the way he thinks they feel about him, the way in which he must approach them in order to obtain respect, their political power, and their reference to his aims. The groups then form a rough continuum ranging from the child, who is thought to like the police, to react to kindness, to have political

[3] See pages 88–95.

power, and to have reference to the aims of the police only in his status as a future citizen, through the better class of people, the slum dwellers, and the Negroes, to the criminal, who is thought to hate the police and to have no political power, to whom force is the only intelligible language, and who is useful to the police as he is apprehended and convicted.

Summary and Conclusions

This chapter has presented illustrations of the public's attitude toward the police; an account of the major types of occupational experience to which the policeman is subjected; a survey of the policeman's interpretation of the public's attitude toward himself; and a description of various categories into which the police divide the public.

A rough sample of 20 lawyers, 14 social workers, 35 prominent Negroes, and 8 union stewards indicated a general condemnation of the police and a characterization of them as ineffectual, brutal, corrupt, and ignorant. This, then, is the framework in terms of which the public is ready to interpret the actions of the police. It suggests that the responses made by the public to police gestures are fundamentally rejective and obviously hostile.

The major types of occupational experiences endemic to police work may be summarized in terms of traffic cases, family quarrels, sex cases, criminals, businessmen, drunks and fighters, courts, and juvenile delinquents. The list is not exhaustive since the research was not exhaustive, but it can be considered sufficiently comprehensive to indicate the broad outlines of the policeman's experience. This experience consists of social contacts in which the policeman interacts with the people of the community. The contacts and the consequent interactions are, however, selective; the nature of the policeman's job brings him into contact with people who are in a state of personal crisis, with people in their sorrow, their degradation, their evil, and their defeat. The selective power of the occupation gives the policeman *qua* policeman a unique series of social contacts, which have in common, however, conflict, hostility toward the police, and situations in which the public immorality is exposed. The interaction can then be expected to possess common and unique characteristics. Each type of situation poses an occupational problem, and because of the commonality of experience, communication within the group, and the consensus generated by a hostile public, they tend to give rise to a series of flexible but collective definitions of the situations, the public, and conduct with respect to the people involved.

The public judgment of the policeman as morally depraved is brought to his attention in his contacts with them in traffic cases, in which the offenders threaten the policeman's judgment and goodwill by refusing to accept his decision and giving excuses, and his integrity by offering him bribes; in family quarrels, in which the participants indicate that they regard the entrance of the policeman as a malicious intrusion; in contacts with drunks and fighters, in which the policeman is accused of dishonesty and brutality. Unable to accept this judgment, the policeman regards the public with resentment and feels himself a victim of injustice. He becomes withdrawn and suspicious, sees the public as hostile to the police, and believes that toughness is the standard for action.

He finds a social justification for his legal right to the use of force in sex cases, in which public pressure and lack of cooperation make this a sanctioned and expedient method; in dealing with fighters and drunks, when it is necessary for self-protection and provocation is intense; and with the criminal, when public pressure for apprehension and public acclaim for conviction make them a paramount goal, an end that justifies the means. A collective sanction for the use of force is thus established among the police.

He comes to see the public itself as corrupt in his contacts with the businessman, who uses favors for leniency and special attention; in the courts, where he sees the privileges of connections and the abridgement of the law; and with the criminal, who makes a living that way. He substantiates this thesis with the type of information that comes to him through his job, information of the numerous cases in which the people try to evade the law or generally indicate a disregard for it. The public support for the law and morality is thus weakened. Morality is defined as less an end than a means, and the public's actions are seen as expediential.

The hostility that the policeman finds in the public is refined to include unfair demands and an uncooperative attitude through his experience with juvenile delinquents, when he sees the public as demanding action on the crimes they commit but at the same time refusing to incarcerate them; with sex cases, when public hysteria and pressure on the police are constant, but so, too, is public refusal to testify or prefer charges; and in the courts, which epitomize the law and the legal tasks of the policeman, and yet repudiate his actions with acquittals. From this experience there grows a definition of the public as selfish, and of himself as a victim of injustice.

The policeman's attitude toward the public and his definition of their attitude toward him is clearly substantiated in a survey of a representative group of 85 policemen. The survey indicated that 73% of the men felt that the public hated the police and was against them, and that only 12% felt that the public liked and supported the police. Two general explanations of this public attitude emerged: (1) that the public was ignorant of the nature of police work and needed to be educated; and (2) that the city newspaper was against the police and misled the public.

In terms of his consciousness of the hostility of the public and his need for public approval and respect, the policeman tends to divide the public into five general categories. These groups form a continuum that corresponds to the degree of respect that the policeman has for the group and the care with which he deals with it. The groups range from children, whom the police conceive to be favoring the police, whom they like, and whom they treat gently, through the better class of people, whom the police see as politically powerful and therefore worthy of respect, and toward whom they act respectfully, feeling that this is the way to obtain *their* respect; through the slum dwellers, whom the police see as politically weak, potentially criminal, respecting only fear, toward whom they act tough and sometimes violently; through the Negro, whom they see as the unapprehended biological criminal who understands only fear, and with whom they generally act very tough and frequently get violent; to the criminal, whom they see as the felon, as having abridged his rights as a citizen, as the object par excellence of their activity and efforts, and toward whom they are ready to use almost any means to obtain a conviction.

In this examination of the occupational experience of the policeman, we have tried to show him as a human being in social interaction with his fellows. We have indicated that because of his occupation the policeman's interaction with the public is colored by, first, an adverse definition of the police on the part of the public and a consequent hostility toward the police and, second, the fact that the policeman's occupation selects interactional situations in which this hostility is intensified. The bias thus introduced will give rise to a complementary bias in the meanings that the policeman derives from the interaction and consequently in his definitions of the world and his own conduct toward it.

The particular definitions of the public and of his conduct that the policeman develops out of this interaction assume a collective and cultural character because the police hold the experiences in common, because of communication among the police, and because of the strong consensual bond developed by the felt hostility of the public.

However, we would like to make explicit that our evidence suggests that this series of collective definitions *does not* possess sufficient coercive strength to act as a firm regulator of opinions and conduct. Rather, the definitions function as a powerful factor in the formulation of police opinion and in the regulation of police conduct. They permit more than they require. Predictively, they should be regarded as tendencies in a given direction.

These tendencies may then be seen as follows: The public is prepared to interpret police actions as evil and theatening; the police are prepared to see the public's actions as hostile, suspicious, derogatory, and uncooperative. These, then, form the frames of reference in which each of the parties will act and interpret the actions of the other. They form the substance of conflict.

The purpose of this chapter was to describe the public attitude toward the police, the occupationally selected contacts of the police with the public, and the policeman's conception of the public. In the course of this description we have suggested various interpretations and effects arising from the policeman's experience with the public. In the chapter that follows we will make these interpretations and effects explicit.

4. The Morality of Secrecy and Violence

The Roots of Morality│Silence, Secrecy, and Solidarity Method for testing strength of secrecy; sanctions for secrecy│**The Uses of Violence** Police powers; police action│**The Identification of Norms in the Legitimation of Action│Legitimation for Violence** Interpretation; legitimation in the maintenance of respect; legitimation in the apprehension of the felon; legitimation in the law; guilt as a precondition to violence; opposition to violence; summary│**Maintenance of Respect for the Police│The Good Pinch│Police Action and the Law│ Role, Morality, and Self-Conception│Summary│**

Policemen find that in order to endure their work they must relate to the public in ways that protect their self-esteem. Since they see the public as hostile to the police and feel that their work tends to aggravate this hostility, they separate themselves from the public, develop strong in-group attitudes, and control one another's conduct, making it conform to the interests of the group.

They insist that all policemen maintain strict secrecy about police affairs; act in such a way as to maintain public respect for the police; and use whatever methods are necessary for the apprehension of the felon. These form broad rules of conduct in terms of which they decide how to act in specific situations.

This chapter deals with these rules of conduct, with the way in which they are articulated in action, and with their impact on law enforcement and the policeman's self-conception, social role, and morality.

The Roots of Morality

The policemen in City X are deeply concerned with the hostility they feel from the public. It is a pressure that they constantly endeavor to alleviate or repudiate. Their job requires that they be in constant interaction with the public — it is an ever-present factor in their experience — and they become extremely sensitive to these public accusations. They lean on one another for moral support; they depend on one another for practical support. Against unpleasant experience they have the bulwark of in-group, interpersonal strength. Even if the public doesn't appreciate them, their fellows do. The public must be repudiated and the group affirmed. "We are only one hundred forty against one hundred forty thousand" is a running commentary on their position, expressing their feelings of affinity against a hostile world. The feeling is a powerful lever projecting the policeman into the group.

Public hostility includes the policeman in his symbolic status. It includes an assessment of collective responsibility or guilt by association, in terms of which every member of the force is made responsible for the actions of the individual officer. The result is that the individual policeman finds that his own interests have been forcibly identified with those of the group. Any action that incriminates or smears a member of the force has the same impact on all the others before the bar of public opinion. In City X the public frame of reference represents the police so negatively that every vice is added to their character and every virtue is forgotten. This is the feeling of the police when they complain so bitterly about the unfair publicity that the city newspaper gives them. It is encompassed in the words of an officer, who said, "You have two strikes against you as soon as you put on the uniform." Almost in spite of themselves, the policemen come to protect the actions of their comrades and to see little in them that is bad. Almost any beating becomes just; even graft becomes permissible. The policeman is thus permitted to breach the law, for to apprehend him would only do the apprehender harm. The prejudice and the stereotype find the police together and give them a common front against the community.

Through the hostility and through the stereotype, the police become a close, social group, in which collective action is organized for self-protection and an attack on the outside world. These become expressed in two major rules. The vehicle of self-protection is the rule of silence — secrecy. The vehicle of attack is the emphasis on the maintenance of respect for the police.

Silence, Secrecy, and Solidarity

The stool pigeon, the squealer, the one who tells, is anathema to almost any social group. He is an outcast among the police. To him is applied the most powerful sanction the group has available — the silent treatment. This is powerful because it deprives the unfortunate man of information vital to his continued success and necessary to his happiness, and because he works alone. This is the penalty for a serious abrogation of the rule of silence. It is a penalty for a threat to the secrecy of the group.

Secrecy among the police stands as a shield against the attacks of the outside world; against bad newspaper publicity, which would make the police lose respect; against public criticism, from which they feel they suffer too much; against the criminal, who is eager to know the moves of the police; against the law, which they too frequently abrogate. Secrecy is loyalty, for it represents sticking with the group, and its maintenance carries with it a profound sense of participation. Secrecy is solidarity, for it represents a common front against the outside world and consensus in at least one goal.

Secrecy and silence are among the first rules impressed on the rookie. "Keep your mouth shut, never squeal on a fellow officer, don't be a stool pigeon," is what the rookie has dinned into his ears; it is one of the first things he learns.

Secrecy does not apply to achievements — these should be publicized. It applies to mistakes, to plans, to illegal actions, to character defamation. Among the police it applies to mistakes in arrests, to the abrogation of departmental rules, to criminal suspects, to illegal actions, to personal misdemeanors. These are important insofar as they represent a breach in the protective coating that the policeman tries to present to society.

Method for Testing Strength of Secrecy. Obtaining concrete data on secrecy among the police represented one of the most difficult problems in the research. The interviewer was at all times an outsider, one from whom secrets were to be withheld. Because of this it was decided to make a frontal attack on the problem by designing a question that would leave every alternative unpleasant. Such an approach had to be limited, however, lest it seriously impede the research project (which it did). Thus, a question was designed, presented to 16 men in a series, and then dropped. Even so, it resulted in a wholesale cancellation of interviews for a period of two weeks, and much persuasion was needed before they could be resumed.

Each man was given the following problem:

I'd like to pose an imaginary situation and see how you would handle it. You and your partner pick up a drunk who is breaking up a bar. While you are patting him down you discover he has five hundred dollars on him. You take him into the station. You drive and your partner sits in the back with the drunk who is raising hell. When you get to the station and check him in with the turnkey the money doesn't show up. The drunk yells for his dough. Your partner says he never saw the money. You realize that your partner has clipped him. What would you do?

When they had replied, a further situation was posed:

The drunk prefers charges against you. In court your partner testifies that as far as he knew the drunk didn't have a cent on him. There are no other witnesses, and there is no further evidence. How would you testify?

These questions "put the men on the hook" because a refusal to answer *looked* incriminating, a failure to report the partner or to perjure oneself *was* incriminating, and reporting and/or testifying against the partner was making oneself a stool pigeon. All the questions were pressed, and most of the men responded. Seventy-

Table 4.1. Proportion of Policemen Willing to Report Other Policemen for Stealing

Response	Frequency	Percentage
Would report	4	27
Would not report	11	73
Total	15	100

seven percent of the men stated that they would perjure themselves. The results are summarized in Tables 4.1 and 4.2.

One man stated that he would both report and testify against his partner. He was a rookie. The last man to be interviewed completely evaded the question by stating:

Why, I have heard about that question. You have to be pretty careful with it. I don't think you know what you are doing. Suppose you are working with a bastard — a real prick. You got to know that. In that case chances are you will make a nine-hole home. But generally the guy who is in on the take he is making a buck regularly and is a swell guy. He is the kind of guy that will come down to the lodge and buy drinks for everybody, real friendly with everybody. Now if you nine-hole a guy like that you are in bad.

Now about this business of a policeman rolling a drunk. That doesn't happen very often. Your partner doesn't do anything without your knowing about it. Of course once in a while you will pick up a drunk and you don't take them all to jail. Might be a nice fellow. Your partner might say, "Let's take him home, he's a nice guy." You will take him home, put him to bed and then you will be driving away. You will leave the guy and be driving away and your partner will reach over and say here's yours, and hand you a twenty dollar bill. Well when that happens very often you begin not to trust that partner because you know it may be that if he is giving you twenty dollars he probably took a hundred because a guy that will steal from a drunk will steal from you.

The full significance of the responses becomes apparent only if it is realized (1) that the support and enforcement of the law is the basic legal function of the police, and they are quite conscious of the fact; (2) that the policemen themselves maintain that biased testimony only leads to trouble in the long run; and (3) that the detection of perjury by the authorities would result in the suspension of the man from the force, causing him to lose

Table 4.2. Proportion of Policemen Willing to Testify Against Other Policemen

Response	Frequency	Percentage
Would not testify	10	77
Would testify	3	23
Total	13*	100

* Two men refused to answer the question.

both his job and his pension time, would seriously hinder him in any future profession, and would make him liable to imprisonment.

From the responses it is clear that in spite of these dangers the illegal action is preferable to breaking the secrecy of the group, to being categorized as a stool pigeon. Undoubtedly, the verbal responses cannot be correlated with the actual actions. If they were faced with a perjury charge, many would probably change their minds. However, this does not diminish the significance of the responses, which represent a choice among alternatives. We would suggest, therefore, that the data are indicative of the strength of two characteristics of the police force: (1) secrecy constitutes one of the most important definitions and is represented in the rule of silence; and (2) law enforcement is subordinate to the ends of the group.

Sanctions for Secrecy. The strength of the rule of silence is again emphasized in the statements of some of the respondents when they tried to indicate what they thought would happen to them if they did report or testify against their partners. The following are representative statements:

1. You would get the name of a stool pigeon in the first place. In the second place if you did give testimony you would be putting yourself on the spot because you had to turn the man in in the first place. If you were a stool pigeon you are an outcast on the police force. Nobody wants to say anything to you. Nobody talks to you. Nobody wants to be around you and you never get to know what's going on in the department.

2. If I did say that I saw the money he would get the sack and although everybody would think I was right they would always remember that I had been down on my buddy, but I would not say anything. I would always remember, though, that he had

rolled the drunk, and one of my rules is that if we make a dollar we split 50-50. Now I don't take that kind of money but I don't think anybody else does. But you make a dollar now and then. Suppose for example that somebody gave my partner a reward and he didn't tell me about it. I'd feel pretty mean if I found anything out about it.

3. If I turned the man in everybody would be out to get me. They wouldn't talk to me. They would go out of their way to get me in trouble. When you are on the police force you can't afford to have a man against you. There are too many situations in which you have got to depend on him and you would work with him unless you knew he was spoiling things completely. If a man will turn you in for one thing he will turn you in for another. That is what they all figure and that is what I figure.

Interviewer: How serious would a crime have to be before you would turn a fellow officer in?

Answer: I wouldn't turn him in for anything. When you are on the job police stick together. If it is off the job it might be different.

4. I know that the other policemen would treat me with contempt. They would regard me as an unsafe officer.

One policeman who first stated that he would report his partner said a few minutes later:

5. I want you to put down that I think I was wrong. I wouldn't turn a policeman in for anything short of murder. When I think that I have seventeen years to go on the force before I get my pension and having those fellows look at me that way I wouldn't turn any man in. I have made a buck in my time from the speeders and even if I saw a policeman breaking into a store I'd run the other way. I'd never see him.

These statements indicate the nature of the sanctions that would be applied, or that the men thought would be applied, should they break the group rules. These include a program in which the culprit would be an outcast, isolated from social relationships so that nobody would talk to him, so that he wouldn't know what was going on, so that the other men would go out of their way to get the man in trouble. Thus, the following specific points are made:

1. The man wouldn't be able to find out what was going on. This would seriously incapacitate him, since the men must have a line to the chief in order to comply with his whims or the current of feelings in the town. There are times when the men can get away with anything, and others when they have to be

exceedingly careful. Word of this comes down through the grapevine. The man who is detached from this source of information is likely to do something that will get him in trouble.

2. The man would be deprived of friendly contacts. This would have important personal consequences for him, because it means a deprivation of the only real source of consolation for the hostility of the community.

3. The other men would go out of their way to get him in trouble. This can be interpreted in two ways: (1) that the other men would feel free to stool on him when he did anything wrong, and (2) that they would fail to support him when he got into trouble with the public or with the administration.

One man told of an experience in which he was tested to see whether he was the leak. He stated:

It is a good idea to keep your mouth shut about what happens in the department. Not long ago I had a man test me out.

When we were in a restaurant he told me a really terrific story about an incident in which a number of policemen were involved. Boy, it was really something. I could hardly wait to run over and tell my partner about it. But then I got to thinking and I decided to keep my mouth shut and later on it turned out that he had told me the story just to see whether or not it came back to him. It wasn't true. He had been having some things come back to him and he wanted to find out if I was the guy.

Interviewer: Do you ever have anyone tell you that some man is a stoolie?

Answer: No, I don't. You have to trust a man to tell him that. Some of your close friends will tell you something. Some of them will talk. But otherwise it is too dangerous.

This case illustrates the extent to which the men feel that the rule of silence has to be enforced. This man wouldn't even tell his partner about it. This in spite of the fact that the buddy or partner relationship is one of the closest on the force. When asked about whether he had ever been told who the stoolies were, he stated that only close friends will tell you something — "otherwise it is too dangerous."

While discussing the same subject, another man described an experience similar to the one posed in the question.

Oh, there are ways of keeping you in line. The men ask to be assigned to another car rather than work with you and they would not fraternize with you. Let me tell you about an actual case, somewhat like that, that I was involved in. Another fellow and I were doing some off duty work, keeping order at a dance. The other fellow went down to the basement and some of the boys were playing craps. There was about fifty dollars in the pot and he just walked over and snatched up the money and put it in his pocket. Well, when the fellows told me about it and asked me what they should do I just gave them a lot of pointless answers. I didn't want to handle the case because I felt that he really had done it and I didn't want to get him involved. Because he was a policeman I didn't want to pinch him. I knew he would lose his job. So I tried to point out to them that they were in the wrong. Convinced them that they were the guilty parties for playing craps in the first place. But I was mad at him for putting himself on the spot.

In this case the respondent at once indicated that you could be kept in line by refusals to work or fraternize with you and that he had been willing to protect his fellow policeman from possible suspension by convincing the public that they, not the policeman, were wrong.

The whole rule of silence, and the need for the maintenance of secrecy, tends to generate a set of reciprocal suspicions among the men. This is reflected in the words of one respondent, who stated:

It's more or less a rule that if you have any beefs you keep them in the family. Don't start talking to people outside. If you are in the department for a while you eventually develop that survival of the fittest attitude. Everybody does. Then you have to watch yourself. Everybody builds a barrier around himself — around his personal affairs. When you work with guys and they get to nosing around they generally get to know too much about your personal life. The way I figure it myself, and the other guys, we are good friends and we will keep it that way.

Part of this feeling arises from the idea that there are unknown stool pigeons among the men, and that if you talk to them you yourself may be labeled a stool pigeon; another part of the feeling is from the fear that if you talk too much people will be able to get something on you. This type of feeling is most prevalent among the detectives, the nature of whose work leads to a considerable amount of competition and a jealous guarding of information. This is also reflected in the following statements:

1. Wait a minute. There was one guy who did tell me the names of some of these stoolies. I tried to find out, you know, because I don't like the idea of trial and error method in a thing like that. But when the guy gave me the names I figured the reason he

gave me the names is because he isn't very much liked in the department and so was probably one of the stoolies himself. Most of the police won't tell you who the guys are. I don't think they want to because they are afraid you will reveal the source.

2. There are some guys you can't trust. They are just looking out for themselves. The men won't tell you who these fellows are. I don't want to work with a man who won't back you up. But actually you know the men don't talk so much about police work when they are together.

Thus, the stoolie is "the kind of guy no cop ever likes to stand for"; he is "just like the TB — you stay away from him, if he comes over while you are talking you just change the subject" — "if you get that reputation you are licked." He is the symbol of the one who breaks the rule of secrecy. His status is the threat behind the rule, which is probably the most powerful rule that the police maintain. It is the principal bond in the solidarity of the police.

The Uses of Violence

The essence of any group norm lies in its permissive or prescriptive regulation of the conduct of the members. Since occupational norms can be considered the product of the problematic areas of social interaction, it is probable that they will control or regulate actions in these areas.

Police Powers. For the police, action in large measure is confined to action toward the people of the community. It involves, on the one hand, the nature of police powers, and on the other, their decisions about using these powers.

Police power has two aspects: the positive, which involves coercion in the power to arrest and to use violence in making arrests; and the negative, which involves the power of withdrawal of protection. Policemen's legal privileges entitle them to the first source of power and forbid them the second. Both are used.

Although the police are legally entitled to certain powers, these powers are utilized for their personal ends as well as in the line of duty.

As a group they tend to use the power that they possess to gain their ends as a group, ends that we have indicated are basically embodied in the maintenance of secrecy, the maintenance of respect for the police, and the apprehension of the felon. In addition to the extension of their legal sources of power, they also tend to draw on certain illegal sources of power which are at their disposal. Principal among these is their power to withdraw their protection. In this sense they come to regard protection as a personal commodity, the extension of which is a reward for compliance and the withdrawal of which is a punishment for noncompliance. This source of power is almost completely reserved for expediting the ends of the police, whatever they may be,[1] and is seldom used to back up their legal function.

Police Action. Police action can be seen as a continuum ranging from letting it pass, or giving a warning, to the arrest and/or a beating. Actions in this range can be legally supported or rationalized. The decision on the part of the individual policeman as to what kind of action to take in a specific situation involves the interrelation of three variables: the enforcement of the law, the maintenance of respect for the police, and the apprehension of the felon, or the making of a "good pinch."

The enforcement of the law, ceteris paribus, will be confined to actions utilizing the legal sources of power and will seldom extend beyond the arrest. Persons involved in misdemeanors, who constitute the largest number of offenders, will generally be treated with respect, and will be warned more frequently than arrested. The speeder, the drunk, the public nuisance, and so forth, are seldom taken seriously by the police. It is only as one or both of the other variables come into play that the enforcement of the law involves more stringent types of action. Thus, when a drunk curses or reviles a policeman, especially in front of an audience, and when the policeman interprets this as demeaning the police, as influencing the public respect for the police, as threatening his dignity, the drunk will be susceptible to the more stringent types of police action — the arrest, and very possibly rough treatment. How far the policeman will go will depend (1) on how threatened he feels, (2) on the current attitude toward the police in the city, and (3) on that portion of the public into which he categorizes the drunk. If the policeman feels

---

[1] Thus, when graft becomes an important end of the police, this source of power is frequently used to force the cooperation of the unwilling gambler, bartender, and the like.

seriously threatened, if the public attitude toward the police has been quiet, and if the policeman sees the drunk as a professional criminal, or a Negro, some type of rough treatment will probably be the result.

This does not imply that there are not legitimate bases on which the policeman resorts to violence; there are many situations in which he may have to choose this course of action, such as when the prisoner refuses to accept arrest, when the policeman is attacked, when the policeman has to prevent someone from injuring another person or from committing a serious crime. However, even in these situations, frequently he can refrain from injuring the offender by overpowering him. Police usually work in pairs, and the situation, therefore, is frequently one in which they are two against one.

In addition, there are individual differences in the frequency with which the policeman resorts to force based largely on propensity and strength. Some men seem to work out their fears and aggressions on the job. Some men are so powerful that they seldom experience resistance on the part of the public, and when they do they can easily overpower the offender. Other men, who are smaller, seem to pose a challenge to the offender because of their very size, and they will frequently experience resistance and have to use the club to overcome this resistance. Nevertheless, the amount of force used by the police and the situations in which it is applied cannot be accounted for fully under the categories of necessity in the line of duty and personal propensities and strength; they appear to be a matter of prescription in terms of ends not thus accounted for.

This, then, affords an opportunity to test our hypothesis that the maintenance of respect for the police and the apprehension of the felon represent major occupational norms of the police.

The Identification of Norms in the Legitimation of Action
Although the prevalence of similar attitudes among a large proportion of the men, and their logical integration with the problems of the occupation, would suggest that these attitudes reflect group norms, it does not demonstrate the point. Similar experiences may generate similar attitudes which have no collective basis. However, the legitimation of action offers an index to norms which does have such a basis. This becomes clear if one

considers the subjective meaning of norms for the men involved.

Here one can assume (1) that a norm regulates action not only because of the sanctions it involves, but also because it represents to the actor the morally correct choice; (2) that any important norm should function as a source of moral authority to the actor so that he will justify his actions in terms of it; (3) that the more extreme the action, the more likely it will be applied toward ends (normatively defined) that are of importance; and (4) that the more subject to criticism the action is, the more likely the man will feel called upon to justify it.

On the basis of these assumptions it was possible to identify the major norms of the police by asking them to justify certain forms of extreme action. The use of force or violence is such an action, since it is both extreme and subject to heavy criticism by the people of the community. Therefore, the ways in which the police justify the use of force would indicate their major norms.

Legitimation for Violence

Seventy-four policemen in Department X were asked, "When do you think a policeman is justified in roughing a man up?" Their responses were essentially prescriptive in that they tried to indicate to the interviewer the type of situation in which they would prescribe the use of force. The situations for which force was prescribed represented those in which the policemen felt its use would be justified; therefore, these situations could be considered as sources for its legitimation.

Their answers frequently had elements in common, and thus it was possible to group them into rough categories which are indicative of the norms they represent (see Table 4.3). Since many of the respondents gave more than one basis for the use of force, their responses are first classified in terms of the major orientation, summarized in the column "primary responses." Each response in this column indicates a separate case. Their remaining rationalizations are summarized in the column "secondary response." Each item in this column represents an additional rationalization advanced by a respondent listed in the primary response column.

Interpretation. 1. The evidence of 39% of the men giving disrespectful behavior as a basis for the use of force supports the thesis that the maintenance of respect for the police is a major orientation of the police.

Table 4.3. Bases for the Use of Force

Basis	Primary Response Number	%*	Secondary Response Number	Total Number	%*
1. Disrespect for the police	27	37	2	29	39
2. Only when impossible to avoid	17	23	0	17	23
3. To obtain information	14	19	3	17	23
4. To make an arrest	6	8	3	9	12
5. For the hardened criminal	5	7	3	8	11
6. When you know man is guilty	2	3	1	3	4
7. For sex criminals	2	3	4	6	8
8. For self-protection	0	0	4	4	5
9. When pressure is on you	0	0	1	1	1
Total	74	100	20	94	

* Percentages computed only to the nearest 1%.

2. That 23% of the men legitimate the use of force to obtain information that would lead to the solution of a crime or the conviction of the criminal would support the thesis that the apprehension of the felon is also a major orientation of the police.

3. That 66% of the men gave as their *primary* rationalization an illegal basis for the use of force (categories 1, 3, 5, and 6) while only 8% gave a legal basis (category 4) would indicate that the group-engendered values are relatively more important to the men than their legal function.

4. The fact that 23% of the men stated that force should be avoided if possible is indicative of the social situation in which the interview took place rather than the feelings of the men. At the time the interviews were being made the chief of police was carrying on a program to reduce the amount of force being used and was applying penalties to deviants; the interviewer was suspected of being connected with the chief. Under these conditions

the safest response was to condemn the use of force. Thus, although some of the men undoubtedly indicated their true feelings, the proportion of 23% probably exaggerates the number. On the other hand, these same conditions would indicate that the proportion of the men endorsing the use of force is biased conservatively.

5. The apparent guilt of the man and his identification as a hardened criminal as bases for the use of force in 15% of the cases does not indicate that these are motivational factors but rather that they represent conditions under which the use of force can take place. They represent the feeling on the part of the men that force must be used with caution because of the possibility of a lawsuit against them.

In support of each of these interpretations, the actual statements of the respondents are more convincing than the number of times they occur. Therefore, we cite at length several typical responses in each category.

Legitimation in the Maintenance of Respect. That 39% of the respondents gave disrespectful behavior as a reason for using force is indicative of the profound meaning that the maintenance of respect has for the police. The responses conveyed this meaning in three general ways: by implication — "You gotta be tough with these fellows"; on a personal basis — "If anybody kicks me you can bet he is going to get it back"; and in terms of the group's needs — "If you don't use force when you have to you can't do your job because it spreads like wild fire" and "as a matter of fact there are a lot of people who know a policeman won't use a gun and they take advantage of the fact and *try* to push him around."

The symbol of disrespect for the police is the "wise guy," the fellow who thinks he knows more than they do, the fellow who talks back, the fellow who insults the policemen. The "wise guy" epitomizes what the police hate in the public. If they think they can get away with it, they will deal with him harshly. He appears in the following response:

Well, there are cases. For example when you stop a fellow for routine questioning. Say a wise guy, and he starts talking back to you and telling you you are no good and that sort of thing. You know you can take a man in on a disorderly conduct charge but you can practically never make it stick. So what you do in a case like that is to egg the guy on until he makes a remark where you can justifiably slap him and then if he fights back you can call it resisting arrest.

This policeman points up the need that he feels to punish the "wise guy," to bring him into line. He formulates possible lines of action. He points out that legally he can't do a thing to the man. He figures out a way to punish the man, to beat him up and not get in trouble, and to hit him on legal grounds.

Many of the responses indicated that the men felt sensitive about public opinion concerning the use of force. They recognized that the use of force was in many instances illegal, that it could get them in trouble. In particular, they recognized that the Negro was no longer so politically impotent and could cause trouble if they beat him up. These points are illustrated in the following cases:

1. The colored people understand one thing. The policeman is the law and he is going to treat you rough and that's the way you have to treat them. Personally I don't think the colored are trying to help themselves a bit. If you don't treat them rough they will sit right on top of your head. The way I look at it is if you think you are in the right use everything including force to straighten it out. If you are in doubt take it easy until you have all the facts. If you are not sure call the sergeant.

It's different on the south side, now, from what it used to be. You can't beat on the colored folks like you used to. They are bringing cases to the courts and that has softened it down a lot.

This man justified the use of force on the Negroes on the basis that it was necessary to make them respect the police. Evidently he felt that such a basis was quite adequate and needed no apology. Statements like these indicate the normative nature of this concept. Also included is the consciousness that one had to be careful because the Negro had means to retaliate.

2. Well, it varies on different cases. Most of the police use punishment if the fellow gives them any trouble. Usually you can judge a man who will give you some trouble though. If there is any slight resistance you can go all out on him. You shouldn't do it in the street though. Wait until you get in the squad car, because even if you are in the right and a guy takes a poke at you, just when you are hitting back somebody's just likely to come around the corner and what they will say is that you are beating the guy with your club.

"If there is any slight resistance you can go all out on him."

This is to say that if the man dares to do other than what the police command, they can and should punish him, they should teach him to respect the police. At the same time the respondent feels that the public won't like such actions, and that they should be confined to areas out of the public sight.

To condone fully the standard of demanding respect for the police, the offender in this area is often reduced to the lowest possible moral level. This tendency appears in the following response:

3. I'd say that the easiest way out is the best way out — either by talking fast enough to get out without too much physical force. In interrogations you don't have to use force too often. I won't say that I have never even spanked a guy. There was a case where a guy had committed seventeen burglaries but I was absolutely certain that he was guilty and that he was lying to me.

If a man shot or tried to whip a policeman he would have to shoot or whip me. *The way we feel about it is that anybody who is out to get a policeman has no respect for law and order and anyone in that category isn't worth a damn.*

Also of course there is a self-preservation idea in connection with it. If it got to be generally known that they could hit a policeman and could get away with it that's a pretty serious matter. If we let some of them get away with that and it got out then we might be lost. If you are in a tough spot and you begin to back down you are lost.

This respondent makes four general points: (1) force is not always the best way to achieve your ends — fast talking sometimes works just as well; (2) there is nothing wrong with using force to obtain important information; (3) the man who resists the policeman by shooting at him or fighting with him "isn't worth a damn"; and (4) the police have to keep the people afraid of them or they won't be able to do their job.

Another respondent stated:

4. Then there's guys on whom you have got to use roughness in order to take them. *After all, you got to remember that a guy who is a cop hater is going to stay one and there's nothing you can do about it. Might just as well kill him.* There are other cases too. I don't know whether you read this article by Commissioner Valentine. It was in *Fortune Magazine* about twelve years ago. In it he pointed out that in 80% of the cases the only punishment a law breaker gets is the punishment that a policeman deals out.

The statement that you "might just as well kill him" reflects the way in which the policeman absolves himself of the responsibility for the brutal treatment of the disrespectful one by categorizing him as permanently inimical to the social interest.

Fundamental to all rationalizations about the maintenance of respect as the basis for the illegal use of force is the idea of the interactional situation in which the offender insults and tries to demean the policeman. These are the situations that the policemen imagine will call for the use of force:

1. Well, a prisoner deserves to be hit when he goes to the point where he tries to put you below him.

2. Well, when a man's language becomes very bad, when he is trying to make a fool of you in front of everybody else. I think most policemen try to treat people in a nice way, but usually you have to talk pretty rough. That is the only way to set a man down — to make them show a little respect.

3. Use force only when it's necessary. I don't believe in force. It's a poor reflection on the police. But if it was a bad crime and I was absolutely sure that I had the right guy I'd work him over good.

If a fellow called a policeman a filthy name, a slap in the mouth would be a good thing, especially if it was out in public where calling a policeman a bad name would look bad for the police.

4. The use of force is necessary to protect yourself. You should always show that you are boss. Make them respect the uniform and not the man. Suppose you are interrogating a guy who says to go fuck yourself. You are not supposed to take that.

5. You have to use force on drunks who talk back but it's not a good idea to use it on ordinary people if you can help it. Of course, if you are after a known criminal then you use anything. It doesn't make any difference.

6. You gotta get rough if the public pushes you around. You can't let them do it.

7. If the police were sure the courts would be hard they would be easier on people. You don't have to have some colored woman spit at you and take it.

These seven responses have in common the feeling that the use of force is called for when the policeman is treated in a derogatory fashion; when he is pushed around, spit at, and made a fool of, called a filthy name; when he is treated in a way that indicates a lack of respect for the police. In addition, two respondents see it as a legitimate device for eliciting information, and one felt that this was especially true if the insult occurred out in public, where it "would look bad for the police."

The trouble with me is that I tend to take my cases home and worry about them. Now just recently there was a case where I got a call about some drunks raising a disturbance and when I got there I found four or five of them, and I told them to get along home. There was one little fellow there, looked to be about twenty-three. Came up to me and started shooting his mouth off, saying, "I know my rights, I am not taking guff of that sort from you, I do what I want to do." I told him to relax and move on and he just stuck his chin out at me and I gave him a littl push and he puts up his hand so I grabs him by the shoulder and bang him against the wall and rough him up a little too. When I let him go he crumpled up on the ground. When I took him to the station I found out he was sixteen years old. I wondered whether I had done the right thing. You may think I was cruel. I wouldn't have done it if I had known he was only sixteen. But it doesn't mean anything. I have had kids younger than that. One of them fired at me with a pistol. Funny thing, it went right between my legs, just didn't hurt me otherwise.

This man states that he feels anxiety about his work, that he worries about his mistakes. He illustrates from his own experience the way in which the policeman who is insulted, particularly by what looks as if he were a criminal, reacts with violence. This is indicated by his response to the boy who talked tough; he threw the boy against the wall with such force that he crumpled to the ground.

The presence of an audience seems to be the ultimate incentive to the use of force in one sense. The policeman who is insulted in front of an audience feels that his prestige is really dropping. Two men illustrated how they reacted in situations of this type.

I am not afraid to bust a guy. Some of the fellows may be but I am not. Like take the other day. We came down there. It was a corner in one of the taverns. It was a bunch of these white chippies. Well, they were raising a lot of hell and all of a sudden this blonde whore comes running out. She really had her machine going. She was plenty excited and she had plenty of drinks in her. We told her she couldn't be coming up like that and she started to get a little sassy, and all those other whores were standing around the corner, watching. So what do I do? I throw her into the car and clear out.

This man was extremely conscious of "all those other whores . . . standing around the corner, watching." He felt this was a good reason to get tough with the offender. He suggests but does not state that he did a lot more than throw her into the car.

However, this in itself constitutes rough treatment, for he meant it literally.

Well, it varies with men. What I can't take is these colored. They call you the worst kinds of names. I don't mind if they all call me a son of a bitch or something like that but this business of calling you a mother fucker — that I don't take. I didn't come on the force for that. If they call me that I just bust them one.

There was another incident of a fellow I picked up. I was on the beat and I was taking him down to the station. There were people following us. He kept saying that I was not in the Army. Well, he kept going on like that and finally I had to bust him one. I had to do it. The people would have thought I was afraid otherwise. But sometimes you hold yourself back. Like there was a time I was in the bus station. A fellow parks his car and I come up and tell him to move it away, then I go back to the station. I come back ten minutes later, and there is the car still in front of the station. I said, "O.K. Buddy, you get a ticket." He starts sassing me out. I got really mad at him. I began to push him a little bit. Didn't hurt him or anything. I asked him for his pencil with which to write out the ticket. He was getting madder and madder. I was getting madder and madder, and boy I was just about to bust him one. He said, "Go ahead, hit me. I don't care." That stopped me. That cooled me right off. Because then I knew he was just baiting me. I wanted to hit him though.

A little while later I met a truck driver who said to me, "I don't see how you can keep your self-control under conditions like that."

But I am kind of big. I don't have to rough them up much. I don't think I have hit but one man in the last two years. But take my partner. Now he is small. He has to rough people up.

This man relates two experiences in which he felt that force was justified, after initially stating that he was "not afraid to bust a guy." In the first experience, he felt the continued insults of the offender would have made the public think that he was afraid if he didn't use force to shut him up. In the second case, he indicates his consciousness of the dangers in letting yourself go by his suspicion of the man's motives in egging him on. There he restrained his impulses and refused to fight with the man.

Legitimation in the Apprehension of the Felon. Twenty-three percent of the men interviewed listed obtaining information as a basis for the use of force. The figures are deceptive, however, since the "third degree" has in recent years received a lot of adverse publicity, and the men were afraid to admit the existence of such a practice. This publicity has reduced the use of the third degree, *in the police station,* to a considerable extent, but it has not been eliminated even there. Out of the station, however, the use of force to make a suspect talk is still prevalent and sanctioned.

The use of force in this area is the product of two general factors. The first of these is that the "good pinch," the apprehension of the felon, or the breaking of a big case is a major source of prestige in the department. A man who makes a lot of good pinches and breaks several big cases has a reputation among the other men for being a good policeman. In addition, the police define the criminal as having abrogated many of his rights as a citizen, and they are therefore willing to use measures they would feel reluctant to use otherwise. The result is that the men, eager to obtain the prestige and having no compunctions about the criminal, feel that the end justifies the means. The group sanctions and the men use, therefore, almost anything they think they can get away with to obtain a confession or to get the offender to lead them to the evidence.

The second factor is the competition between the patrol and the detective divisions. This is mostly one-sided, the patrolman feeling that he doesn't get an even break in the solution of cases and the consequent publicity and prestige. Thus, when the patrolman apprehends a suspect, he is eager to close the case before he has to hand it over to the detectives. He has to act fast to do this, and to him force seems a legitimate way to make the man talk. Besides, he can usually get away with it by saying that the man resisted arrest.

The use of force against the suspect is justified by the men on the basis that they are acting in the interests of the community. They feel that they are only using the methods of the suspect, and that in doing so they frequently apprehend men who are a danger to the people in the community. One cannot overlook this as a form of self-justification for the men involved. Feeling as they evidently did that such an explanation made their actions reasonable in terms of the values held by the interviewer, it is very likely that it likewise served as an answer to those values as they internalized them. Therefore, it is likely that the individual men, faced with specific situations, make their decisions in terms of a complex of factors that are not easily disentangled but among which their desire for prestige, their feeling that they are performing a community service, and their definition of the criminal as having abrogated his rights as a citizen form a substantial basis for the use of force.

In addition, it is important to point out that many of the men hold as a prerequisite to such action the assurance that the suspect is guilty. They see this as a check on their actions, and in reality it probably does have a substantial function of this nature. Nevertheless, the existence of public pressure in a big case, and the eagerness to be the one to make the good pinch, cannot be neglected as an influence that gives the men involved a readiness to find or believe that the suspect is guilty.

The following case illustrates the way in which the use of force on the suspect is a result of the way in which the patrolmen compete with the detectives.

I was a fighter for four years but I didn't hurt anybody. I have never hit a man with my club in four years, but once in a while I will swing a guy and will throw him against a wall or something and slap him but I will never hit him with my club. There are certain guys on the force who use a hell of a lot of rough stuff. One night I saw V use a lot of force when it was not necessary.

Now and then you gotta use it. The chief is really down on the use of force but I'd say that at least thirty percent of the guys are roughnecks. A lot of these young fellows have been using it heavy. But if you use force you have to make a report to the chief explaining why.

One time Y and I found three guys in a car and we found that they had a gun down between the seats. We wanted to find out who owned that gun before the dicks arrived so we could make a good pinch. They told us.

The last paragraph illustrates the patrolman's competition with the detectives. This man and his partner found three men in a car and noticed a gun between the seats. Although it is not stated, they suspected the men of a series of robberies. They wanted to pin something on the men so that they could get the credit for the pinch just in case their suspicions were correct. They therefore forced the men to reveal to whom the gun belonged.

The case that follows brings up public pressure as a basis for getting rough with a suspect.

Every man is entitled to a clean, decent pinch. I wouldn't consider it legal to use rough stuff. You have to use rough stuff sometimes, though. I would rather let a man go than send him up with flimsy evidence. I don't believe in using violence. I won't say that I haven't seen a guy get his face slapped a few times.

If a guy kills a cop and they are sure of it he is going to have a rough time. *Or if it's a big case and there's a lot of pressure on him and they tell him you can't go home until the case is finished then naturally a fellow is going to lose patience after a while.*

Now take that case in Chicago where they hung that janitor by his thumbs. They must have been awful sure of him. Or take a case where some sex pervert kills a little girl. You are not just going to talk to him calmly, especially if you have been talking to the family and stuff like that. Or if you get some guy in who will answer questions by not even telling you a simple thing like the time of day. He will get a slap in the mouth.

This man feels very strongly that a man has to be guilty before force can be applied. He recognizes that using force to obtain information is illegal, yet he feels that it is a necessary part of police work. However, when the police are seriously threatened — "if a guy kills a cop" — it's perfectly all right to go all out on him. When the pressure is on the police, they sometimes lose patience. He feels that the harsh treatment of sex perverts is understandable, that the suspect that does not cooperate with the police deserves a "slap in the mouth."

One man pointed out that using force was sometimes the only way to get results and to help the victims.

No, the police don't get rough. When they do they are pretty sure of their ground. The chief has put out an order that after a man is brought to the station he wants no rough stuff.

Well, once in a while you have to get rough. Now, for example, there was a case I was on recently where a woman was in a tavern and she went to the powder room and left her purse. There were only three other men in the tavern and they had been talking together. When she came back both the purse and the men were gone. Well, this was a clear-cut case. Nobody else could have taken the purse. We picked up the three fellows and they denied knowledge of it, but after we banged them around a bit they told us what they had done with the purse. They had taken the money out of it and thrown it up on top of a roof. Well, in this case if we had not roughed those fellows up that woman would never have gotten her money back.

Notice how this man contradicts himself in the first paragraph. Initially, he gave a defensive response by denying that the police get rough. However, his emotional involvement in this area was so great that he immediately contradicted this statement. The source of his fear, the chief, is apparent. The case that he describes to support his position indicates the types of situations in which the policeman feels that force is not only justified but to be commended — "if we had not roughed those fellows up that woman would never have gotten her money back."

The feeling that if the man is guilty one is justified in using extreme measures to make him talk is reflected in the following two cases:

1. Well, I will give you an actual instance. We got a call about a man being knifed. When we got there this guy was in an alley and he had been stabbed seven times. There was another fellow with him and the other fellow told us that two men had chased this guy and stabbed him and he described one of them quite well to us.

We went out and managed to pick up this fellow and when we caught him he said he didn't know anything. Now, what would you do? What would you do in a case like that, huh?

The implication of this statement was that the man was forced to admit his guilt and that this was for the police the only reasonable course of action. The offender had used violence and it was violence that he deserved in return.

2. Well you have to rough a man up when he won't talk. When you know he is guilty. Like there was a fellow I caught who had just broken into a window. I knew he was a burglar because he had bits of glass in his cuffs. He also fitted the description of a purse snatcher. I had to rough him up a little.

For this man the criteria for the use of force are (1) that the man won't talk, and (2) that you know he is guilty.

The idea is current among the men that certain types of people will cooperate only when force is used. They see force as one of a number of possible methods for eliciting information. This appears in the following two cases:

1. The thing I dislike most is when I have to beat up a man.
Interviewer: When have you had to beat up men?
Answer: A couple of times, to get information out of them. But you know, mostly it's easier to just mix them up. Talk to them quiet-like and then shoot a question at them.

This man indicates that he dislikes to use force but sees it as one of the possible methods for making a man talk, one that is sometimes necessary.

2. It depends on the guy. On some guys it won't do any good. On others a good slap is the best thing to make them talk. But the policeman don't beat up a guy just for the sake of beating him up. Take a fellow like yourself now. They would never beat you up. But take a guy from the slums. He is tough. Sometimes you need a little slap to loosen him up.

Here it is felt that whether or not you use force depends on the kind of person you are dealing with. It is effective with the tough fellow from the slums who needs "a little slap to loosen him up," but is of no use with the "better class of people" into which the respondent classifies the interviewer.

The protection of the people in the community as legitimation for the use of force is evident in the following case:

The third-degree methods are justified in certain cases. For example, four potential killers pull a job. One is caught. The freedom of the other three is a menace to the community. In that case third-degree methods are essential in getting the other three men.

Legitimation in the Law. The policeman is legally entitled to the use of force in the performance of his duty. He has to and does use force in this connection. In making an arrest, in defending himself, in maintaining the peace of the community, the policeman frequently finds himself in situations that require that he use force to perform his duty and to go about his job. This legal entitlement is the basic refuge that the policeman has whenever he uses force for whatever reasons. He can always say that it was in self-defense, or that the offender was resisting arrest.

Seventeen percent of the men mentioned their duty as a basis for the use of force. This came up in two forms: to make an arrest and for self-protection. Only 7% of the men felt that force should be limited to cases involving these characteristics. The following are representative cases:

1. On this force business you have to use it. Like this case where we caught a fellow. He was a drug addict. He was fighting us all the way. I put him in the car. He lashed out with his feet and caught me in the face. We had to work him over and we opened his scalp a little bit. You have to work men over like that. They may be dangerous. You often have to do it to get things done.

2. When he resists arrest any time. That lets you use force enough to complete an arrest but the amount is up to you.

3. Force is legitimate only when necessary to make an arrest.

4. The average man has to use force only once or twice a year. Of course, there are individuals who never have to use force because they never bother about arresting anybody.

Guilt as a Precondition to Violence. The policemen, aware of the community's condemnation of brutality and of the legal dangers in the misuse of force, tend to utilize the apparent guilt of the offender as a basis for escaping both. They feel that if the man is guilty, they are doing the people of the community a favor by forcing him to confess, since this protects the community against his further depredations. The more serious the crimes attributed to the offender, the more likely they are to feel this way. In addition, they feel that the necessity for using force to apprehend the felon who is found guilty is more believable and at the same time more excusable. This is the structure of their rationalization. We do not question its validity in terms of effective police work; however, its illegality and misuse are obvious.

The rationalization does not, however, incorporate or reveal two other factors that underlie and are important in police actions of this type. Both of these involve the prestige of the policeman. As we have previously indicated, the solution of a crime, the making of a "good pinch," is one of the most important sources of prestige for the policeman on the police force and in the community. Second, the relationship between the policeman and the criminal is one of conflict. The policeman pits his wits and resources against those of the criminal. The failure to obtain a confession or a conviction, therefore, represents a kind of defeat in which the policeman's own competence is threatened. The lower the status of the offender, the greater the threat.

The responses of the police indicate that guilt is attributed in three general ways. That is, the policeman has confidence in any of three factors as indicating the guilt of the party: personal observation or unimpeachable informants, a criminal record, or sexual depredations. Two of these factors need explanation. The man with a criminal record, who has done time in prison, the policeman sees as the "pro" or the "hardened criminal." Policemen feel that the previous record predicts the future. The sex criminal has, in the eyes of the police, such a low moral status that they are willing to believe anything of him.

Twenty percent of the men interviewed listed the guilt of the offender as a basis for using force.

The characterization of a man as a hardened criminal or a "pro" is illustrated in the following two cases:

1. *On a pro* they would be doing the public a favor. If it was a felony, I surely would believe in it but if it is a little misdemeanor, no.

This man articulates the idea that the action is justified because "they would be doing the public a favor." He points out, however, that the action would have to fall in the felon class (good pinch category) before he felt it would be legitimate.

2. In making an arrest I don't believe as some police do in striking a prisoner any more than is necessary. I'll take quite a bit of back talk, more than most officers, but after a man is *a hardened criminal* I think a certain amount of force could be legitimately used.

In spite of his scruples this man believes that the use of force on the "hardened criminal" is justified.

The feeling that the sex criminal deserves a beating appears in these cases:

1. Well, one thing, when he resists arrests. Two, if he fights me. Three, sex criminals. Four, professionals or robbers who we are sure of being guilty. Then we will beat him up to make him spit out his guts.

This man also adds that in the case of the professional criminal whom they know is guilty, he is certain that they will beat him to make him "spit out his guts."

2. One of the most hated things is sex crimes and the funny thing about them is most of them resist arrest.
Interviewer: What other cases do you think the policeman is justified in punishing a man for?
Answer: Well, if the man was engaged in some serious crimes. I believe that the end would justify the means.

This man points out how resisting arrest is used as a protective device by the officer who uses force for other reasons.

3. If I saw a guy beat up a sex criminal I'd figure the guy had a good reason for it. If the guy is no Goddamn good and he has information you need, I think it's all right to rough him up.

The question might be raised as to how guilty a man can be. For the policeman the ultimate guilt arises out of an attack and injury to a policeman. To be suspected of this crime is to endanger one's life, as this case clearly indicates.

The only case where I'll rough a man up is when I see him do it with my own eyes and there is no other witnesses. That is the only case I will be sure he did it. Then I'll rough him up to get a confession. Then I'll climb onto him — if I see him with my own eyes. If he killed a cop I'd beat him with a two by four. I'd break every bone in his body. Put him in the hospital for six months.

This man felt willing to extort a confession from a case that he had himself observed and about which he was therefore certain of the offender's guilt. In the case of the "cop killer" he felt that no penalty was too severe.

All the cases point to the general feeling that the policeman's conviction of the guilt of the offender is sufficient protection so that violent methods can be used to obtain a confession.

Opposition to Violence. Twenty-three percent of the men interviewed stated that they were opposed to the use of force, that it was not necessary on the job, that it should be avoided if possible. Many of these men were quite sincere. Many of them had deliberately taken jobs inside the station, positions in which they wouldn't have to use any force. However, others were merely playing safe with the interviewer and giving out the official line on the use of force. The men conceived of the chief of police as being very tough on those men who used too much force. Several men had been called before the chief and reprimanded during the past few years for using too much force. The men felt that the chief had a lot of power over their lives, the assignments they would get, and possible promotions. The result was that they had good basis for feeling that it was not wise to say anything that would indicate that they in any way differed with the chief's policy. Many of them took the position that it was not going to do them any good to talk to the interviewer and that it might possibly do them much harm. These conditions should be kept in mind in assessing all the responses to the questions on the use of force.

The following cases are representative of the responses that indicated a sincere opposition to the use of force.

1. He is never justified in roughing a man up. A man is not guilty until proven so. Besides there is no point in hitting a man. You can get just as much out of him without it. That's the way the police work gets a bad name. We fellows have to work to set a good example. It may not happen in my generation but if we keep at it another twenty years or so, people will have a lot of respect for the police department. The thing is to get the individuals and get your man and leave the rest of it to the courts. If the policeman sells himself to the public, they will know how good he is. You can't just tell them you are good, you got to show them.

2. I hate roughness in any form. I will take a lot to have peaceful relations. That's why I drifted into the clerical part of this work, but I'd like to see effective police work done to protect life and property. I'd like to teach police work. I could spend hour after hour doing it according to nationally recognized methods. Men should constantly have in-service training. They should learn how to enforce the law legally.

3. I hate the use of force and I guess that is why I prefer the juvenile job.

4. You should never use force in interrogating because you have the man at a disadvantage. There are other ways. For example, when the two men can work together. One guy can pretend to be tough and the other pretend to be easy. That way they will talk to the easy one. As for beating a confession out of a man, it's against the law in the first place and against my conscience in the second place.

5. Well, I guess it's all right if a guy is professional, a hardened criminal and you need to get some evidence, but they don't do much of that sort of thing any more. Now you take Capt. X. He is a good police officer and told us in school, and I have heard around the department, that he has got a heck of a lot of convictions on many different fellows, and has never had to use roughness.

These five responses were elicited without insistence from the interviewer. They are representative of those cases in which the respondents were probably indicating their true feelings. They describe arguments that the policemen advance against the use of force: (1) the law can be enforced legally; (2) it is a bad public relations policy to use too much force; and (3) using the psychological approach accomplishes more than using force.

The following responses typify the elusive reply. The first man replied quickly and enthusiastically, but obviously was trying to present a favorable picture of the police. This is evident in the attempt to treat the question abstractly rather than indicate his own feelings. The remaining replies were all elicited under pressure, the question being repeated and sometimes rephrased. The bulk of the answers in this opposition category were of this type, difficult to elicit and laconic upon arrival.

1. Force is almost never used in interrogations, but the policeman is supposed to be getting smarter.

There is a feeling of this in going over from the political days when a policeman got results or else.

Now take this case that I had. There was a boy that killed another boy. We had him in the station. He wouldn't say a word. There were lots of dicks around. He was just plain scared. So I took him out by H and we just sat by ourselves and I talked to him about everything — about school, about baseball, about something — anything he wanted to talk about. After about an hour and a half he told me the whole story.

2. There should be absolutely no brutality used even though a man kills a cop. If he is rough you can rough him up.

3. If a man shot at and missed a policeman it wouldn't make the man angry enough to beat him up.

4. I don't feel that brutality is called for or needed. I never use it. I don't believe in it.

Summary. The preceding examination of the situations for which the police prescribe the use of force indicates that maintenance of respect for the police, apprehension of the felon, and law enforcement are the major ends of the police. Since law enforcement is a formal objective of the police, its appearance is self-explanatory. Therefore, we leave that point and go on to consider the other two factors in their normative aspects.

Maintenance of Respect for the Police

The listing of maintenance of respect for the police as a basis for the use of force by 39% of the men interviewed indicates that this is a prime value of the police. It is a value oriented to the experience of the policeman, experience that consists primarily of interaction with a public that is conceived to be hostile, in a role that is unpleasant to the public. In terms of this experience, the value gains meaning. It represents a form of individual and group action in opposition to a threat of personal and group degradation. That it operates normatively, as a regulator of conduct, is apparent in the emphasis it receives in the initiation of the rookie, and in the way in which the police define their actions toward different portions of the public — the better class of people requiring psychological treatment and the slum dwellers needing fear. In each case the definition is aligned in terms of what will make these different publics respect the police. In addition, the department formally is making an attempt at a good public relations policy.

The Good Pinch

The apprehension of the felon also appears as a major value of the police in that 23% of the men interviewed gave it as a basis for the use of force. This received further support in the responses to another question, which otherwise has no significance.

Fifty policemen in Department X who formed a roughly representative group were asked, "What gives you the most satisfaction about the job?" and "What is your biggest gripe?" All the men responded, but not all of them answered both questions. In general, the responses were idiosyncratic; that is, except for one point no more than two or in a very few cases three men listed the same likes or dislikes. However, on one point, a form of satisfaction, there appeared to be considerable consensus.

Fifty-nine percent of the men who answered the satisfaction questions replied that making a good pinch or some variation thereof gave them the most satisfaction. Some typical responses follow:

1. A good pinch is one of the most satisfying things. If a policeman catches a burglar and he doesn't get the credit he is unhappy. It's funny that way because it's the only real part of his job, but I guess that's human nature. A good pinch is if a guy did something outside the routine. Of course a lot depends on where you are located.

2. I find satisfaction in the type of case that gives you prestige in the community. The businessmen cater to you for the favors they can get out of you, and the women shine up to you. Besides that you are working from the time you hit the street.

3. Making a good arrest gives me the most satisfaction, that is, an arrest for a felony where there is no doubt in your mind about the guilt of the party.

4. The thing I enjoy most is outsmarting a son of a bitch and making him tell about the jobs and then clearing them up. The thing I dislike most is working with juveniles.

5. The thing I'd like most to do is crime work, that is doing police work. I'd like to be in a crime detail.

6. The thing I like most is a good pinch. That is, to catch a burglar or a hold-up man.

7. The most satisfaction I get is to break a case and do good police work. Any time you arrest a man for a felony it is considered a good arrest.

8. Working on felonies. Just a while back I stopped a fellow trying to break into a place. I enjoy that sort of thing.

These responses indicate that the good pinch is the felony, the major crime; that it is work of this type that is considered to be real police work; and that the men like it for this reason and because it gives them prestige in the community. The apprehension of the felon thus represents for these men a source of prestige in the police department — "It's real police work" — and in the community; a job on which they can work hard with an expectation of satisfaction; and an area in which there is little in the way of community repercussions. Many of the men see the good pinch as a source of promotions. They find that when they solve a good case the chief is obviously pleased, because it shows up the department as a necessary and efficient organization. That the good pinch appears as the major source of satisfaction to the men further supports our thesis that it forms an important group value for the police.

Police Action and the Law

Law enforcement is the legal job of the police. Theoretically, this, with the protection of the community and a host of other services, constitutes the function of the police. Yet there are strong grounds for believing that for the police themselves, law enforcement is only an incidental function and is frequently utilized not for the community but to further the ends of the police.

The contacts that the police have with the courts soon teach them that the law is not inviolable. They see it used to further political ends; they see it available for purchase; they frequently find themselves punished for its enforcement by undue time spent in attempts at prosecution. They tend to lose respect for the law.

In his contacts with the public, the policeman finds that law enforcement is not popular. He sees great numbers of people operating their businesses and conducting their lives in disregard of the law. He finds reflected in the eyes of the community a lack of respect for the law. When he does enforce the law, he receives only insults from the public that takes the trouble to let him know what they think — the offenders.

It is not surprising, therefore, that the police, who are referred to as the pillars of the law, should see its enforcement as an end of dubious value. They recognize that it sets limits to their actions; they recognize that a too-obvious flaunting of negligence would result in the loss of their jobs; they recognize that it is fundamentally what gives meaning to their job; they recognize these things, and the recognition exerts sufficient pressure on their behavior so that their function is far from a mockery. Law is thus, in a very real sense, an end of the police. Yet, when contrasted to other ends, it plays a subordinate role. The substantiation for this point appears in several ways:

1. When the men were confronted with the alternative of breaking the law by perjury and breaching the secrecy of the group by testifying against their partners, most of them chose to break the law. Thus, for these men the law is subordinate to the maintenance of secrecy.

2. Sixty-six percent of the men felt that the extreme form of police action — violence — was to be used for illegal but group ends, and only 8% of the men felt that violence was to be reserved for their legal ends. This would at once indicate a subordination of law enforcement to the ends of the group and a willingness to break the law to achieve the ends of the group.

3. When 12 men were asked how they would feel and act if the chief issued informal orders directing them not to enforce the law in such areas as vice and gambling, the activities of the gun mobs, or shoplifters, 11 men replied that they would go along with the chief, and one replied that he would continue to enforce the law. The 11 men stated that they would go along with the chief not because they had faith that he was acting in the best interests of the community, but because:

1. If that's the way the administration wants it, then that's the way they get it. I am looking forward to my pension and I don't want to be fired for something I have no control over anyway.

2. There is no sense in being a martyr. You don't know so much they can't replace you. If you want to be a martyr, you are a chump. When you act that way you are going to get the crappy end of the stick. Don't overstep your bounds. You are just a little pea in a big pod.

3. As a policeman I feel that what we do depends on the policy issued by the chief. It is like the Army. You do what they tell you.

4. I think I'd ride along. I think I'd have to pay attention to the department orders first. After all, as an individual it is your job

and you got a wife and baby to support. What the hell, I figure that if they want to get you out of there they can get you out of there anyway. The only thing Civil Service does is to give you a chance to fight.

One man replied:

5. Well, as far as I am concerned I wouldn't take any orders to lay off. If the town was wide open I'd try to make life miserable for the gamblers and the prostitutes. They would probably move me to some nice quiet place but then I'd find things to do.

The replies indicate 11 to one willingness to comply with the orders of the department, even in the face of the law. They are indicative of a general feeling that the maintenance of themselves on the job is more important than the enforcement of the law. Although this cannot be represented as a group-oriented rule of behavior, it lends support to the primacy of the other group rules, particularly that of silence, by diminishing the strength of an important opposition principle, the enforcement of the law.

4. It is not infrequent for the police to abrogate this basic function by withdrawing their protection when it serves their ends. This is illustrated in a story told by one of the men:

If you get some tavern owner who is always sassing up the police, you know this ——— club, the place down on ——— and ——— streets. Well that guy, he is a wise guy. He is always trying to get the police to do things for him and then is always spitting on the police. Well the police always have it in for a guy like that.

Suppose, for example, they should get a call that there was a fight on. Well, maybe they would only be two blocks away. But they wouldn't hit the place right away. They would drive the car around the block for two or three minutes. Then they would park the car in front of the club and then they would take it real easy going in. Well, you know how a fight is. You got to stop them right away or they do a lot of damage. Only takes thirty seconds — couple of minutes — to wreck a place. That guy would have plenty of damage in his joint.

The example is not unique and is amply documented in the research. Unfortunately, the details cannot be presented here without revealing the identity of the department.

Together, these four sources indicate quite clearly that although the police are not oblivious to their responsibilities with respect to law enforcement and of their role as agents of the state, the law is for them a secondary end to be enforced when it is convenient. Thus, when the enforcement of the law conflicts with the ends of the police, the law is not enforced; when it supports the ends of the police, they are fully behind it; and when it bears no relationship to the ends of the police, they enforce it as a matter of routine. For example, when the people of the city are aroused about some point of law enforcement such as traffic violations or vice and gambling, the police will put on a drive in those areas and the law will be enforced rigidly; for in this situation it is to the interests of the police, in line with a maintenance of respect for the police in the community, to enforce the law. Again, the apprehension of felons carries a prestige value for the police individually and collectively, and law enforcement in that area is quite vigorous. On the other hand, generally, the rigid enforcement of vice and gambling laws is an unpopular measure; many people resent it, and there are likely to be strong political repercussions; thus, except for the aforementioned instance, the vice and gambling laws are not enforced.[2]

This evidence of the way in which the police tend to disregard the law has been cited to indicate the relative strength of the group-defined ends of the police, to point out by contrast the extent to which these group definitions are rooted in the life of the police, and to indicate their strength in regulating the conduct of the members of the force.

Role, Morality, and Self-Conception

The materials presented in this and the two preceding chapters now permit a brief statement of the policeman's conception of his social role, and the relationships between this role and his morality and self-conception. Our observations on this point are frankly speculative, the result of a deduction from other characteristics of the police and of talking to the policemen themselves. They should be considered in no other light.

Social roles can be considered as a perspective on life from which the world, the self, and conduct receive their definition. They can

[2] Naturally, the fact that the police are a politically oriented body, under political control, has much to do with their attitude toward law enforcement. The chief of police is a political appointee and must fulfill the political obligations of the party in power. He is able to do this because his authority enables him to make the life of any member of the force exceedingly unpleasant should he so desire, and there are therefore few rebellious ones. However, we would like to point out that political control is a factor superimposed on the basic occupational orientations of the police, which in themselves give the police this orientation toward the law.

be thought of as a segment of the person's self and integral to his self-conception. How large a segment of the self a particular role represents will to a large extent depend on the degree to which the person's life is oriented about it. As a segment of self, it implies an involvement of the self in the role-oriented interaction. As one plays a role, his interaction with others will to some extent involve the defense of his self-esteem and a form of self-assertion. Again, to the extent that the role dominates the self-conception, it will dominate morality and discriminate good and evil. Role, morality, and self-conception are thus inextricably interlocked.

The policeman's involvement in his role is very great. The pension ties him to the job for 20 years. It is a shackle that few are willing to throw off. The job dominates his time. He works eight hours a day, six days a week. He puts in a lot of extra time in the courts. The job disrupts his life. He works on shifts, and working in this fashion sleeps when other people work and works when they sleep. He is thus cut off from establishing social contacts with other people. He is emotionally involved in the job. Feeling that the good pinch is a high value, many are willing to spend some of their off hours planning how to present a case in court or attempting to break a big case on their own. The job isolates the man and his family. The disrupting shifts make social participation difficult. The rule of secrecy keeps his family and himself from talking about that in which he is most well versed and most interested. The isolation, the time allocated, the emotional involvement, make the job a major, if not the most important, influence in the policeman's life. Accordingly, it constitutes an important part of his self. Furthermore, as he is a social stereotype and a public servant, the community obligates him to continue in the role even in his off-duty hours. They come to him with their troubles and their complaints. In the bar and in the tavern he is beset by those who want to tell him what an unfair deal they got from the police and by people who want him to do them a favor. The neighbors hold him responsible for the maintenance of the law in his territory. If the neighbor's child's bicycle is stolen, the policeman is held responsible, and he is expected to do something about it. The only refuge is isolation, to make certain that one does not become too friendly with the neighbors. Even so, he cannot escape the continued definition of his role. He is not allowed to have a job on the police force, he is forced to be a policeman, a particular kind of a man. With resentment and with complaints, the policeman adapts himself. Finding that he is no longer a Catholic, a house-owner, a father, he becomes a policeman. The role, then, is a large element in the self, and the deep involvement of the self in the role produces a consequent involvement of the self in upholding the role. Other men in other occupations can keep their jobs relatively anonymous. The blue uniform going down the street and into the house, the blue uniform in the streetcar and in the restaurant, makes it difficult for the policeman to escape definitions and makes the periods of anonymity relatively scarce. Other jobs do not so completely categorize the man, and the job-holder is likely to be considered apart from the job. The policeman, like the Negro or the Jew, is a stereotype, however, in which the label identifies the morality and the personality. He is more ominous, however, than either for he carries a gun and a club, and is known to use them. Therefore, for him it is exceedingly difficult to dissociate the set and the role.

Policemen *qua* policemen find themselves in a hostile environment. They feel that the public is hostile to them, and they expect antagonism in response to their every gesture. They feel that the public is watching them, looking for a way to get them in trouble. They feel that they are misunderstood and that they are persecuted. They feel that they have to protect themselves from this hostile public. They feel that they must keep silent about the things they do and stick together, supporting one another. Finding it necessary to deny the public definition of them as corrupt, brutal, and ignorant, they respond with a demand for respect. They feel that the public must be wrong, that the public must lack understanding; and as with children who insist on acting improperly, they feel that one must be firm, one must teach them to respect you. The instrument of correction depends on what public one faces. Some understand politeness, some understand only the fist. The public is at worst evil and dangerous, at best misguided and ignorant. The attempt to repudiate the public and its opinions is not entirely successful, however. Too much time is spent in dealing with the public, the public is too influential in the policeman's life, for him to escape their opinions. Unable to completely repudiate the public, the policeman partially repudiates himself. He carries a residue of guilt about his own behavior and insecurity about his own self-esteem. This is nowhere better illustrated than in the policeman's repudiation of the occupation in his aspirations for his children. Like the workingman who wants his son to go to college *and become successful,* who thereby admits his own failure, 70% of the 54 policemen interviewed were definitely opposed to their sons' becoming policemen and wanted them to do something more successful (see Table 4.4). This is an admission of failure, an admission of degradation, which cannot but effectuate a partial denial of one's own worth, however much it is rationalized. Its effect is to leave a man without dignity.

They wanted their sons to go into professional work — doctors, lawyers, and ministers (9 cases); to get a college education (9 cases); or to get into some job where they would be more successful and make more money (6 cases). They gave replies like the following:

1. No, I wouldn't want my son to be a policeman because it isn't highly skilled or a trained job. Anybody can do it. You can take a man off the streets and after a few months he can do the job. He doesn't need any education or particular skill.

2. I wouldn't want my boys to be policemen because there is too much chance for them to become crooked. I would like my boys to go to college. I wouldn't want them to become a lawyer, though, because that has no security.

3. No, I don't want my son to be a policeman. I don't think there is any sense in two members of the family taking the shit I have had to contend with.

Table 4.4. Would You Want Your Son to Become a Policeman?

Answer	Frequency	Percentage
No	38	70
He must make his own choice	6	11
Yes	10	19
Total	54	100

4. I wouldn't want my boy to be a policeman. I don't think it is good. It is a rough deal. You get criticism on all sides whether you are right or wrong.

5. I don't want my boy to be a policeman because he would see too much of the seamy side of life. It makes a man very skeptical and cynical.

6. I think I'd like my son to be a businessman. The average policeman is not a college graduate or a well-educated man. He is just an average citizen. You see a lot of misery and cussedness. Besides, I'd want him to have a better education.

The policeman is a cynic. Faced with the duty of keeping the people in line, and believing that most people are out to break the law and do him in if possible, he always looks for the selfish motive. The byword is "What's in it for him?" The good action is for the policeman a relative one; it is good insofar as it indicates a respect for the police and an appreciation of the policeman; but it is bad in that it is sure to have a selfish motive. The world for him is a jungle; everybody is looking out for himself and, to use their terms, "out to make a buck." In such a world, self-preservation and success demand that one look out for his own interests and not be "taken in" by the fast-talking advocates of altruism.

The policeman's vision of the world puts an emphasis on immorality. The radio he listens to tells a tale of sorrow, of misery, of crime, of terror, of the cheap, the sordid, the vicious. Among the people he meets, the belittlers of morals and the breakers of law loom large. The position he occupies exposes him to the manipulations of power and shows him the cheapness of the law. The judge who does a favor, the lawyer who defends the criminal, the businessman who profits from illegality, the minister who sells his soul, all come to his attention. His occupation selects his contacts and defines his experiences.

The police force for him is an island in a hostile community. The interests of the police are his interests through a community assessment of responsibility. He finds himself a partner to crime and brutality, but even for these he finds group support and a collective meaning. The shock of a hostile community absolves their evil and renders an alchemy of integration. Being one with all, against the universe, the rules sink deep. Secrecy, the good pinch, the maintenance of respect, the definitions of the publics, the necessity for violence are fused as a defense against hate. They constitute the role of the policeman in its most profound sense. Role involvement being large, they constitute a morality. The job being a way of life, they structure the self-conception.

The role of the policeman, then, is defender of the police, apprehender of criminals, agent of the law. His obligations are primarily to the police and secondarily to the community. His privileges, authority, and right to violence are too few for the community goat and the martyr. So he sees it.

Morality is oriented to prestige and power. It is ethnocentric, revolving about the police, good and bad being a relationship to their ends. So the discrimination is made.

The self is conceived of as a victim of injustice, as the ordinary person on a job, doing a job, who is misunderstood. The self-esteem is insecure. Dignity is absent, for the self is corrupt and failure is apparent, for there is no faith in the work. So he feels.

Sociologically speaking, two factors may be identified as contributing to a relationship between the occupation, the morality, and the self-conception. These are the social definition of work and the occupational selection of social contacts. We refer these to the police.

A man's occupation usually involves an important part if not the best part of his time, and a large part of his life. An occupation is part of a man's identity. People use it as something with which to characterize the man, and being a looking glass, to use Cooley's phrase (1902), they reflect the self. Therefore, the way people define his occupation is something a man must reckon with. It is something he must integrate into his life organization. For the policeman this is a definition of derogation. It is a definition with which he experiences a major involvement. It constitutes a threat to his self-esteem which he cannot accept nor reject. It forms a self in personal conflict.

A man's occupation involves a selection of his social contacts, an emphasis on a part of the world, and a meeting with people in a special series of roles. The laborer meets the laborer, the boss, the union organizer; the physician meets the patient, the nurse, the hospital staff, his colleagues; the janitor meets the tenant, the owner, other janitors, and the agent. Each meets in these contacts a series of roles in which people are acting a part, a part that defines the interaction. In turn, the person plays a series of roles. Each of these contacts poses for him a problem in relationship and decisions concerning how he must act so as to carry out the ends of the occupation and at the same time maintain his self-esteem. These are the problems of an occupation. Their solutions form its norms. In addition, the occupation is likely to bring its members into contact with a particular segment of the population in a particular state of mind. The laborer finds himself largely involved with people at work, discussing work, thinking about work; the physician meets people in their physical misery, sick and complaining — he meets them in crisis; the priest meets people in devotion and in their immorality — he hears of immorality, he is conscious of irreligion. Each of these, then, constitutes an important vision of the world. One sees its work, one sees its sickness, and one sees its immorality. Each sees more of its own than the others. Each therefore sees its own as a more prominent characteristic of the world. This has its impact on the self and morality. The self-conception can be but a relative concept, a comparison of one's self with society. Morality can but refer to people, and what one considers good and bad must have roots in the way one conceives people to be. Thus, the defense of one's occupational norms and the vision of the world to which they are intimately related blend and can be said to constitute an occupational morality and an occupational self-conception.

The policeman's most significant contact is with the law-evading public, which defines him as a malicious and dangerous intruder into their business and acts accordingly. His resolution of this problem includes an insistence on his will and on obtaining respect, by the use of violence, if necessary. He tends to meet those portions of the public which are acting contrary to the law or using the law to further their own ends. He is exposed to public immorality. He becomes cynical. His is a society emphasizing the crooked, the weak, and the unscrupulous. Accordingly, his morality is one of expediency and his self-conception one of a martyr.

The norms and the vision of the world operate in the atmosphere of the social definition of the job. The self-conception engendered by the social definition can be reinforced or contradicted by the norms and vision. When the major contacts are with the public, the social definitions have a powerful impact on the interactional roles. If the occupation is low in social status, the member is likely to be faced with people taking a superordinate role, and vice versa. Each will pose a particular problem for the worker, although the solution is not predictable. For instance, low-status occupations may engender an orientation about the problem of self-assertion.

The policeman, faced with a hostile public, given the status of a pariah, finds that he is constantly being degraded or subordinated. This intensifies the rejection engendered by the public definition of him as a malicious and threatening intruder, and consequently intensifies his need for self-assertion, which becomes articulate as a need for maintaining respect for the police.

Summary

The preceding materials would indicate that the police in City X possess the characteristics of a social group in having as collective ends the maintenance of secrecy about public affairs and the maintenance of respect for the police by the people of the community; in having a consensus on these ends, developed through a community of experience and discourse resulting from their occupational experiences; in having a set of norms that guide conduct and sanctions to enforce the norms represented in the rule of silence and the use of the silent treatment for offenders, the rule of maintaining respect for the police and the use of ridicule to punish offenders, and in the rule that the means justify the ends in the apprehension of the felon, a rule maintained by the reward of prestige; and finally, in their possession of organized action bodies as represented by the Fraternal Order of Police and the Police Ex-Servicemen's League, to which 88% of the men belong and attend an average of ten meetings a year.

This should have implications for other occupations, since the social group characteristics are in large measure the result of its being an occupational group; the social definition of work should give many occupations a basis for collective action. Common work experiences and common occupational problems, as a part of this experience, should provide the basis for a community of experience and discourse with which to generate consensus and norms when the members of the occupation come in contact with one another.

The importance of secrecy to the police in City X is evidenced by the fact that of a sample of 13 men, 77% indicated that they would prefer to perjure themselves rather than testify against another policeman. They indicated that should they break the secrecy rule, they would be labeled a stool pigeon and have an outcast status; that they would receive the silent treatment, which would cut them off from important sources of information and from social contacts with other men. The existence of these powerful sanctions indicates that secrecy has a normative status among the police. That secrecy is felt to be so important, and the degree of consensus on this point, would indicate that it functions both as a collective end and as a solidarity mechanism for the police as a social group.

Secrecy among the police can be traced to the social definition of their occupation as corrupt and brutal, and may be seen as a protective mechanism against this attack. It functions as a shield for actions that may be criticized but that the police feel are necessary to their ends. As such, it should be true of many occupations to some extent. To the degree that members of an occupation or a social group feel it necessary to engage in actions in conflict with the dominant values of the society, or defined as evil by the society, secrecy should prove a necessary bulwark to criticism. Again, since secrecy functions as a mechanism of solidarity in giving the members a sense of mutual involvement and possibly of importance in the belief that they then have special privileges, it should prove convenient to any group.

The police conceive of violence as an instrument to be used for the support of personal goals, and only incidentally as a restricted source of power given to them to facilitate their legal function. Corollary to this is the indication that law enforcement itself is conceived of as an incidental function, to be pursued when it supports group ends or has no reference to them. Law enforcement is subordinate to the maintenance of secrecy, the maintenance of respect for the police, and the apprehension of the felon. Policemen's position on the use of violence was demonstrated in their willingness to use it illegally to force respect and to elicit information, and the group endorsement of this procedure. The subordinate position of law enforcement appeared in the relatively limited degree to which it was used to legitimate violence in comparison with the maintenance of respect and the apprehension of felons; in the willingness to abrogate it to achieve other ends, as evidenced by the withdrawal of protection for this purpose; and in the willingness of the men to cease enforcing the law if the chief of police indicated such a desire.

The significance of this point lies in the suggestion that the most important goals of an occupation's membership are those that involve the self-conceptions of the members. Thus, it is likely that those aspects of the job that affect the self-conception will receive the greatest attention, to the detriment of others.

The maintenance of respect for the police is demonstrated as an occupational norm of the police in its utilization by a large percentage of the men as a source of moral authority in terms of which they legitimate violence. It is meaningful in terms of the policeman's interaction with the public when he feels that his competence is constantly being threatened and his personal value is in question.

The apprehension of the felon appears as a major value of the police in their indication that it is the major source of satisfaction that they gain in the occupation. The rule that "the end justify the means" in the apprehension of the felon is demonstrated as an occupational norm of the police in its utilization as a basis for legitimating violence. This is supported in the policeman's conception of the criminal as a person who has abrogated his basic rights as a citizen, and as a personal challenge to the policeman.

Policemen consider themselves to be persons without particular worth and to be failures when they state that they don't want their sons to become policemen, that they want them to become successes.

5. On Becoming a Policeman

The Recruit School|**Contacts with Colleagues**
Personality factors; reception by the group|
Insecurities About Action|**Experience — the
"Reality Shock"**|**The Data — Ten Case Histories**
Summary of case material|**Group Definition of the
Initiate**|**The Role of the Initiate**|**Summary of
Initiation Process**|**Analysis of Phases in Initiation**|
Mechanisms of Social Control Expediency;
categorical reaction; application of sanctions;
maintenance of personal integrity|**Conclusions**|

The rookie is a stranger to the force, and each regards the other with caution and suspicion. The rookie feels some fear and ambivalence, for he is bound to feel that to be a policeman is perhaps not a happy thing. The force welcomes the rookie but still sees him as a threat, to be tested and treated with caution. So the man and his new world come to interact.

This stranger must be transformed into a friend, and the most important part of the young policeman's experience with the force consists of his interaction with the older men and what their feelings say to him about the nature of this new world and his place in it.

This chapter follows the rookie policeman into the force, searching out the important experiences and the reasons why they transform him into a policeman. It is meant to provide an understanding of police norms and action in terms of the experience of the man.

We shall begin with the police school and then describe the unfolding of the drama of experience that shapes the man into the policeman.

The Recruit School

The first real contact that new policemen have with the force generally consists of a session in the recruit school. Here they are introduced to the basic technicalities of police work — a rough outline of the laws, their duties, ways to handle themselves in various situations, the use of the club, the proper method of gathering evidence — and to the officially approved standards of morality. The last point is of interest to this investigation since it represents the logically organized attempt to shift the attitudes of the new men.

In the school the men first begin to think of themselves as policemen; they feel a growing sense of identification with the professional ideals, a sense of importance. They are led to believe that things are tough in this school. The captains who teach the school try to approach the tough FBI methods. During the sessions an FBI man will come in and tell the doctrine of professionalization, "You are now an officer of the law . . . never think or speak of yourselves as a cop or coppers . . . a policeman has an important job and heavy responsibility." He blends into his speech a sufficient number of off-color jokes to make the recruits feel that they are all men together. The school gives the rookie a vague feeling that he is a policeman; that policemen have to stick together to do a great job. The longer the school session lasts, the deeper imprint it will have. The men are quick to learn the advantages of being a policeman, and among them the theme is security, a steady job, and a pension. Integrated into many conversations are such statements as, "Why, after twenty years on the job you can retire as your own man and live out the rest of your life on what you get. . . ." "Why, the pension alone is worth thirty-five thousand dollars; just try and buy an annuity for less." Most of the men work hard in the school. This is the first time they have been in a classroom for years. It is a break in the routine of life and an opportunity to find out something about a job that they are a little afraid of. The men are ready to accept a new system of ideas. The police school in Department X doesn't give it to them, but it puts them in a state of readiness for change — it functions as a sort of *rite de passage*.

In almost every session something of the reality of police life will creep in. The captain will absentmindedly or purposely answer an awkward question. One man reports that a question as to brothels and gambling places in town was answered with the statement that the mayor was a politician and he made his own deals when he was elected, that it was the job of the department to do what the mayor wanted. Themes of solidarity are introduced along the lines of the brotherhood of policemen, the danger of the work, and the need for cooperation. Most of these ideas have little real meaning for the ordinary recruit; they are frequently misinterpreted. They are introduced without purpose, almost by accident, so to speak, as a result of the perspectives of the men who are teaching the course. The instructors themselves are so much a part of the perspectives that characterize the police that illustration and logic follow those paths. Thus, the line between formal and informal tradition is thin and diffuse.

The formal controls on behavior refer to the more socially approved areas; that is, a policeman must not speak to anyone about police matters as it may result in the criminal obtaining information that will obstruct the operations of the department. However, this is but part of the powerful and general definition of silence, which extends into a host of areas in which secrecy has no operational basis. Thus, gossip with outsiders about the other members of the force is prohibited, in spite of the fact that there are no formal sanctions against it and it does not fall within the realm of necessary secrecy. Although the basis for this definition may be obvious in terms of solidarity and peace within the group, it also exemplifies the strength of the occupational bonds arising from this work.

The recruit, as he passes through the police school, thus comes in contact with the more informal definitions by implication and suggestion. The needs of the instructing officers appear in what they select and what they emphasize. No recruit could explain this to the observer, but the fact remains that the school is his first contact with policemen and the police force, and through it his picture of the world of police work and the role of the police officer begins to develop. For the man himself, the most important function of the school is to provide him with a set of temporary behavioral definitions — that is, whom to arrest, how to quell a disturbance, how to direct traffic, and so on — which are acceptable to the other members of the force and which he can therefore utilize until he begins to direct his actions through experience and the homely axioms of his fellows. Thus he can hesitantly and amateurishly act his new part in the social drama. He can follow these cues and be accepted by society and tolerated by the older men. A little zealousness is humorously accepted, since everyone expects him to take himself seriously *at first,* but he will not obtain the trust and confidence of the other men until he begins to see the formal rules as they are and to send them back to wait for the new man.

It is difficult to make an objective assessment of the function of the recruit school in initiation. However, as the foregoing impressionistic account shows, there is little doubt (1) that it detaches the new man from his old experience and prepares him for the new; and (2) that the recruit learns the rough outlines of his job as it appears on the books, and with this he can work until he knows better.

Contacts with Colleagues

Traditionally, the procedure for integrating the new man into the force is to put him on the job with an older and more experienced partner. This was done before police schools were seriously thought of and is still followed today when the new man leaves the school. Generally, this is done with the idea of moving the man about until he obtains some concept of the operations of the department. Variations from department to department are great, ranging from a thorough training program in which the new man is carefully guided through the entire department and has a chance to work at every job, to those in which he is thrown with one older man and forgotten. Department X is irregular in its recruit training, but generally moves the new man from district to district every few days. He manages to work in a patrol car and on the foot beat. His experience is confined, however, to the patrol divisions, and he seldom, if ever, works in the station.

Personality Factors. As he leaves the school, with its security of procedure and clarity of definitions, the recruit tends to operate in terms of his own way of dealing with society. The aggressive and confident man will try to teach the older officer, will try to act with initiative and force, to apply the things he has learned in school. The man with a disposition to withdraw will listen and observe, saying and doing very little. Most of the men are exceedingly self-conscious, ill at ease, and slightly fearful. Past experience has told them to expect rough treatment at the hands of their fellows; they are therefore wary. The uniform is a shock; they are conscious of people looking at them. Men have been known to carry their uniforms to work and put them on in the locker room for weeks before they have the courage to leave home so attired.

Reception by the Group. Their reception is not what they expect. There is no hazing. They are received warmly, with advice and tolerance. All the rookies in Department X were enthusiastic about the warmth of their reception by the older men. On the beat and in the car they were instructed as to the characteristics of their territory, the eccentricities of its inhabitants, the procedures of the job. They were regaled with tales of past exploits. They were warned against the stoolies, the politicians, the women. They were gathered into the group with warmth and swiftness unusual to an initiation. This was their feeling and their response.

Eight hours a day, six days a week, around the clock, they talked with their partners. Long hours between action have to be filled; and the older men, hungry for an audience, use them to advantage. Here the experienced man finds an opportunity to talk about himself as a policeman, about his hardships and happinesses. Here he is expected to talk. His talk makes him feel good — more important. Here is someone to whom he is an expert; here he finds none of the boredom of his wife, or the derision of the public, but an eager, subservient listener. Thus, amidst an incessant barrage of warnings as to silence, the recruit is initiated into the experience of the man, the history of the department, the miseries of police work, the advantages of police work, and the gripes and boasting of a long series of men. The older man, who had been long bottled up, who is insecure about himself and the worth of his job, who faces from day to day an unfriendly world, exploits the situation to the full. The rookie proves a psychological asset. This is the training and the initiation.

The primary colleague experience of the rookie is with his older partners. He is likely to be placed with many different men during his first two months on the job. The long periods of time he spends with each man permit rather intimate acquaintance, provided that the rookie plays his role well. It is primarily from these older (more experienced) partners that he learns the right way to act, to pick his way through a host of delicate situations.

Insecurities About Action

Family quarrels, irate storekeepers, impudent teen-agers, taunting drunks, ingratiating storekeepers, all pose situations for which the police school offers little help. The rookie faced with these situations, and a host of others, finds himself in a perplexing situation. His prepolice experience offers little in the way of instruction; for him the role is unique. Thus, he casts about, seeking for a way to act. He learns to distrust his own inclinations. He finds that he never had to examine the world so attentively and he is astounded at what he sees. He is anxious and insecure. He knows that he is supposed to act, but action is blocked for lack of a habitual pattern of action. He has to think — that is, cast about and imaginatively examine possible alternatives — but how is he to know which of them will be the correct one? He cannot afford to make mistakes, for he is the law and the law is right. The pressure on him is great. Next to him, however, walks or sits a good, safe solution, his partner. Thus, he watches how his partner acts, and the next time anything happens he does the same thing. From his partner he is receiving a constant stream of explicit and implicit definitions of behavior: "See that fellow over there — he's drunk but he won't give you any trouble. Just tell him to go home and he'll do it quietly.[1] Most of them are that way, but you'll meet a bad one now and then . . . you don't have to take anything from them though, just pull them in . . . if there is one thing I hate it's a guy who is too soft . . . that sort of thing never does the force any good." And from these explanations and assertions the recruit gets his actions defined. In fact, he is overwhelmed with such explanations and scarcely has time for a thought of his own. From them he gets a general orientation, which is concretized as he gets involved in police action. It is from these primary contacts with his partner, however, that most of his conception of his role as a policeman is developed and his conception of man and society is subtly altered.

In his contacts with his colleagues, through his work with his partners, the new policeman thus shapes his conception of the policeman's role and his relationship to the group. The warmth of his reception, repeated assertions of the necessity to stick together, pointed references to the differences between the police and the public — "Everybody hates a cop . . . You gotta make them respect you" — result in the rookie's amalgamation into the force and his setting himself apart from the public. At the same time, the rookie begins to accept these rules of thumb, which represent the operational values of the police. He learns to make his own (group-defined) judgments about when the law is in force, how to deal with the public ("You gotta make them respect you"), but these have yet to gain emotional force; they represent only plausible instructions — they need experience for support, to weld the rookie into a policeman.

Experience — the "Reality Shock"

The rookie policeman learns about the problems that the police face from his partner. He is told about how hostile the public is to the police, about the difficulties of working with the public and getting them to cooperate, and about what a hard life the policeman has. He does not really believe these things, however, and it is only as he begins to experience them that he realizes

[1] City X has a municipal ordinance against being intoxicated on the street.

that they are true and what meaning they have in the life of a policeman. This realization is what E. C. Hughes (1952) has called the "reality shock."

Coincidently with his contact with the older men and his acquisition of knowledge about the police, the rookie gradually begins to assume responsibility for his own actions. Gradually he begins to act, to attempt to resolve problematical situations in line with his duty. As he does so, he comes in contact with the public. He experiences this contact as one of rejection and hostility by the people he is serving. He is prepared to interpret most contacts in this light by the things he has heard from his older partners. He begins to experience what the older men have experienced, to be unjustly treated, to be hated, to be jeered at.[2] He reexperiences what has produced the definitions of behavior that the police hold.

As the rookie experiences these contacts with the public, he becomes emotionally involved with the maintenance of the informal rules of behavior. For the protection of his self-esteem he begins to believe that "you gotta make them respect you." He generally formulates this rule as a duty to make the public respect the law. He begins to recognize emotionally that his interests lie with those of his fellow officers, and he begins to differentiate himself from nonpolicemen by defining them as enemies. Thus, the stories and instruction that he received from his older partners, which he first held only as logical constructs, as reasonable positions, deepen and become empowered with the emotional force of bitter experience. The rookie has then become a cop, and the group has gained a new member.

At this point it would be well to examine this experience as the rookie policeman sees it.

The Data — Ten Case Histories

All the police rookies contacted in the research were asked to give an account of their first day on the job and to describe the things that the older men had told them and their experiences since they had been on the job. At the time the interviews took place, the rookies had been on the job from two to four months. Their descriptions of their experiences can be regarded as case histories

[2] Typical experiences of this type are cited in Chapter 4.

of initiation. Each case history is cited in full and followed by an analysis.

Case 1 In school I met all the different officers in the department. They treated us very nice. I liked the other fellows. The first day on duty I was expecting almost anything, but all went well. The old police were very cooperative. I am finding out that all police like their jobs. Policemen generally cooperate with each other and will go out of their way to help each other. They are very frank. They tell us things it would take us years to find out by ourselves. They trust us.

Interviewer: What do you mean, they trust you? What did they tell you?

Answer: Well, they tell you that if you arrest certain individuals, if they are involved in minor infractions, well you just don't pinch them. For example, an older fellow and I saw a man in a car drunk. He was so drunk that he could not drive the car. The older man told me that if we took this fellow down to the station he will be out right away, so instead we took him home in a squad car. He then thanked us.

The same old fellow would point out the various men who were drunks and would be harmless and quiet. They wouldn't bother anybody. He said it is not good for public relations in the police department to arrest a drunk every time you see one. Try not to make arrests if you can help it because every time you make an arrest you make an enemy.

Two of my partners have told me that what happens between you and I is strictly between you and I. Everybody on the police force tells you that you shouldn't talk about police work off duty. I don't even talk about it to my wife. You know about Z, don't you? Well, maybe I shouldn't tell you about that.

The other men tell you that you are a police officer and you cannot back down verbally or otherwise because if you do it is a bad thing when the word gets around. Pretty soon everybody is getting smart. Mind you, when I say rough them up I don't mean beat them up badly. I mean just crack them a few times. A lot of times the policeman's got no choice. For example, we had a fellow two weeks ago, brought him into court and the case was disposed of for a dollar and costs. We got a call saying there was a fight at such and such an address and when we got there there was a man and a woman standing at the door of a private residence using the most obscene language you ever heard of. They were just yelling at the door. There were lots of school kids just standing around in a crowd listening to them. They had smashed in all the windows of the storm door. The fellow is a one-armed man. His hand was all cut and bleeding and he was covered with blood. I grabbed the one-armed fellow and told him to take it easy and not to use that language. My partner grabbed the woman. If that fellow had had two arms I would have gotten hold of one of them and twisted it behind his back and put a little pressure on him just to stop the language, but I would feel kind of funny doing that to a cripple.

Well, here's another case. My partner and I picked up a drunk, and like all drunks he says he knows somebody in the department. He was pretty drunk and was raising a lot of fuss and so I think we had better take him to the station and let him cool off and not book him. So as we were riding down in the car we search the guy and I recognize his face. It turned out he worked in the mill same time as I did. He was still working there. So he was quiet, didn't raise a fuss, didn't say much, just talked. We got to the station and took him in to the turnkey to have him checked in and as he was turning in his stuff he yanks a dollar out of his pocket and looking at us he says, "Well, here's one dollar you won't get." We had never touched the guy. But when he says that the turnkey said to him, "That's all, brother. If you were not booked before, you are now." And just about that time a detective comes down and he knows the guy. He goes over to me and says that he knows the guy, he is a quiet fellow and maybe we should let him go home. That he will take the responsibility.

And then the turnkey tells the detective what the drunk had said and the detective says, "Book him. I'll have nothing to do with him."

I felt kind of funny when it was over. I kind of wanted to say that we hadn't taken anything but you just can't say that. I would have wished they had gotten the drunk to admit he was just kidding us or something.

Analysis. This man was unusually cooperative and gave a full and quite frank account of his experiences. In examining this experience the following points are of importance:

1. The man was enthusiastic about his reception by the more experienced men, whom he found warm and friendly.

2. The man was acquainted with the rule that the policeman must maintain respect for the police, through the use of violence, if necessary. This appeared in two places: (1) he was instructed not to make too many arrests because "it is not good for public relations in the police department"; and (2) he was told that a police officer cannot back down because "it is bad if the word gets around"; and this latter instruction evidently carried an implication as to the use of violence, which appeared when the man stated, "Mind you . . . I don't mean beat them up badly."

3. He was acquainted with the rule of secrecy; he had been told to keep his mouth shut and not talk about police work.

4. He experienced some "reality shock," which was the beginning of his "acquaintance with" the meaning of the rules, (1) in his experience with the one-armed man whose case "was disposed of for a dollar and costs," and (2) in his experience with the drunk who falsely accused him of robbing him. In the one case he was prepared for a disillusionment with the courts and a belief in the need for punishment at the time of the arrest, and in the other he found the public just as hostile, bitter, and unjust as he had undoubtedly been told.

Case 2 On the first day they put me on a beat with an older man. I walked from 1st to 4th along Broad Street. The other fellow had been in the department about five years. He's a real nice guy.

I found one thing out about all the police. They all try to help you. They seem to realize that they have gone through the same thing. He showed me what his duties were on the beat, places to watch for, like the ———— restaurant on 4th and Broad Street. At that place they have a lot of teen-age kids and frequently they cause trouble. When you are on the beat you make a point of dropping in to see that everything is okay.

I remember that on that night we found a kid 19 years old in the washroom drinking wine. We just happened to wander in there and there he was. We took him and sat in a booth with him for some time and talked to the kid. He told us he was married and had a family. He also told us the liquor store where he had gotten the wine. Well, after we sent the kid on his way we called in a detective and went to the liquor store which was run by a Greek or a Jew, I think. He admitted selling the wine to the kid and that he had done so only on the basis of an identification card which did not have any evidence of the kid's age. We took his license. At the station they told us that they had had several complaints about that fellow.

That night I was all ears. Us police don't talk. We just observe. If anything comes up we talk it over with our partner. Every complaint you get and every call you make is different and this is where we learn because our partner explains it to us.

Interviewer: What else does he tell you?

Answer: Well, there's drinking. I don't care for beer. When you go to a place you are supposed to set an example. The only time you are supposed to go into a tavern is when you are called into one. He told me that when you go into a place you should be the boss and make them show respect; make them respect the uniform.

He would tell me things like there is a certain man who is a habitual drunkard and he is harmless. He will go home when you tell him to. When you go into a tavern and there is a fight on, go to the center of the fight. Move right into the center. If there is a big crowd there grab one of the fellows who are fighting, the fellow who started it if you can tell. Keep from using force unless it is necessary.

He told me that in the white districts you got to treat people psychologically but in the central district you have to use a rougher voice and show more authority because they don't understand. But mind you, it isn't this way with all the Niggers. Those that have moved out of that district you can talk to like anybody else.

You are not a judge, you can't make decisions. Don't try to decide who is right, that is, in things like a family fight. Of course you have to make up your mind whether a man is breaking the law or not. In a family fight the only thing you can do is to break up the dispute and if they insist on your making an arrest advise the complaining party to get a warrant. Fifty percent of the people down there in this job you have to use a lot of common sense. They can't tell you in school how to handle every situation.

I remember that several of my partners during the first three weeks emphasized that you don't complain about your work partner; that you just don't talk about what happens between the two of you. The best policy is to go along in the car and forget about it when you get out.

They also tell me about getting excited. That if you get excited stop because when you get excited you won't act properly. The older men also remind you of the techniques you learn in school. They tell you about how to make an arrest and how to use the radio, the siren, and the lights.

Another thing the fellows tell you is about not talking. I had people pointed out to me as stoolies.

Interviewer: Any consistency?

Answer: Well, three or four men out of the thirty I have been with have pointed out different people to me as stoolies. They told me that this or that fellow talks too much, that he is a general fucker.

In general I think that it is a good idea that the new men are in the cars. I remember I was out that night when they had that big fire. We didn't have any uniforms yet. First they had me on the corner directing the traffic away and I felt kind of funny. I had never directed traffic before but I just told some of the cars to go this way and some to go that way and didn't have any trouble with them at all. But later when the traffic patrol got there they had me keeping the pedestrians back and this was tough. In the case of cars they don't care whether you have a uniform on or not, they will listen to you and obey you. But those pedestrians. I would go over and tell them to move off and they would not pay any attention, they would just stand their ground. That is where a uniform counts.

Analysis. This man was cooperative and frank. During the entire interview he was relaxed and interested. He showed very little tendency to protect himself or hide things. He made the following important points:

1. He was warmly received by the more experienced men. He felt that this was because "they seemed to realize that they had gone through the same thing."

2. That this man was made conscious of the necessity for maintaining secrecy about police affairs was apparent when he stated

(1) that "us police don't talk"; and (2) that his partners told him "you don't complain about your work partner . . . you don't talk about what happened between the two of you. The best policy is to go along in the car and forget about it when you get out"; and (3) that "they told me that this or that fellow talks too much, that he is a general fucker."

3. He was familiarized with the rule that the respect for the police must be maintained at all times, as evidenced in his statements: (1) "He told me that when you go into a place you should be the boss and make them show respect; make them respect the uniform"; and (2) "He told me that in the white districts you got to treat people psychologically but in the central district [slum area mostly populated by Negroes] you have to use a rough voice and show more authority because they don't understand."

Case 3 Well, on the first day I was assigned with an older man in a car. We worked Broad Street and East. We only had one call all day. Some woman wanted to move her clothes out. She was leaving her man and when we got there we saw that she had been badly banged up. She had her nose busted and her face cut and teeth out. I was all for running right out of that apartment and pinching the guy but the older guy held me back and when we talked to her and the guy we found that she had been shacking up with another guy and that this guy had found out about it, though she had been shacking up with him too but for a longer time. So then I felt sorry for the guy, but all of this didn't affect the older fellow and he taught me not to take one person's word for it; not to take a flash impression seriously.

This older guy, he taught me to be calm and he used this incident as an example, pointing out that if we had pinched the guy, nine times out of ten she wouldn't file charges and we would be the horse's neck.

On that day this fellow taught me the district, how to check stores, see whether doors are locked and that if I was around and assigned to a district that I should get to know everybody and that I should memorize their faces; that the more people you know the better it is for you. He said that the best way to get along is to let the older man take the lead. He told me that the majority of the fellows on the force get on there the same way I did, through their merit, through Civil Service, without political affiliation, and that the majority were a regular bunch of fellows.

I was a little afraid at first because I expected some kind of a hazing but nothing happened. They all try to help you. Some of them told me about their own mistakes so I wouldn't make them. Stuff like making a bad arrest. They told me that whenever I was around women to watch myself, especially during working hours, but even off duty. That if I took a drink on duty to take only one and to make sure I did it when nobody could see me, but I don't ever remember taking a drink with any of the men or seeing any of them drink.

We go in for coffee all the time but I always offer to pay. The fellows teach you where you can get your coffee, that is where you go back to and buy dinner, but I haven't found any stores where you get a free steak yet.

Interviewer: What else did they tell you?

Answer: Well, several of them told me that what goes on in this car today finishes today and you don't take it into the station or family. Everybody works a district differently.

I asked about stool pigeons and the police said that is something you will have to find out for yourself. As far as I am concerned I believe that if the stool pigeon talks to the captain, the captain will come right back and eat him out. It is my opinion that there are no such things as stool pigeons. If stool pigeons exist it is a reflection on the higher ups. They should tell the stoolie off. These sergeants know who is working the districts and who drinks and things like that. They don't need anybody to tell them.

Analysis. This respondent was cooperative but very nervous during the interview. An analysis of his case brings out the following points:

1. The man was surprised at his warm reception. He expected a hazing but received only help from the more experienced men.

2. He was informed of the rule of secrecy, as evidenced in his statement that "several of them told me that what goes on in this car today finishes today and you don't take it into the station or the family." It was also evidenced in his concern with stool pigeons.

3. He was taught to mistrust his own impulses in his experience with the household quarrel. Thus, he learned that his previous experience was not adequate for the problem that the police met.

4. He was told how to break the rules of the department — that is, to make sure that nobody saw him when he was taking a drink and always to offer to pay for the coffee which he mooched.

Case 4 The first day I was not in uniform. When I did get into uniform later I noted a difference. The way I figured it, is was an easy job. We would have nothing to do. The first day I figured I knew everything about police work and as more time went on I became more ignorant, so to speak. I noticed it when they put me out in ———— by myself. I was pretty jumpy. I called the car out three or four times on false steers but the fellows were pretty nice about it.

Interviewer: What sort of things did the men tell you in order to help you get along with the other men?

Answer: Just about every man I have been with since I have been on the force has told me not to squeal on another policeman and about the value of getting along with them all. They told me to forget personal differences while I was doing a tour of duty. You know, all policemen are more or less lodge brothers and if a policeman is assaulted by a criminal that is taken into consideration in the interrogation, no matter what police force they are on.

Interviewer: How did they justify that?

Answer: The way they justify it is that if a prisoner treats one policeman that way he is going to treat another policeman in the same way, with the same kind of contempt. At least, this is the way they told it to me and I agree. They told me also that the policeman is actually a public relations man. He has to sell the police to the public.

Interviewer: Did they say anything else about using rough stuff?

Answer: They feel that it's okay to rough a man up in the case of sex crimes. One of the older men advised me that if the courts didn't punish a man, we should. He told me about a sex crime, the story about it, and then said that the law says the policeman has the right to use the amount of force necessary to make an arrest and that in that kind of a crime you can use just a little more force. They feel definitely for example in the extreme cases like rape, that if a man was guilty he ought to be punished even if you could not get any evidence on him. My feeling is that all the men on the force feel that way, at least from what they have told me.

Analysis. This man was very ill at ease during the interview and extremely nervous. He spoke rapidly for a short time and then stopped abruptly. He made the following points:

1. He had the unusual experience of being alone on the beat shortly after he joined the force. He stated that he was very nervous and called the cars three or four times on false steers. He illustrates the inadequacy of his previous experience and school training in providing him with definitions of behavior adequate to the problems he would face on the job.

2. His acquaintance with the rule for maintaining respect for the police is evidenced when he states that if a prisoner is going to treat one policeman that way he is going to treat another policeman in the same way with the same degree of contempt.

3. His familiarity with the rule of secrecy about police affairs is demonstrated in his statement, "Just about every man I have been with since I have been on the force has told me not to squeal on another policeman."

4. He is being trained to accept the use of violence on a personal basis, as evidenced in his statements about sex criminals.

Case 5 On the first day I was on the job they told me that I couldn't go according to the law all the time, that I had to use my own judgment. Things like that you are not supposed to go in without a warrant but sometimes you do, or you are not supposed to question a man without arresting him but you do that lots of times.

Like there was a guy in ——— district who we knew had a record and the police told me to keep an eye on him. I saw him down in my district and stopped him and questioned him and then I saw that he took the bus over to ——— district. Well, you never know what that guy might have been up to if we hadn't stopped him.

Lots of times when you are working midnights you see a guy standing around and you have to question him.

They said that force goes according to the class of people. Some people you can't use enough force on. Some of those rubes in the central district want you to use force, but with the people in the better districts force is an insult.

We had a case a couple of days ago. We came by and a car was parked with parking lights on and we figured it was a couple of lovers so we drove on and then when we came back an hour later and the car was still there and we thought this was funny because if they had been lovers they would have had time to finish so since it was an area where I lived I told my partner to go up to them and tell them to move along because I didn't want to get a reputation of sneaking up on people in my own area. I though it might be somebody I'd know.

He went up there and pretty soon he called to me and there were a couple of fellows in the car with their pants open. I couldn't understand it. I kept looking around for where the woman could be. They were both pretty plastered. One was a young kid about eighteen years old and the other was an older man. We decided with the kid so drunk that bringing him in would only really ruin his reputation and we told him to go on home. Otherwise we would have pinched them.

During the time we were talking to them they offered us twenty-eight dollars and I was going to pinch them when they showed the money but my partner said never mind, let them go.

Another time we got a call that there were two guys fighting. The wife had made the call I guess. When we got there they were arguing all right but one of the fellows said that it was his house, that he didn't want us there, that he was the owner and we said okay, but as we were on the way out we heard him say to the other fellow, "Well you had better mind your own business or I will call the police." That is all they want to use us for is a threat.

One time I saw my partner beat up a drunk pretty badly but he had cussed him out. I was a rookie and I didn't want to say anything so I didn't say anything, I just went back in the car and sat there and then I didn't talk to my partner.

Analysis. This man was very cooperative but seemed unwilling to say much about what the older men had told him. An analysis of this case shows the following important points:

1. He was acquainted with the rule requiring a maintenance of respect for the police, as the older men told him about the use of force, and he stated, "Some of these people you can't use enough force on."

2. He was told that a policeman couldn't go according to the law

all the time and that "I had to use my own judgment." He was informed that the policeman has to break the law in order to do his job. Thus he was being initiated into the secrets of the group.

3. He had three experiences that gave him the "reality shock." These were (1) his experience with the homosexuals who tried to bribe him (and thus challenged his integrity); (2) his experience with the family quarrel, when he found that the public was using the police to further its own ends; and (3) his experience when he saw his partner beat up a drunk who talked back.

Case 6 They told me don't get too excited. Stand by and watch for three or four months. Don't say anything.

On my first day on the department I walked the beat with an older man. He told me that the biggest part in being a policeman was just using common sense. Not to try to show too much authority. He introduced me to everybody on the beat.

He said that a good policeman is a fellow who does things according to rules and regulations.

The first time I had a free cup of coffee the fellows told me that there were some fellows who had consistently not paid and they had gotten in trouble because of it. They told me always to offer to pay.

The public don't have respect for the work we are doing for them. They think that you are bad if you ever pinch anybody.

The fellows tell you that once you back down you are not a good policeman any more.

Analysis. This man was very uncooperative. He stated that he couldn't remember his first day on the job and that the older men hadn't told him a thing. It was only after considerable urging that he made his laconic statements. The analysis of the case reveals the following points:

1. He was acquainted with the rule that respect for the police must be maintained, as he was told that "once you back down you are not a good policeman any more."

2. He was told how to break the rules by always offering to pay for a cup of coffee.

3. He had become conscious of the hostility of the public.

Case 7 Well on the first day I was with an older man in a patrol car and we were in the north-side district. That was really a day. The car I was in takes care of the hospital emergency calls and I saw some things that day that I never believed could have happened. We got one call to go to the hospital and there was a Negro woman and she had chunks of flesh taken out of her the size of a half dollar. Just right out of her — regular holes — just chunks. She told us that her husband had bitten them out of her. Besides the hospital calls we had a lot of routine calls and then there were houses to check for people who were out on vacation and things like that.

The older men want you to ask questions, like what would you do in this case or in that case. Most of them told me to take it easy the first nine months to watch my step and not to try to clean up the city. They said you would be just sticking your neck out. There are only certain things that you can do. I remember that on that first day out I did get all the radio signals and I learned the use of the siren, the red light and the stop light. The fellow I was with talked about the district. They said don't try to be an eager beaver and when you get a call try to talk the person into behaving. Try to keep him out of jail. You make more friends that way.

They tell you that there is a certain fellow, they don't name him, who tells everything to the chief, and that if you find anything going back to you just remember who you told it to. They never tell you who they are.

They tell you not to go out on the streets on the outskirts of town looking for petting parties in the summer time. That you should check over your territory all right but you shouldn't go out there looking for much, and not to go into the station too early when you are coming off, and not to go into a tavern unless you are called into it.

I remember one time when we got a call to a place which had been burglarized. When we got there we got out of the car and I saw that the other fellow had drawn his gun. He went around one side of the house and told me to go around the other. I didn't have my uniform on but I drew my gun too and as I was going around the corner of the house I met two men from the uniformed patrol who had also come in on patrol, and they had their guns out and boy, for a minute I was afraid they would shoot me because they didn't know me. I don't like that business with the guns.

Another time we got called out on a murder call. We picked up the guy and took him to the scene of the murder in a hotel room. He confessed everything and they reconstructed the crime. Then evidently they wanted to talk things over and they told me to take the fellow out in the hall and guard him. Well, I think that was a hell of a thing to do. Since they told me to guard him I figured I wasn't taking any chances so I drew my gun out and held it on him all the time I was out there.

Analysis. This man was talkative but evasive. He was trying to give the impression that he was cooperating but it was evident that he was withholding a lot of things and was being careful about what he said. He made the following points:

1. He was acquainted with the rule of secrecy, having been warned about the people who bring things back to the chief.

2. He experienced some degree of "reality shock" in his contact with the hospital cases, when he "saw things he never believed could have happened." He thus began to see people and the public in a different light and was being prepared for a set of definitions in which they were defined as different from and in conflict with the police.

3. He was let in on the trade secrets when he was told not to make too many arrests and not to go out on the trails looking for petting parties.

4. He indicated his own feelings of inadequacy with respect to police work in the two stories he told about the burglary and the murder call. Thus, he indicated that his previous experience and training did not prepare him to handle these situations.

Case 8 During the first day of work I was pretty ill at ease. I felt kind of conspicuous riding around in a squad car. The first call was for a prowler. When we got there we entered the house together. You know usually one man goes around each side of the house. The older man was more interested in my security than in catching the prowler and we never did catch the party.

Interviewer: What did the older man talk to you about?

Answer: Well, he talked to me about my job and how to be careful of women and drinking. I asked him questions on these investigations and if he couldn't answer he told me to ask the desk sergeant. He never did shut me down like some fellows did by saying, "Why do you want to know that?"

He mentioned that what you see in this car keep it here and don't mention it in another car.

Interviewer: Did many of the men you were with during the first month tell you that?

Answer: About nine out of ten fellows made a point of telling me that. I found this to be a wise thing to do because some of the fellows didn't get along and because if you talk you are more or less of a squealer and you never hear anything of what goes on in the department. There are certain people in the department to whom certain persons won't talk, but I don't think that there's anybody who nobody will talk to.

They say drink but don't make a habit of it. That if it is cold you can go in for a fast shot. The first night I was out I only had cokes. I was afraid it was going to bounce back. I had drinks with a couple of fellows. I think they were watching me to see whether I was going to tell it to anybody else. I always make a point of going to the back door and regardless of whether I know the fellow or not I try to pay. I think they will think more of you and appreciate it if you do try to pay. And besides then you are not obligated. Tavern owners have a habit of calling on you for minor incidents, things which really aren't in the line of duty.

Analysis. This man was uncooperative. He really didn't want to talk to the interviewer, but he seemed to be afraid not to talk. He took a long time to say what he did and it was only the coercion of silence on the part of the interviewer that kept him going. An analysis of his case indicates the following points:

1. He was impressed with the rule of silence by most of the older men he had been with; and he had accepted the definition that if you talk you are more or less of a "squealor."

2. He was beginning to learn how to break the rules, and thus was being initiated into the secrets of the trade. This is evidenced in his statement that "I always make a point of going to the back door [to get a drink in a bar] and regardless of whether I know the fellow or not I try to pay."

Case 9 On my first day on the job I walked the south side beat from 29th to 35th. I was in civilian clothes and I was amazed to find that the public was friendly but cautious and suspicious of the policeman. I never realized what there was in that area. The worst kind of drunks and bums. I didn't even know there were people like that in X. I guess I am soft-hearted but I feel sorry for them. I wished I could help them. I was just amazed to see how the other half lives, the way the women talk and the language and phrases they use.

I was amazed at the knowledge these people have of the law. For example if they take a beating they know that they have to swear out a warrant before the policeman will arrest the other man. Nobody in Park Manor knows that.

I was also amazed at the restrictions on a police officer, the things he can and can't do and the things he has to do to make an arrest stick.

I found that the old officers were awfully soft-hearted, that the minute they get a guy they start feeling soft-hearted. The average public doesn't realize that the police officer has a job to do. They think you are out to get them in trouble. It seems to me that about ninety percent of the public is against the police. I think it's the idea that they don't like being restrained. If we can convince the public that the policeman wants to help them I think that's the thing.

The older men tell us how to go about making arrests. They say that the main thing was to use common sense. To use your head. Don't do things on the spur of the moment. When a police officer is on duty he has to do in four or five minutes what it takes the courts two or three weeks to find out. You have to decide whether or not a man is guilty. Everybody tells you, "Don't get arrest happy." They impress on you the idea that the police officer who makes the most arrests is not necessarily the best officer. I think I have heard it a dozen times if I have heard it once about the guy on the Cleveland police force who spent twenty years on the force and retired without ever having made an arrest.

They also tell you to keep your gun in your holster. Everybody emphasizes that.

They tell you to be polite and to never use force until the last resort, and you have to take an awful verbal beating. The old timers tell each rookie to keep his mouth shut and not to agree or disagree. Because of my brother being a policeman I know a lot of old timers and when I first went into the force I spoke to any of them when I heard anybody criticizing any of them but I was told to keep my mouth shut and mind my own business. Policemen are pretty clanish. They will criticize a brother policeman but if any outsider says anything against a policeman that outsider is wrong. Policemen have to stick together. In X there are a hundred and sixty policemen against a hundred and forty thousand people and if we didn't stick together we would all be lost. Police officers on the whole are anxious to be helpful and are not glory hunters.

Interviewer: Do you worry about your cases when you get home?
Answer: Yes, I am like that. I do it quite a bit. Sometimes I will sit and think four or five hours and then still have it on my mind when I get up in the morning. Recently we had a funny case. This woman side-swiped another car. Well, we caught up with her and put her in the squad car. She was pretty drunk. She just sat there and she had a nice little dog, holding the dog in her lap and crying and saying she was so sorry and she had never done anything like this before, the first time she had been in trouble, she didn't know what her husband would say, and I felt like letting her go right then and there, but since she had busted this guy's fender we took her into the station, and as soon as we got in the station all the old timers knew her and called her by her first name. She had been in a hundred times if she had been in once. But I felt silly.

Analysis. This man was cooperative but evidently (from the interview material) seemed to be taking care that he said nothing that would look bad for him. He seemed to be giving out the official line on what the rookie policeman learns. He made the following points that are of interest to this study:

1. He was extremely conscious of the need for the policemen to stick together against the public, as evidenced in his statement, "In X there are only a hundred and sixty policemen *against* a hundred and forty thousand people and if we didn't stick together we would all be lost."

2. His experience with the drunken woman indicates his awareness that he couldn't resist his own impulses and that he had a lot to learn.

Case 10 The fellow I first worked with had only been on the force about six months. We walked the south side and I never did get out of there since then. He told me where the call boxes were, not to be pinch happy, to give the men a break, but if they were snotty bring them in, you have the right; not to let them make fools of you; to use my common sense. He told me how to shake doors to see if they are locked and what to look for. He pointed out people to me, mostly those bums who slip around there to try to come up and make friends with you. During the first month I had to work one or two nights and then I had to be in a car for three or four.

They said that if a fellow stepped out of line a bit he never heard the end of it. Those police were like a bunch of old washwomen. As for the older men, each of them was trying to whitewash himself.

After working a while you meet one or two of the fellows and gradually you get a group which sticks together and then they tell you things about who is a stoolie and stuff like that.

The old timers would tell you to keep your mouth shut and that what went on in the car was between the two of you. They told you that what we do or where we go is between us. Don't say anything about it to the next man. I have had fellows pointed out to me and had said about them that if you work with them you just watch what you say.

Analysis. This man was cooperative but laconic. He was anxious to get the interview completed. The analysis of his case indicates the following points:

1. He was conscious of the rule emphasizing the maintenance of respect for the police, as evidenced in his statement that the older man had told him "not to be pinch happy, to give the men a break, but if they were snotty bring them in."

2. His awareness of the necessity for maintaining secrecy about police affairs is indicated in his reference to stool pigeons.

Summary of Case Materials. The preceding case materials are not equally extensive and informative. The informants varied in the degree to which they were cooperative; however, the cases represent the viewpoints of almost 50% of the rookies in the department at the time the study was made. As such, they are considered to represent a significant description of the initiation of the rookie policeman into Department X.

These cases delineate the initiation experience from the viewpoint of the men. They indicate that initiation in Department X involves an interaction with the older men and experience with the public in which the rookies are informed as to the importance of maintaining secrecy (6 cases), the need for maintaining respect for the police (7 cases), and the laws and departmental rules which can be broken (4 cases). They indicate that the rookie is warmly received by the other men and that he experiences no hazing; that he finds that he must mistrust his own impulses and that there is a lot to learn about the job. They indicate that the rookie finds that he can't go according to law all the time and must use his own judgment in many of the problems he meets; that he finds the public to be hostile to the police; and that he recognizes the need for solidarity among the police.

A few of the cases describe situations or experiences in which the men experienced "reality shock" in finding that the bad things in police work were just as bad as the other men had told them they would be. However, most of the cases emphasize the transmission of knowledge about police work, arising from the contact of the new man with his colleagues, and fail to mention anything in connection with the "reality shock." This is because these men had spent most of their time on the force with older and more experienced men, who absorbed the shock, so to speak. It is in the personal experience of the rookie, when he is alone or responsible for his action that he really becomes "acquainted with" police work. This experience is dealt with extensively in Chapter 3, and therefore needs no further discussion or documentation at this point.

The preceding cases restrict the description of initiation to the viewpoint of the initiate; however, his is only one part of the interaction that takes place between the newcomer and the group. It is necessary to investigate the viewpoint of the experienced men toward the initiate in order to gain a full comprehension of what this process involves.

Group Definition of the Initiate

In an effort to determine how the group looks at the initiate, and how they believe he should act in order to get along, 40 experi-

Table 5.1. Desirable Behavior in the Rookie as Indicated by 40 Experienced Policemen

What the Rookie Should Do	Frequency
Listen to the older man	22
Keep his mouth shut	17
Don't be cocky or an eager beaver	13
Respect the older man's feelings and cooperate	13
Don't be a stool pigeon	5
Do his job	4
Find out the bad ones (stool pigeons)	3
Remember that police work is common sense	2
Mind his own business	2

enced men were asked, "If you were talking to a new man and you wanted him to get hep, to help him get along with the other men, what would you tell him?" They responded in the manner summarized in Table 5.1.

The replies indicate that there exists a general conception of how a new man should act. In other words, they indicate that the rookie has a role that he is expected to play. This role is defined in the next section. Here, however, is a series of responses, chosen at random, which illustrate how the experienced men replied to the question.

1. To get along pay attention to the older men and follow suit. Follow the rule book. You have twenty years to do and do the job well. Don't let it become a personal thing.

2. To get along I'd say go along with the older men and let them take the first step. Keep your eyes and ears open. That way you will learn more and gain the respect of the older man by being a good partner. Once in a while you find a guy who thinks he knows it all. That's bad. The best thing is to go along because then the older man will teach you a lot of things. Cooperate and keep a cool head.

3. To get along be observant of the senior partner and don't be too cocky. Don't go sounding off just because you just got out of school. It takes so much more than schooling to be a policeman and don't stool on another policeman in any way to be in good.

4. If I wanted to get along with the other police I'd recommend that you do a lot of listening. Let the older fellow make the decisions. Don't act as if you knew what it is all about. Remember that police work is good common sense.

5. To get along with the other men I'd say keep your mouth shut and keep your ears open. You know that the first two weeks on the job is what sticks with a man. If he is a wise guy he gets that reputation and it will stay with him for the next twenty years.

6. To get along tell a man to keep his eyes and ears open, and his mouth shut. Don't try to tell the older men what to do if you want to get along. Wait until you get your feet on the ground and the guys will talk to you.

Police work is something that requires experience. Give me an older man over some young college student.

If you want to get ahead study and get along with the other men. You've gotta have guts and be conscientious.

7. To get along with the other men keep your mouth shut and listen for a long time. When you get the drift of things it's okay. I don't care much for the guys who are loud.

The Role of the Initiate

The role of the rookie is that of the listener, the inactive one. He learns his role in interaction with the older men — it is never fully explicated. It is a problem in action and reaction. His sensitivity to how the older man reacts to his gestures will determine his popularity and his success. Questions about the work are welcomed; statements about the work are frowned upon. According to definition, the rookie is a fellow who has a lot to learn, and he can only learn it from experience. School is a good thing — every policeman could use a lot of it; *but* you can learn to be a policeman only on the job. Asking questions about the other men on the force is dangerous, for the older men don't trust a rookie, they don't know what he will spill. If he keeps his mouth shut with them, they figure he knows how to do it. Then maybe it is safe to tell him a thing or two. If anything happens, the rookie should stand aside and let the older man handle it; if he tries to handle the situation, he will usually mess it up and it would prove that he thinks he is smarter than he is. They expect the worst of such a fellow. If he makes a mistake, then they are good fellows and help him out — show him that policemen stick together. If he thinks he is smart, they answer his questions, when they are about the work, but let him figure the rest out himself. Thus, in the rookie's training the first thing is to learn how to act like a rookie. The socially sensitive man learns this quickly, and with it he learns important things about the force. He learns who are the "stoolies" and thus knows for whom to watch out.

Interviews indicated that the men who were most at ease in the interviewing situation inevitably knew more about the stoolies and who they were. All the rookies who were interviewed knew that a policeman should keep his mouth shut. All of them knew about stoolies, the guys who tell. But only a few, the most relaxed, had the stoolies pointed out to them. These men had a greater chance of success. Knowing who the stoolies were enabled them to know when to be careful and kept bad reports from reaching the captains and the chief.

Summary of Initiation Process

The initiation into the police force in City X can be divided into the three experiential stages: recruit school, contact with colleagues, and experience with the public. In school the recruit obtains a temporary definition of the situation, which will permit him to operate until he becomes oriented. In addition, he is brought into contact with the atmosphere of police work, with the themes of group solidarity, with the concept of being tough, with the need for maintaining and raising the prestige of the group. Leaving school with this set of temporary definitions, the recruit begins his work in the company of an older and more experienced man. In this relationship he is expected to play the role of rookie — the quiet one, the listener. From this older partner he receives technical information and the rules of the game, explicit and wrapped in stories and homely wisdom. The older man enjoys the paternalistic expert role, provided that the younger man plays the role of recruit, a role he learns from interaction with the older man. From the older man he learns the importance of the police "sticking together," the need for making the public respect the police, the need for being tough, the difference between the police and the public, the public condemnation of the police. He receives these ideas verbally and sees them demonstrated in action. Faced with problematical situations, he observes their solution in the actions of his partner — actions made in terms of the group definitions of behavior held within the police force. Thus, the younger man finds the group solution an easy, socially sanctioned one and is ready to follow it when he has occasion to act. At this point in his initiation the rookie holds these definitions of actions as reasonable and easy, but feels little in the way of emotional involvement, and therefore his adherence to these definitions lacks conviction. It is in his experience with the public that he becomes emotionally involved with identifying himself with the group and upholding its values. He finds the public uncooperative, unpleasant, and antagonistic. He finds that the maintenance of his own integrity and self-esteem is linked with the maintenance of respect for the police. He begins to defend and follow the group-defined rules of action with conviction. He has become a policeman.

Analysis of Phases in Initiation

Sociologically speaking, this initiation indicates certain phases of importance in understanding initiation in general.

1. The initiate role is an essential part of integration into the group. It is one of a pair of counterroles: the initiate vis-à-vis the paternalistic expert. The initiate must act his part in the drama of experience versus inexperience if the older man is to function as teacher, for it is only in that social situation that the older man derives the ego satisfactions that encourage him to teach the younger man. When the initiate breaks out of the role and attempts to indicate abilities of his own, he threatens the knowledge of the older man and deprives him of his ego satisfactions. The initiate will then be defined as "too smart for his own good" and will be deprived of access to the informal rules. When he is unable to observe rules of which he is not cognizant, sanctions will be applied.

Although the initiate role as previously described has reference to the police, it has its analogies in other occupation groups: in the shop, in the hospital, in the army, and so forth. These other areas may differ as to the content of the role, but the form persists.

2. In the initiate-expert counterrole context, the new man is familiarized with the content of his occupational role. Although varying from occupation to occupation, this content will consist of a self-conception that identifies the individual with the group and differentiates him from others, a definition of the others, a set of status-orienting values, and specific or general rules of action with respect to recurrent occupational problems. This content is transmitted to the new man through specific directions, through illustration in story and proverb, and through example and demonstration in action. This, however, is *knowledge about*

group membership and occupational role, and it leaves the recruit without the emotional participation that would make him a member of the group.

3. Following or concurrent with the acquisition of *knowledge about* his role, the recruit begins to have *acquaintance with* or sympathetic knowledge of the rules or values. He obtains this through the "reality shock," personally experiencing the problem areas of the occupation. For the policeman this is represented in his contact with the public. He experiences the antagonism of the public, is properly embittered, realizes the meaning of many rules like "you gotta make them respect you," and finds that the interests of the police department are his interests, that it is in his interest to uphold the interests of the police.

Thus, the role of the initiate permits the transmission of knowledge about the informal rules of behavior, and the experience with occupational problems brings an acquaintance with or emotional involvement in these rules.

The foregoing analysis has indicated the stages and processes involved in the incorporation of a new man into the occupation of police work. Essentially, the analysis has been of the dynamics involved in a shift of group perspectives, or "generalized others." Mead (1947) saw such a shift in the group perspective of the individual as the crucial aspect of a social control, which he believes to be self-control. Our analysis has therefore emphasized the personal or subjective aspect of the shift in group or occupational orientation. At this point we should like to analyze the same phenomena from an objective standpoint.

Mechanisms of Social Control

Objectively, the integration of a new member into an occupational or social group can be described in terms of four principal mechanisms or processes of varying degrees of reasonability. We have labeled these expediency, categorical reaction, application of sanctions, and maintenance of self-integrity. In the heuristic utilization of these four concepts, our problem is to comprehend sympathetically why an individual will internalize the new group rules so that he voluntarily and almost unconsciously conforms to the action patterns of the group. The concepts as used will apply only to voluntary groups in which one can conceive of the individual as desiring to become a member of the group, or to succeed in the occupation. It is such an individual, entering an occupation through his own volition, who actively participates in his own initiation. The question is how he comes to decide that the specific cultural modes of behavior are the most desirable, and how it is that he transfers his allegiance to the new group?

Expediency. By the term *expediency,* we refer to the way in which a new member is likely to solve the problematical situations that he faces as a part of his participation in the new social or occupational group. The basic idea is that a person entering a new occupation is seeking ways to behave; that is, as part of the ordinary course of his activity, he will meet with new and problematical situations inherent in the occupation, for which he will have to seek a course of action. To the extent that the occupational experience differs from his previous experience, he will lack a defined way of acting in the new situations. When we point to expediency as a force controlling the behavior of the incoming member, we refer to the fact that he will not possess solutions to the problematical situations that he encounters; he will then take the path of least resistance and follow the prescriptions of the older men — the rules of the group. In the case of the rookie policeman, situations in which he must make an arrest inevitably require some rule of thumb to make the decision; how to deal with a recalcitrant and aggressive citizen body and other such problems are not things that the rookie ordinarily knows how to handle. In most instances he will turn to the older man for advice or will act as he has observed the other men do. What we are trying to say is that a powerful factor in the social control of group members is that they meet identical problems. Thus, the new man does not have to be forced to act in a certain way. More than likely he will find the group's way convenient and expedient. The individual, being anxious to get ahead or do well in the occupation, will himself gulp down the prescriptions he finds.

Categorical Reaction. By the term *categorical reaction,* we mean the situation in which the individual finds himself a social stereotype and realizes he is involved responsibly with all others of his kind. Lippman (1922), Simmel (1950), and others have pointed out the tendency of people in modern society to treat one another as members of a category. Simmel in his *Metropolis and the Mental Life* indicates this to be a necessary attribute of urbanizations, of the multitude of contacts in the social densities of the city. In this connection we should like to point out that the individual who is treated categorically finds that he is responsible for and has the reputation engendered by the actions of others in his category.

For the policeman the categorical reaction is very strong. In City X the police department has a very bad reputation, as it does in most cities in America, with the result that the public has a very low level of tolerance for its misdemeanors. Here, in a real sense, the bad policeman characterizes the whole force.

A citizen may observe one policeman beating up a drunk (and it happens), and immediately all policemen are considered brutal. The good policeman is thought of as an exception. Mind you, we are not at this point stating or even suggesting that the characterization of policemen is wrong; we are not interested in a defense of the police, but rather in the explication of the effects of categorization on the subject.

The first ostensible basis for the categorization of the policeman is his uniform. This immediately marks him and differentiates him from the remainder of the population. Second, he is powerful — a disciplinary symbol. Third, he bears a bad reputation. Fourth, his business is to intrude into other people's business, and to interact with other people. Hence, he is differentiated from other uniformed figures: the soldier, the postman, the doorman. The uniform is only one of the possible bases for categorization, but its importance lies in its visibility. Because of its visibility, the policeman seldom escapes his category. Thus, even when he is off duty, the neighbors will recognize his profession by seeing him enter his apartment or house in uniform. They will continue to treat him in terms of his category and will feel free to harass him with their own troubles, to call him into their apartments to speak to the maids who they think are stealing, to accuse him of malfeasance when the neighbor's boy's bicycle is stolen, to accuse him of laziness when they see him in his backyard on his day off. Because of his high visibility, because his activities are exciting, because he is a personally threatening figure, because he is in constant contact with the public, the policeman is highly conscious of his category. The public categorization forces him into the group. It forces him to identify his life chances with those of the group. Policemen always tell stories about how Joe Cop killed a man one day and how everybody gave him a dirty look the next day. In this sense, every rookie sooner or later has the experience of being made responsible for the actions of his fellows before the bar of public opinion. Once he is conscious of this, and once he begins to identify his fate with that of his fellows, a powerful emotional basis for the personal observance of the group dictum has been established.

Application of Sanctions. This is a subject that has been well developed in the literature and needs little discussion here. The general idea is that the individual moves into an organized and unorganized system of rewards and punishments which guide his behavior and gradually structure his perspectives. A word is in order, however, about the initiate in this respect. Naturally, the initiate, who is ignorant of the rules of behavior, cannot be held responsible and cannot be punished in the same degree as the experienced person. Thus, the work novice who breaks the rule is not considered in the same category as the experienced person who makes this mistake. Among the police the initiate is permitted to make mistakes; there is tolerance attached to the role. The eager-beaver rookie who does his job too well and the rookie who backs down from a gang of young toughs are seldom dealt with severely by the other men. Light sanctions may be applied, advice will be given, but the primary idea is to help the man out of the difficulties he gets himself into. This is done as long as he plays his role of rookie. When he departs from this role he assumes the responsibility for his own actions, and sanctions will be applied. For the police, a crucial area in this respect is the maintenance of the rule of silence. The rookie coming out of school frequently has ideas about police conduct which are out of line with the prevailing definition. He may tell his troubles to one of the captains. However, if he plays his role, he will be dealt with gently; some older man will give him hell — but he won't be defined as a "stoolie." Should he fail to play the rookie role, however, he will be regarded as a sneak — possibly even as a stoolie. He won't be trusted, and the penalty of the silent treatment may be applied. This is the primary sanction among the police. The men who are not liked, the stoolies, find that they are shut off from sources of information, that their partners will not gossip with them, that groups will stop talking as they approach. This is a very severe sanction among the police for two reasons. First, information about what is going on is essential to one's own success and protection. Perhaps the chief has decided to tighten things up — if you don't know about it, he may catch you smoking on duty. Second, one of the few sources of prestige for the policeman is that he knows what is going on in the world of crime and can talk authoritatively to the public on this subject. Some friend may ask him if they caught such and such a purse-snatcher. The policeman's ability to give a full account of the case and its present stage of development is one of the few ways he can obtain ego satisfaction in his relationship with the public. To be deprived of this information, therefore, is most trying.

A second type of sanction, which is frequently applied concurrently with the first, is the refusal to work with the man concerned. Thus, a man will find that his partners are always asking to work with someone else.

Maintenance of Personal Integrity. This is perhaps the most subtle and difficult of all the processes to delineate. Empirically, it is nearly impossible to substantiate; therefore, it is offered only as a hypothesis. The general idea is that the individual will struggle to maintain his self-esteem, and that when he moves from group to group he finds that the behavior patterns in which he is rooted are such that they present an uncomplimentary self-conception. Thus, the policeman drawn from a population in revolt against authority, condemning brutality and graft, frequently finds that he must be authoritative and use brutality and take graft if he is to be successful in his job. At first, he will think badly of himself for acting as he does. Perhaps initially he might refuse to act in this way. However, as he continues in the work and the temporal distance from his previous group experience and previous "generalized other" increases, their force weakens and he finds himself less and less able to justify his opposition to the new modes of behavior. If the new group of which he is a member is in conflict with his former society and if he is inclined, therefore, to be opposed to the old society and depend on the new for his self-justification, the pressure increases. As he begins to participate in the new group more and more completely, he begins to internalize (at first) those group values which do not conflict with the values he previously held. But the values are likely to be closely interconnected, and in accepting some of them he finds that he is committed to the others. Thus, he may for a period work in a state of conflict between his old values and his new actions. The conflict is unpleasant, however, and the unpleasantness is likely to be attributed to the old values. Since the conflict is painful, he will endeavor to resolve it. Generally, only two resolutions are possible: to cease acting as he does, thus quitting the new group, or to discard the old values. A few men accept the first alternative; still fewer continue in the state of conflict; most of them accept the new values.

This particular mechanism is important in our analysis since it represents a pressure or force distinct from the others, which must, in a sense, be added to the others if we are to understand the completeness with which a new member is integrated into some social groups.

With respect to the police it should be pointed out that few men ever achieve a complete resolution of the conflict. The larger society, with its antithetical values, is ever-present in the lives of the men, and try as they may they are unable to forget it. This leaves a residue of guilt. A high degree of integration does take place, however. On this level of the maintenance of self-integrity, the crucial point in the shift of values for the policeman occurs when he recognizes that he as policeman faces a hostile society and then conceives of himself in conflict with that society. Once this idea permeates his thinking, he is ready to discard the values of the larger society; for in accepting the idea that the larger society is evil, he easily conceives of its values as being evil. Naturally, most of the men upset the old values by a slightly different rationale — by saying that the old society does not really know what it is talking about, that it does not really know what is going on. But they clearly define it as evil by emphasizing those sectors that they can most easily attack — the businessman, the entertainer, the newspaper people, the lawyers, in each of whom they empirically can detect evidence of corruptions, for their very trade brings them in contact with this type of evidence; and from what they know, they generalize and feel satisfied. The most prominent mechanism in this connection is one of projection: they point out that all kinds of people accept tips for services and thus justify the traffic shakedown; they point out that everybody is out to make a buck and that most people don't care how they do it; and so forth. Conflict with the public brings with it conflict with the values held by the public — so the policeman accepts the values of the police.

Conclusions

The foregoing description and analysis of the initiation of the rookie policeman indicate that the rookie policeman passes through three general experiential phases: recruit school, contact with and instruction by his more experienced colleagues, and experience with the public. The first phase functions to detach him from his previous life pattern and prepare him to accept a new one, and to provide him with a set of temporary definitions of behavior with which he can function until he becomes more thoroughly oriented. The second phase involves the interaction of the rookie with the more experienced men, and the communication, directly and indirectly, of the secrets and customs of the police. The third phase involves the rookie's taking responsibility for his own actions and learning that the public is everything that the older men said it would be. In the third phase the rookie becomes emotionally involved in upholding the values of the group because he comes to recognize them as involving his own self-esteem. At this point the rookie becomes a policeman.

An analysis of this material indicates that if he is to be trusted by the group and told the rules and the secrets, the initiate must play a role — the role of the initiate — which, for the police, is the listener, the one who does not initiate action. It suggests that four mechanisms are responsible for the rookie's acceptance of the rules of the group: (1) expediency, or the need for a way to act in view of the uselessness of previous definitions and the acceptance of the safest and most available channels of action — this involves the imitation of the actions that the rookie sees around him; (2) categorical reaction, or the response to being stereotyped, which involves the knowledge on the part of those involved that their life chances lie with those of the group, and which leads to their upholding the values of the group on this basis; (3) application of sanctions, which refers to the system of the rewards and punishments provided by the group that guide the newcomer's behavior and structure his perspectives on the basis of a hedonistic response; and (4) the maintenance of personal integrity, or the tendency toward self-consistency, in which the individual tries to maintain a homogeneous generalized other, in which he has self-esteem. As the value of the new and old groups conflict, this tendency forces a selection, which, if the member continues in the new group, leads to a rejection of the old values and an acceptance of the new.

6. Postscript 1970: A Shared Fate

The tension between order and change corrodes and destroys many people and their ways, while blowing life into others. It has a vortex of anxiety, excitement, fear, and perhaps of madness. In the center of this vortex, one finds the police. They are the agents of order, and to survive they must routinize miracles, passions, and even violence. Change and dissent are their enemies, and these have the sympathies of discontent and guilt. Against all these the police must fight. As change escalates, they must band together, and in doing so they withdraw from the community, build a wall of secrecy, and live by their own rules.

As far as we know, policemen have always lived in such a changing world, sometimes abused by corruption, sometimes used by political force, but seldom gathered into the heart of the community.

As simple men, like all of us, they have found, as Gilbert and Sullivan wrote, that their "lot is not a happy one," and they have struggled against such a fate. But since their hope is yoked to order, it has dimmed with change. Time, which has been kind in bringing them better pay, better training, and more pride in their work, has also brought greater tension between the police and the community. Order seems ever more fragile, and the police are obviously fighting back. As they fight, they are forced away from the community. With the deepening hostility between the police and the community to which they are symbiotically related and inevitably a part, their need for approval and secrecy must mount and their joy in work and life fade.

We cannot permit this to happen. Rules have meaning only as they are acted out, for in enactment lies their sustenance and growth. The police are our agents of rule enactment in the most important way that any rule is dramatically affirmed, the day-to-day decisions of ordinary life. Within the day-to-day life of the community, as they interact with the people, they assert our rules — both formal and informal ones. To an important degree their actions are our rules, and they become a sensitive part of our everyday life. Thus, to maintain a liberal, democratic society they, above all men, must be liberal democrats, feeling respect and hopefully affection for their fellow citizens.

Our police are precious to us, and we need policemen whom we can trust and respect, who will act in ways giving us confidence in the liberalism and democracy of our community. Just as life in the family is the crucible of personality and man's freedom inside himself, the law in action spells out and affirms man's freedom in the community. It's time we saw this role of the police with clear eyes and planned the hard work necessary to make them part of our community, respected by and friends with all of us. Training, high pay, and social status, and most of all full democratic participation of the police in the life of the community are all essential to this end.

Appendix A:
Interview Sample, Interview Structure, and Data Gathering

Interview and Sampling Categories The interview sample; structure of interviews│**Data and Techniques**│**Responsibilities of an Exploratory Study**│

Interview and Sampling Categories

Forty-seven percent of the men in the department were inter-viewed. In order to assure a sample that was representative of the categories that might influence attitudes and actions, quotas were drawn from the following categories, which had been chosen dur-ing the first and second stages of the research:

Basis of appointment: The men in this department had obtained their appointments on two bases. If they had joined the depart-ment before 1940, their appointment had been made on a politi-cal basis. If they joined after that date, their appointment had been made through competitive Civil Service examinations. Every other category was split, therefore, so as to represent these dif-ferences.

Rank: In addition to the chief, the department contained four ranks: captain, sergeant, detective, and patrolman. Each rank was sampled.

Job in the department: The different jobs within the depart-ment were in large measure correlated with the ranks. In a few cases in which this was not true, such as the desk sergeant's job, the records department, and the bureau of identification, care was taken to include men from these areas in the respective rank samples.

Experience: Time in service was considered to represent expe-rience. To a large degree this correlated with the basis of appoint-ment. Thus, the men who had 11 or more years of experience had been appointed on a political basis, and the men with 10 or fewer years of experience had been appointed through the Civil Service examinations. Within these categories an effort was made to maintain representativeness by two-year categories, but this was not completely successful owing to problems in interviewing. In addition, the experience sample had to include the rookies, the men who had just joined the department and who were on pro-bation. They were therefore established as a special experience category.

Race: The department included 16 Negroes, all but one of whom were patrolmen. Care was taken that more than half of these Negroes were included in the sample.

The Interview Sample. Although it was thought to be desirable that the sampling be random within the categories of selection,

Table A.1. Representatives of the Interview Sample

	Political Appointees			Civil Service Appointees			Entire Department		
Rank	Total	Sample No.	%	Total	Sample No.	%	Total	Sample No.	%
Captain	5	4	80	0	0	0	5	4	80
Sergeant	10	5	50	4	2	50	14	7	50
Detective	20	9	45	12	8	67	32	17	63
Patrolman	39	14	36	82	40	49	121	54	45
Rookies	0	0	0	22	10	45	22	10	45
Total	74	32	43	120	60	50	194	92	47

this was found to be impossible because of the difficulties in reaching the men, who worked on varying shifts. The sample therefore consisted of the men as they could be reached. Table A.1 indicates the degree to which the sample was representative of the department as a whole.

Structure of Interviews. The contacts for the interviews were made by telephone, and whenever possible the interviews took place at the home of the policeman, where it was felt that he would feel more free to talk, and where it was possible for the interviewer to observe something of the home life of the police-man. Each interview lasted approximately two hours and was so structured as to include the interviewer's filling out of a face sheet,[1] which requested pertinent data about the policeman's background, experience, and life pattern, and the discussion of the following general points, which were developed from the "get acquainted" period: (1) preceding occupational history; (2) aspirations for children and whether they would like sons to become policemen; (3) personal aspirations held in high school; (4) reasons for joining the police department; (5) how to get along with the others on the police force; (6) solidarity and reasons for its existence; (7) use of violence; (8) conceptions of a good police-man; (9) conceptions of an ideal police department; (10) how they think the public pictures them; (11) most disliked duty; (12) most gratifying experience; (13) how their wives feel toward the work;

[1] See Appendix B.

(14) definition of the criminal; (15) attitudes toward the Negro as a crime problem; (16) experiences in and attitudes toward the courts; (17) graft; (18) conceptions of a policeman's job; and (19) degree to which they would accept police policy deviating from the law.

The actual introduction of these subjects, the way in which they were introduced, and the extent to which they were pressed depended on a number of factors:

1. A particular subject was dropped within an interviewing category (e.g., Negro patrolmen) when and if consensus was evident and nothing was being obtained.

2. Some men were presented with dilemma questions in areas of high sensitivity, for example, "Suppose you discovered that your partner had clipped a drunk for five hundred dollars when you were bringing him into the station. Would you turn him in? What would the men think of you if you did? If you didn't turn him in, the drunk pressed charges, and your partner testified that he had never seen the money, how would you testify?" This line of questioning was continued until a strong reaction set in and interviews began to be cancelled. The question then might be reformulated to appear innocuous, or dropped, depending on whether or not consensus was evident.

3. The degree of rapport obtained had much to do with whether or not a question was pressed. This was of strategic importance, because policemen are under explicit orders not to talk about police work with anyone outside the department; there is much in the nature of a secret society about the police, and past experience has indicated to policemen that to talk is to invite trouble from the press, the public, the administration, and their colleagues. The result is that when they got the slightest suspicion that anything was not on an innocuous level, they became exceedingly uncooperative, and the rest of the men caught on in a hurry. As a matter of fact, the principal obstacle in the research was to avoid being defined as a spy. This was more difficult than it seems, since it sometimes required walking up to a policeman, amid a hostile group, seeing fear in his eyes, and shaking his hand (which he tries not to offer), while at the same time maintaining an appearance of joviality and unconcern. The research required a continuous campaign of personal propaganda in order to meet

repeated waves of suspicion and consequent lack of cooperation. This meant a constant search for ways to define oneself that would be acceptable. Some of the most successful definitions were those of the man in trouble and the policeman's friend. Each definition seemed to wear out in time, however, and a fresh one had to be constructed.

Data and Techniques

The data and reports of 92 interviews with policemen in a single police department were supplemented by extended observation of the operations of the department. The interview data were of two types: (1) quantitative data concerning the policeman's background, occupational history, experience, and habits; and (2) the account of a general discussion concerning specific aspects of police work and the policeman's experience. The latter part of the interview material can be considered as a series of personal documents whose validation rests on the following assumptions:

1. All statements were made with a conservative bias. The men interviewed were all conscious that they might get into trouble by saying what they did. Many of them deliberately lied in order to present the best possible front. On this basis it was assumed that statements that were detrimental to the police and tended to incriminate the man were valid, provided that they also fulfilled the following two conditions.

2. All statements that indicated a high degree of consensus from interview to interview were considered valid. This second assumption might be called inter-interview consistency.

3. All statements that were consistent with the observations were considered to be valid.

In addition, the three bases of validation listed by Allport (1942, p. 128) were also used:

Nonquantitative indications of validity are three in number. (1) As in everyday life the general honesty and credibility of the report can be relied upon; this is the ad hominem test. (2) The plausibility of the document in terms of our own past experiences, as they are relevant, can be considered; even if our past experience is meager we know something of the range of human potentialities by which we can judge the probable truth of an account. (3) The test of internal consistency or self-confrontation has to be widely relied upon. A document that hangs together, that represents a structured configuration of human life and harbors no impossible contradictions has at least prima facie validity.

In the analysis of the interviews, each case was checked for these points of validation, and the statements were appraised accordingly. In cases of doubt on the more important points, the statements were checked by actually going to the police station, conducting a general inquiry among the men contacted, and, if possible, attempting actually to observe the actions concerned.

The general techniques of collecting data were two: personal observation and intensive interviewing. These were the techniques of research. In the analysis, the major technique was a rough quantitative analysis of the interview responses, and a summary of them in terms of percentages. Relatedness was tested through the cross-tabulations of the factors that were thought to be related. In every case in which responses were categorized, one or two techniques were used to indicate the validity of the categories: (1) the categories were made so narrow and so frequent that they represented the full range of responses; and (2) extensive case materials were presented representing the types of responses that fell into the particular category.

A basic problem of the research was the identification of certain individual perspectives as norms or customs. In order to make this identification it was assumed that when persons were asked to justify or legitimate unpopular actions to a stranger they would do so on the basis of what they felt was a moral authority, and that their bases of legitimation would then represent a rule or custom of the group; that is, these bases would represent a rule if the following conditions held: (1) that there was considerable consensus on the basis of legitimation; and (2) that the bases of legitimation were different from or in contradiction to the mores of the larger society. On the basis of this assumption, the police were asked to justify the use of violence, and their legitimations were considered to represent the norms of the police if they fulfilled the given conditions. We mention this technique because we feel that it may be useful in research on other social groups.

Responsibilities of an Exploratory Study

A person making an exploratory study has the responsibility to communicate as fully as possible the full range of his ideas and hypotheses, to an extent that would not be justified in more definitive studies. To do this, the researcher should include any materials that he feels are relative to the full understanding of the area studied and the problem under consideration even if he cannot validate his statements. This is vitally necessary if an exploratory study is to provide the basis for further research in the area, by suggesting hypotheses and orienting the future research worker. The restriction of the report to findings that the researcher has full confidence that he can defend and validate results in the loss of much valuable material and thus should be avoided.

This is not meant to imply that the researcher does not bear a full responsibility for the assessment of his data and the clear indication of its value. He, more than anyone else, is most conscious of deficiencies and adequacies of the work, and these should be so indicated.

In composing this report we have kept these considerations in mind and with one exception, which follows, we have included everything that we considered to be relevant, regardless of how well is could be validated. In addition, however, we have taken care to differentiate clearly those aspects of the study that we feel are adequately validated within the range of the case study. The conclusions of the study are restricted to these results, except as we have indicated otherwise.

The one area we have not reported on is one that was literally "too hot to handle" in the research, and one in which we gathered only scattered data. This is the area in which the police are connected with the political machine and are involved in the vice and gambling activities of the community. This information was not essential to the ends of the study, which had reference in large measure to the police as an occupation. It has been withheld because the information cannot be documented adequately and would necessarily identify the men involved.

Appendix B:
Interview Face Sheet

Name: Address:

Rank: Years in dept.:

Pre or post civil service: Race: N   W

Age at last birthday: Place of birth:

Marital status: S M W D   No. yrs. school completed:

No. of children: Occupation of wife:

Birthplace of parents:

Occupation of father:

Occupation of mother:

Occupations of relatives in vicinity:

Sibling position, with relative ages:

Do you own your home?   O   R

To what clubs or organizations do you belong?   Attendance?

Name   Attend   Office

1.

2.

3.

Veteran? yes   no   Unit: Yrs. service:

What books have you read in past two years?

To what magazines and newspapers do you subscribe?

To what radio programs or commentators do you listen?

Appendix C:
Social and Attitudinal Backgrounds

Occupation of the father; job aspirations;
reasons for job choice; job histories; ethnic
background; previous employment; education;
the policeman's family; home ownership; television
and radio ownership; reading habits; religious
preferences; associational membership; part-time
work.

Occupation of the Father. The father's occupation was felt to be of significance in the son's choice of an occupation because of his use as a model, and because it was felt that mobility aspirations would be regulated by it. Table C.1 indicates that only four men followed their fathers' occupations, i.e., protective services, and that the majority of the men experienced downward mobility from their fathers' occupations in choosing police work. The results would suggest that police work is appealing to men from families of manual workers (69.7% of the men came from such families), but that there are many intervening factors in the choice of the occupation. The disproportionately low percentage of the fathers in the operative category, as contrasted to the crafts and the laboring categories, suggests that many of the men exaggerated their father's occupation.

Job Aspirations. Aspiration (Table C.2) was considered a significant basis in the selection of police work as an occupation, since it would indicate whether the choice represented a fulfillment or a disappointment in terms of the aspiration. Assuming that any

Table C.1. Occupations of Policemen's Fathers*

Occupation	Frequency	Percentage
Professional and semiprofessional	4	4.5
Proprietors and managers	14	15.5
Clerical and sales	3	3.5
Craftsmen and foremen	25	28.0
Farmers	3	3.4
Protective services	4	4.5
Operatives	7	5.6
Service workers (nondomestic)	2	2.2
Laborers	29	32.7
Total	91	100.0

* Classified according to the categories used by the Bureau of the Census as they appear in United States Department of Commerce, Bureau of Census, *Alphabetical Index of Occupations and Industries* (Washington: Government Printing Office, 1940). Categories are arranged in the order of social prestige as evaluated by Hatt and North from an N.O.R.C. nationwide survey and reported in Cecil C. and Paul K. Hatt, "Jobs and Occupations: A Popular Evaluation," included in Wilson, Logan, and Kolb, William L., *Sociological Analysis* (New York: Harcourt Brace and Co., 1949), p. 467.

Table C.2. Occupational Aspirations*

Occupational Aspiration	Frequency	Percentage
Professional	19	21
Semiprofessional	10	11
Sports	6	7
Clerical and sales	2	2
Craftsmen	2	2
Protective services		
Soldiers	3	3
Policemen	5	6
None	43	48
Total	90	100

* With the exception of the sports category, which belongs among the semiprofessional group, categorization was made on the same basis as Table C. 1.

category from sports down would in the minds of the men represent an equivalent choice, 68% of the men can be said to have chosen an occupation that was equivalent to their aspiration in success terms.

Those listing a particular aspiration wanted to be doctors (3), lawyers (4), priests (3), engineers (4), accountants (2), artists (1), musicians (2), college graduates (40), singers (1), actors (1), embalmers (1), foresters (1), draftsmen (3), baseball players (4), athletic coaches (1), and boxers (1).

Cross-tabulations with father's occupation and with years of education completed were made but showed no significant relationship.

Reasons for Job Choice. Security was the most frank response received to the question as to why the men joined the police department (Table C.3). This category also included responses to the effect that it had a good pension or that it was a steady job. Included in the category "It was a good job" were responses of the following order: "I had always wanted to be a policeman" . . . "I hated the mill and wanted something else" . . . "I thought I would like it; it was a good job and my friends talked me into it." Some responses included both categories, in which case the first reason given was the one used.

Table C.3. Reasons for Joining the Police Department*

Reason	Frequency	Percentage
Security	25	35
A good job	25	35
Needed a job	7	10
None	15	20
Total	72	100

* Cross-tabulations with age on entering the department, aspirations, education, and father's occupation indicated no significant relationships.

The results indicate that security is a major factor in the choice of the police as an occupation. The interviewer's impression in talking to the men about the occupation and in listening to the conversations between the men was that security is a great deal more important than the direct responses would indicate. In the conversations the men made frequent allusions to the good pension, the fact that there were no strikes in the police force, and the fact that the police continued to receive their pay even during the depression — all suggesting the importance of security in their conception of the worth of the job.

Job Histories. Twenty men were asked to describe their experience from high school to the police force. The resulting job histories were very uneven in detail and continuity, and, since they were not chosen to be representative, the results cannot be generalized to all the men in the department. One characteristic of these histories appeared so persistently, however, that it deserves special mention.

Of the 20 men, 18 had held three or more jobs before joining the police department. Thus, irregularity of employment would *seem* to be a significant characteristic of men who choose to become policemen.

Although most of these job histories were depression histories, which would suggest that the irregularity of employment was the result of losing jobs, this was not entirely the case. Most of the men stated that they had left many of the jobs voluntarily.

For illustrative purposes, we have chosen three job histories for detail and continuity:

Case 1 I did go to high school. Flunked algebra three times. The fourth time I got it. I was an A student. Played in the band — saxophone. Play almost any kind of a wind instrument. After school I was usually in a movie theatre.

When I got out of high school I worked in the mill as a messenger. I wanted to study chemical engineering, so I worked nights. I went back to high school to pick up my physics and chemistry, then came a slack period and all the messengers were laid off. I decided to study music. I went to Kentucky Teachers College, in Bowling Green. After four months I decided that was not the place for me. So I went back to City X and back to work in the mill. I operated a glorified mimeograph machine. After three months of that I wanted more money. Then I got a job in the ——— Mill as a laborer, low class. Then I decided that labor was not good for me. I went to the ——— Works as a shipping clerk with less money but it was a clean job. Then I went on the police force.

When I decided to be a policeman I was a conscientious fellow. Well, it paid a higher wage and there was a pension to look forward to. I believed the people were good and I wanted to become a policeman and fight crime. At the time I came on the department they had just had a big shake-up with a complete reorganization. Most of the men at the department were old timers who were politically appointed, had lots of political connections in town. With them it was a matter of everybody for himself. They didn't trust the new fellows and most of them feared that if we learned anything they would be out of a job. We were lucky that we had six weeks of school. It was a really intensive course and they gave us a lot more than new fellows get. I learned most of my police work in the Army.

Right after I finished my probation period I was drafted into the Army. I went into the MP's as a company clerk for a year and a half. Then they put me in CID, and I began to learn gradually about police work. By the time I returned to the department it had dawned on me that my faith in people was all gone. For a long time my daily chant was that people were no damned good.

Case 2 I played football and basketball, was on both teams and I worked weekends as a garage mechanic to make spending money.

While I was in grammar school I had a paper route. I didn't do much dating while I was in high school. There was a group of three or four of us and we all worked and saved our money to take trips during the summer. Once we took a trip to Mexico City. We financed it all ourselves. We bought a car and saw a lot of the country.

When I was in high school I wanted to be a doctor. I thought that I would like to help people and work with them. Generally I liked high school. I had a good time. But you know how it is, everybody wants to get out and get on his own. That was the way it was with me.

When I got out of high school, that was in 1937, I got a job in the mill. I still wanted to be a doctor but things were pretty rough then and I was lucky to get the job. I suppose I could have gone to college but I wanted to be on my own.

I was laid off at the mill in 1940 and on the advice of the superintendent I went over to the Works and I worked there from 1940 until February 1st of this year when I went on the police force. While I was working there I did odd jobs outside of the mill. I worked in the garage on weekends, helped my brother-in-law fix his house, and stuff like that.

I went on the police department for security. I didn't feel secure in the mill. Just didn't have that feeling of security because in the mill you worked six months then they would lay you off. I remember that the old timers told stories of the number of times they had been laid off in various periods, and this always had me worried. It was not that I wasn't doing well in the mill, because the superintendent and the bosses like me real well. I just wanted a job in which there were no lay-offs. I applied for a job in the police department in April, 1949.

I knew a couple of men in the department. They have a very good pension plan. During the depression I remember the policemen were never laid off. They didn't get too much money but when you average it for a period of ten years it's as good as they make in the mill. That's the way I figure it.

Case 3 Well, I got out of high school and I enlisted in the Army. This was during the first World War. I served two terms in the Army and then after I got out I mined coal for a year. Then I went into the mill for five years and then I went out and did some contracting on my own. Then during the worst of the depression I worked for one of the oil companies.

My brother, he was in politics and one time there just was a fellow running for mayor and my brother said he would like me to meet him. So I went down and met the fellow and liked him real well. So I did some work for him on the campaign. Well, it comes around that he is elected and I happened to be in his office one day and there was a whole lot of fellows standing around outside talking about the kinds of jobs they would want to get and they asked me what I wanted. I said I hadn't thought about it. They said, "What do you want? Fire department? Police department?" So I says, "Police department." Well, it was funny that day. One of the fellows in there he sneaked in to see the mayor and he figured on getting in good with him — get himself a good job. He told the mayor that the boys in the outside room were making up a list of the jobs they wanted. Well, the mayor said he was just delighted, and then he threw that guy out of his office. The fellow never did get a job at all.

And then I saw the mayor and he said he saw I was down for police department and a couple of days later he called and told me to come up there. A couple of police officers got me and we went up before the security board or something like that and I saw the mayor in with the members of the board. He looked at me and told me to raise my right hand and I was a policeman.

The preceding materials suggest that men who decide to join the police department are drawn from large, working-class families, have a relatively low level of aspiration, experience a high rate of turnover in their prepolice jobs, and emphasize security as a major reason for joining the department.

Specific data as to acceptance and rejection by the civil service board were not available. Three factors available from the study data were thought to have some bearing on the type of men selected. These were ethnic background, years of education completed and previous occupation.

Ethnic Background. The results shown in Table C.4 strongly suggest that there was little if any ethnic basis for the selection of new members, since no particular nationality group, other than the native-born, is strongly predominant.

Table C.4. Birthplaces of Policemen's Parents

Country	Both Parents	One Parent
Czechoslovakia	7	0
Austria	5	0
Poland	5	1
Ireland	4	1
Hungary	3	3
Lithuania	3	0
Yugoslavia	2	1
Italy	2	0
Canada	2	0
England	1	3
Norway	1	0
Serbia	1	0
Germany	0	2
Total foreign-born		36
Total mixed foreign-born and native-born		11
Total mixed and foreign-born		47
Total native-born		44
Total		91

Previous Employment. The results in Table C.5 indicate that 60% of the men on the police force were previously employed as skilled, semiskilled, or unskilled laborers. They suggest that previous occupations, with the possible exception of military service, were of no effect in the selection of the personnel. The large number of men coming from the laboring categories is undoubtedly a result of the selection of the occupation by these men, as discussed in the previous section.

Education. The median years of education completed for 91 men interviewed was 10.6 years. Many of the older men had not finished grammar school; all of these men being political appointees. Fifteen men, or 17%, had one or more years of college. Two men had completed college.

The Policeman's Family. Of a sample of 91 men, representative as to race, rank, position, and experience, 76, or 88%, were married. Of those married men, nine, or 13%, had previously been

Table C.5. Previous Occupations*

Occupation	Frequency	Percentage
Semiprofessional	5	6
Managers and officials	1	1
Clerical and sales	16	18
Craftsmen and foremen	13	15
Operatives	27	31
Service		
Protective	5	6
Other nondomestic	9	9
Labor	11	14
Total	87	100

* Categories used were those employed by the United States Government Bureau of the Census. Categorization was made either on the basis of the last job held before entering the police force, or, where further data were available, on the basis of the job of longest duration held before entering the department.

Table C.6. Residential Status

Type of Residence	Number	Percentage
Living with parents	9	13
Owns small house	28	41
Owns medium house	12	17
Owns large house	1	1
Rents small apartment	17	25
Rents small house	2	3
Total	69	100

divorced; four, or 5%, had previously been widowed, and one had been divorced twice previously. Of the simple men, two had been married and divorced.

The median number of children in the policemen's families was 1.97; 17% of the married men had three or more children. **Home Ownership.** The homes of the policemen were scattered all over the city, with no concentration in particular types of neighborhood, although none of the policemen lived in the slum areas. Most of the policemen lived in small homes with approximately two bedrooms, probably worth between nine and eleven thousand dollars in terms of 1950 values. Most of them had mortgages on their homes.

The interviewer visited 69 policemen's homes. On a strictly informal basis these have been classified into three types: small homes are those with two bedrooms, living room, bathroom; medium houses are those with three bedrooms; and large houses are those with four or more bedrooms or the equivalent. Table C.6 gives a detailed breakdown.

Those policemen who lived with their parents were invariably young, unmarried men. The interviewer's impression, from memory, was that those owning small houses mostly lived in new developments on the outskirts of the city.

Television and Radio Ownership. Of 92 men interviewed on this subject, all had radios and 49% had television sets. Their program preferences were as shown in Table C.7.

Many of the men stated that they had purchased the television sets either to keep their children at home or in order to see the baseball and football games. They all stated that after obtaining the television sets they seldom did much reading or radio listening.

Reading Habits. Ninety-two policemen were asked what books they had read in the last two years, what magazines and papers they read regularly, and whether they managed to do any reading about police work. Their responses indicated the following:

1. Fifty-four percent read no books at all; among the remaining

Table C.7. Radio Program Preferences

Type of Program Preferred	Number	Percentage
Mystery stories	26	28
Music	26	28
News and commentators	24	26
Sports	23	25
Comedies	19	21
Plays	13	14

46%, most of those who did any extensive reading were members of some book club.

2. All except two of the men subscribed to the town paper and read at least two additional papers on Sunday.

Table C.8. Associational Memberships

Association	Number Belonging	Percentage Belonging	Median Number of Meetings Attended Yearly
Fraternal Order of Police	78	85	7.5
Police Ex-Servicemen's Club	27	30	6.3
The American Legion	22	24	2.6
Masons	15	16	6.5
Veterans of Foreign Wars	6		
Sportsmen's Club	6		
Elks	4		
Holy Name Society	3		
Knights of Columbus	3		
Isaac Walton Club	2		
Men's Social Club	2		
Eagles	2		
Slovak Political Club	2		
The Billiard Club	2		
Amvets	1		
Rifle Club	1		
The Tall Cedars	1		
Law Fraternity	1		
Carpathian Union	1		
St. Michael's Club	1		
The Sobols	1		
Polish National Alliance	1		
West Side Lithuanian Club	1		
Scots' Club	1		
Croatian Fraternal Union	1		

3. Eighteen of the men read no magazines, and the remainder read a median number of 2.8 magazines a month. The most popular magazines were *Time, Newsweek, The Reader's Digest, Life,* and various sporting journals.

4. Only 15% to 16% of the men did any reading in their field of specialization. Even for these men this reading was very little, consisting of no more than one book every two years or one pamphlet a year; the chief sources of reading on police work were the F.B.I. magazines and pamphlets on homicide investigation or police work in general. None of the men subscribed to or read any of the criminology or police journals.

Religious Preferences. Eighty-two men were asked to state their religions and whether they attended church. The responses indicated that 34, or 41%, were practicing Catholics; 4, or 5%, were nonpracticing Catholics, 17, or 21%, were practicing Protestants, 24, or 29% were nonpracticing Protestants, and 3, or 4% were without religious preference.

Associational Membership. Ninety-two men were asked what

Table C.9. Additional Jobs Carried by Policemen

Type of Job	Frequency
Protective jobs	6
Odd laboring jobs	4
Gas station attendant	3
Labor in steel mill	2
Credit investigator	2
Student	2
Dry cleaning plant (part-owner)	1
Butcher	1
Woodworker	1
Welder	1
Truck driver	1
Bricklayer	1
Shoe salesman	1
Radio repairman	1
Farmer	1
Owner of riding stable	1

clubs or associations they belonged to and approximately how many meetings they attended yearly. The responses are summarized in Table C.8.

The median number of organizations belonged to was 2.5. Eighty-eight percent of the men belonged to at least one police organization, 62% belonging to one and 26% to both.

Part-time Work. Sixty-two men were asked whether they did any other work in order to supplement their incomes. Forty-eight percent stated that they did do some kind of part-time or full-time work in addition to their duties on the police force. Some carried full-time jobs, some carried regular part-time jobs, and others worked whenever they had the chance. The types of jobs they did are summarized in Table C.9.

Bibliography

Allport, Gordon
The Use of Personal Documents in Psychological Science. Social
Science Research Council Bulletin No. 49. New York, 1942.

Becker, Howard
"The Professional Dance Musician in Chicago." Unpublished
Master's Thesis, Department of Sociology, University of Chicago,
1950.

Best, Herbert
"Why the Police Fail." *Harpers,* January 1933, pp. 204–210.

Blumer, Herbert
"Sociological Theory in Industrial Relations." *American Sociological Review* XII (1947): 272.

Byrnes, Asher
Government Against the People. New York: Dodd, Mead &
Co., 1946.

The Citizens Police Committee
Chicago Police Problems. Chicago: University of Chicago Press,
1931.

Cooley, C. H.
Human Nature and the Social Order. New York: Charles Scribner's
Sons, 1902.

Cotrell, Fred
The Railroader. Stanford, Calif.: Stanford University Press, 1940.

Durkheim, Emile
The Division of Labor in Society. Glencoe, Ill.: The Free Press,
1947.

Fosdick, Raymond
American Police Systems. New York: The Century Co., 1920.
European Police Systems. New York: The Century Co., 1922.

Gold Raymond
"The Chicago Flat Janitor." Unpublished Master's Thesis, Department of Sociology, University of Chicago, 1950.

Goldman, Nathan
"Police Selection of Juvenile Offenders." Unpublished Ph.D. Dissertation, Department of Sociology, University of Chicago, 1950.

Greer, Sarah
A Bibliography of Police Administration and Police Science. New
York: Institute of Public Administration, 1936.

Hall, Jerome
"The Law of Arrest in Relation to Contemporary Social Problems." *University of Chicago Law Review,* April 1936, pp. 345–
375.

Hall, Oswald
"Informal Organization of Medical Practice in an American City." Unpublished Ph.D. Dissertation, Department of Sociology, University of Chicago, 1944.

Hopkins, Ernest J.
Our Lawless Police. New York: The Viking Press, 1931.

Hughes, E. C.
"The Chicago Real Estate Board." Unpublished Ph.D. Dissertation, University of Chicago, 1928.
"The Work and Self." In J. Rohrer and M. Sherif, *Social Psychology at the Crossroads*. New York: Harper, 1951.
Men and Their Work. Glencoe, Ill.: The Free Press, 1952.

Lavine, E. H.
Cheese It — the Cops. New York: Vanguard Press, 1936.

Lippmann, Walter
Public Opinion. New York: Harcourt, Brace, 1922.

Lohman, J. D.
The Police and Minority Groups. Chicago: Chicago Park District, 1947.

Lortie, Daniel
"Doctors Without Patients. The Anesthesiologist, a New Type of Medical Specialist." Unpublished Master's Thesis, Department of Sociology, University of Chicago, 1949.

Mannheim, Karl
Man and Society in an Age of Reconstruction. London: Routledge & Kegan Paul, 1948.

Mead, George Herbert
Mind, Self and Society. Chicago: University of Chicago Press, 1947.

New York State Legislature
Report of the Joint Committee on the Government of the City of New York (Hofstadter and Seabury Commissions). New York. 5 volumes in 2, mimeographed, 1932.

Park, Robert E., and E. W. Burgess
Introduction to the Science of Sociology. Chicago: University of Chicago Press, 1922.

Reitzes, Dietrich
"Collective Factors in Race Relations." Unpublished Ph.D. Dissertation, Department of Sociology, University of Chicago, 1950.

Simmel, Georg
The Sociology of Georg Simmel. Translated by Kurt Wolff. Glencoe, Ill.: The Free Press, 1950.

Smith, Bruce
Police Systems in the United States. New York: Harper, 1949.
Sutherland, E. H., and C. E. Gehlke
"Crime and Punishment." In The President's Research Committee on Social Trends, *Recent Social Trends in the United States*. New York: McGraw-Hill, 1933, p. 1122.

U.S. National Committee on Law Observance and Enforcement
Report on the Police. Washington, D. C., Government Printing Office, 1931.

Vollmer, August
The Police and Modern Society. Berkeley, Calif.: University of California Press, 1936.

Weber, Max
General Economic History. Translated by Frank Knight. New York: Greenberg Publishers, 1927.
"Bureaucracy." *In Essays in Sociology*. Translated by Hans Gerth and C. Wright Mills. New York: Oxford University Press, 1946.
The Theory of Social and Economic Organization. Translation by Talcott Parsons. New York: Oxford University Press, 1947.

Whyte, William S.
Street Corner Society. Chicago: University of Chicago Press, 1943.
Woods, Arthur
The Policeman and the Public. New Haven: Yale University Press, 1919.

Index

Beat men, 31, 34, 35, 49, 89
Blumer, Herbert, 9, 12n
Brutality, justification of, 62–64, 68, 73–76, 90–92, 99, 104, 106, 148, 149, 152
  cases of, cited, 124–142
  see also Violence
Byrnes, Asher, 2

Chicago, 3–5, 12
Citizens Police Committee, Chicago, 4, 5
Civil service, 20, 22, 23, 27
Communications section, 32–33
Community, background of, 19–22
Controls, structure of, 8–11
Cooley, C. H., 148
Criminals, 65–70, 89, 90, 105, 106, 110, 151
  use of force against, 128–140 *passim*
Custom, as group control, 8–11

Desk sergeant, 31, 32
Detectives, 31, 36–43, 49, 63
  and patrolmen, 38, 56, 129, 130
Drunks, 89, 90, 105, 106
  see also Fighters
Durkheim, Emile, 9

Family quarrels, 60–61, 89, 105, 106
Felons, *see* Criminals
Fighters, 72–76, 89, 90, 105, 106
  see also Drunks
Force, *see* Brutality; Violence
Fosdick, Raymond B., 2, 3, 5

Gehlke, C. E., 10
Goldman, Nathan, 7, 8, 85, 97
Graft, 4, 33, 57, 88
Group identification, lack of among detectives, 39
  of police, 110, 111–118

Hopkins, Ernest J., 4
Hughes, E. C., 9, 160

Informants, 40–42
Interviewing, as stage in research, 12
  detailed description of, 195–201

Juvenile delinquents, 82–86, 89, 91, 97, 105, 106

Kefauver Committee, 5

Law, as societal control, 8–11
  as legitimation for violence, 133–134
Law courts, 7, 64, 76–82, 89, 91, 105, 140
Law enforcement, 119–120, 140–143, 151
Lawyers, 50–52, 55, 105
Lippman, Walter, 184
Lohman, Joseph D., 9, 14, 16

Mannheim, Karl, 9, 10
Mead, George Herbert, 9
Men on the beat, *see* Beat men
Metropolis and the Mental Life (Simmel), 184
Morality of police, 8–11, 143, 148, 149
  roots of, 110–111
Municipal police, development, 2

National Committee on Law Observance and Enforcement, (USA), 5
Negroes, 4, 53–55, 105
  as police public, 99–104, 107
New York City, 3, 5
New York Tribune, quoted, 3

Observation, as stage in research, 12–13

Patrol cars, 31, 35–36
Patrolmen, and detectives, 38, 56, 129, 130
Peel, Robert, 2
Pittsburgh, 7
Police chief, 22–30
  authority of, 24–29
  responsibilities of, 23–24
Police Department, 16, 30–32
  Detective Division, 36–43
  Patrol Division, 34–36, 43
  Personnel, 43–45
  Records and Communication Division, 32–33